Gender Policies in Japan and the United States

Gender Policies in Japan and the United States: Comparing Women's Movements, Rights and Politics

Joyce Gelb

GENDER POLICIES IN JAPAN AND THE UNITED STATES
© Joyce Gelb, 2003

First published 2003 by
PALGRAVE MACMILLAN™
175 Fifth Avenue, New York, N.Y. 10010 and
Houndmills, Basingstoke, Hampshire, England RG21 6XS
Companies and representatives throughout the world

PALGRAVE MACMILLAN is the global academic imprint of the Palgrave Macmillan division of St. Martin's Press, LLC and of Palgrave Macmillan Ltd. Macmillan® is a registered trademark in the United States, United Kingdom and other countries. Palgrave is a registered trademark in the European Union and other countries.

ISBN 0–312–29355–0 hardback
ISBN 0–312–29356–9 paperback

Library of Congress Cataloging-in-Publication Data
Gelb, Joyce, 1940–
Gender Policies in Japan and the United States: comparing women's movements, rights, and politics/Joyce Gelb.
        p. cm.
    Includes bibliographical references and index.
    ISBN 0–312–29355–0 (cloth)
    ISBN 0–312–29356–9 (trade pbk.)
    1. Feminism—Japan. 2. Feminism—United States. 3. Women's rights—Japan. 4. Women's rights—United States. 5. Women in politics—Japan. 6. Women in politics—United States. I. Title.

HQ1762.G37 2004
305.42'0952—dc21   2003051188

A catalogue record for this book is available from the British Library.

Design by Newgen Imaging Systems (P) Ltd., Chennai, India.

First edition: December 2003
10 9 8 7 6 5 4 3 2 1

Printed in the United States of America

For My Japanese Friends and My Family

Contents

Preface

This study has its origins in a fellowship program, the "Japan Initiatives," based at City College in New York City, my home campus, and Tokyo Metropolitan University in Japan, funded by the Japan–United States Friendship Commission in 1987. I was fortunate to be selected as an exchange professor that summer and, while in Japan lecturing, I was able to take a preliminary look at the state of the feminist movement there. That began a fifteen year odyssey, with frequent research trips to Japan, usually at least once a year, sometimes more often. Professor James Shields and then Dean of Social Science Arline McCord were responsible for the program and my participation in it. I am grateful for their confidence in me and their support then and afterward.

A long time student of feminist politics in comparative perspective, I became interested in the 1985 Japanese Equal Employment Opportunity Law and began to research and write about it. The last fifteen years have provided me with a unique opportunity to learn more about and study Japanese politics and society, a topic initially new to me.

I have developed numerous close academic and personal relationships in Japan, without which this research effort could never have been possible. First and foremost, I owe an extraordinary debt to Kubo Kimiko of the Ichikawa Fusae Memorial Association. She worked tirelessly for over a decade to help me set up contacts and appointments, gather data and gain a greater understanding of the Japanese political system. We have collaborated together in several endeavors, including a workshop at the Beijing Women's Conference in 1995. In conjunction with her close associates and my good friends, Yamaguchi Mitsuko and Nuita Yoko, as well as my own institution, in August 1998 we cosponsored a conference entitled Japan-U.S. Women's Dialogue: Empowering Women in Politics, which brought together state and local legislators from both nations. That conference proved to be significant in a number of ways, including its emphasis on the topic of violence against women, reflected in this volume. In addition, the conference demonstrated the importance of comparative policy analysis, a legacy that is the focus of this book.

I owe enormous gratitude to many others as well. My initial host professor at Tokyo Metropolitan University, Kawamura Nozumu, has remained a close academic and personal friend. My landlords and dear friends, the Morises, housed me on numerous stays in Tokyo. The opportunity to teach in the Associated Kyoto Program (AKP) in 2000 enabled me to spend an entire semester in Japan. I was able to use part of that memorable time to do preliminary research for this book.

I have so many wonderful colleagues and friends that I hope the list I am about to present does not exclude anyone. Koedo Shizuko of the Working Women's Network, Osaka, has introduced me to numerous working women's groups; we have participated in international workshops together as well. It has been a treat to experience her "*genki*," or spirit, and drive during these past fifteen years. Hayashi Hiroko of Fukuoka Law School has been an invaluable colleague during the years. Nakanishi Tamako, former Diet member and present head of the Women's Solidarity Foundation, has also been a collaborator in a number of wonderful international venues. Ueno Chizuko, of the University of Tokyo was my host professor during the fall of 2001 during an extensive research study visit; her office assistant Kozai Mayumi provided cheerful assistance during that period as well. Asakura Mutsuko of the Tokyo Metropolitan University Law School gave tirelessly of her time and wisdom in the fall of 2001, when she went far beyond the role of host professor at her university. Others who deserve special mention are Hashimoto Hiroko of Jumonji University; Kaino Tamie of Ochanomizu University; Ogai Tokuko; Tsunoda Yukiko; Kuroiwa Yoko; Hayashi Yoko; Nakajima Michiko and numerous other lawyer/advocates. Many Diet members have given their time and support to this research; their names are listed in the interview section of this book. Moriyama Mayumi has been generous with her time and assistance, first in her role as Diet member and then as Minister of Justice of Japan. A group of American lawyers, advocates and scholars were invaluable in supplying information on the current policy situation in the United States. All of those whom I have interviewed over the years have earned my deepest appreciation for the efforts they made to patiently explain issues, movements and policy to this avid listener.

My former editor, Deborah Gershenowitz at Palgrave Macmillan provided editorial comments that were invaluable in preparing manuscript revisions. Other colleagues and friends who reviewed all or part of the manuscript, Heidi Gottfried, Marian Palley, and Eileen McDonagh, have my heartfelt thanks for the time and effort they put into their helpful evaluations. Tony Chambers has provided continuing encouragement for this project. Frances Rosenbluth of the Yale University Department of Political Science has given me useful feedback on numerous occasions.

Thanks to Tanaka Michiyo and Mittelman Kyoko for translations of Japanese language materials. Other excellent translators/interpreters were also invaluable in the research process. I owe special appreciation to my skillful research assistant (now Dr.) Kobayashi Yoshie in Tokyo during the fall of 2001 and summer of 2002 (with many, many e-mails in between and after). Tan Megumi, an MA candidate at City College, vetted the Japanese language material in the manuscript before publication. Shimotakahara Setsuko of the Japanese Consulate Office of Information in New York has been a tireless source of data for me on my occasions. Tanya Vajk has provided thoughtful and invaluable assistance in formatting and editing the manuscript.

Portions of the research have been presented at conferences, including the American Political Science Association and the Association for Asian Studies. I am grateful to the participants in those sessions for their comments and feedback, as well as to the audiences at lectures at different institutions, including Columbia University, Arizona State University, Marist College, John Jay College of the City University of New York, the University of Toronto and the University of California, Berkeley. A special note of thanks to Professor Robert Kagan of the latter institution; participation in several conferences there, largely at his invitation, proved seminal in my thinking about some of the underlying concepts of this book.

Appreciation also is due to those who have supported portions of this research during the last several years. They include Grants for Advanced Research on Japan from the Social Science Research Council; continuing support from the Professional Staff Congress / CUNY Research Grants of the City University; and funding from the National Science Foundation/Japan Society for the Promotion of Science and the Northeast Asia Council of the Association for Asian Studies.

I have also been appreciative of the continuing encouragement I have received from my departmental colleagues at the Graduate Center and City College, City University of New York. I have been grateful for the excellent support provided by the Graduate Center Mina Rees Library, particularly the Interlibrary Loan Department.

Finally, an immense debt of gratitude goes to my husband, Joe, who patiently endured numerous absences while I pursued research in Japan. He provided input and support throughout the lengthy period during which this book was completed. My son Andrew and daughter-in-law Kara, who resided in Tokyo during much of the period of this research, always encouraged my work. Visiting them was another wonderful benefit of this scholarly effort. My son Jonathan deserves my thanks for his wise counsel during the course of this endeavor and in general.

All Japanese proper names appear Japanese style, with the family name first.

Introduction

Why Study Gender Policy Making in Japan and the United States?

Why focus on a study comparing Japan and the United States? The United States and Japan are the two leading economic and industrial powers in the world today and both are democratic post-industrial societies. They both play leading roles in world politics. Japan has been influenced by the West throughout the twentieth century, both before World War II and after, as a result of the post-war occupation of Japan and its political reconfiguration along American lines. Superficially, the countries bear some similarities, particularly due to Japan's U.S.–sponsored constitution. It includes the equivalent of an Equal Rights Amendment, Article 14, which states that Japanese men and women are equal under the law, although this clause has never been fully realized.

The following comparative analysis is based on case studies conducted in each nation on similar policies. The analysis involved reconstructing the role of women's movements in shaping gender-related policies and assessments of policy outcomes in the post-war period through extensive interviews and use of other source material. The case studies examine the processes of agenda setting, policy adoption and implementation, and analyze legislative and other policy histories in order to create a full account in each instance of the factors producing policy change.

I initially chose three gender-related policies for the comparison: equal employment, reproductive rights, and domestic violence policy. The study also compares "family friendly" policies intended to aid in balancing women's family and work roles in Japan and the United States. These have been placed on the policy agenda in both nations in recent years, sometimes through very different approaches and with distinct outcomes, making them particularly good issues for comparative analysis. Consideration is also given to the Japanese Basic Law for a Gender Equal Society, passed in June 1999. The enactment of this law was the result of persistent demand from Japanese feminists. It does not have a direct United States equivalent but is noteworthy as a recent development related to gender in Japan that may influence other policy developments. It is my hope that the policies compared in this book will provide a useful window into women's roles as citizens, workers, mothers and clients of the state in two of the world's most highly developed postindustrial democracies (Siim, 4).

The Gender Empowerment Measure of the United Nations Development Project (UNDP) ranks Japan forty-first and the United States eleventh. These ratings take into account such variables as income, female administrators, parliamentary seats held and share of income. The data suggest that women in Japan are engaged in a far more difficult struggle to gain true equity. Nonetheless, Japanese women do not simply reflect a later version of western and American feminist movements: feminism has existed for over a century in Japan and has developed its own concerns rooted in culture and societal traditions. "It would not be fair to say that the contemporary Japanese feminist movement, which emerged in the 1970s was a simple transplant of its Western counterparts," although it was influenced by "what was happening in the U.S. and other western nations" (Mikanagi, 211). While most feminist agenda concerns are shared across the globe, national factors do produce differential approaches to them.

This study was undertaken with two primary goals in mind: to provide the first comprehensive comparison of policy processes and change in Japan and the United States, particularly in the area of domestic and social policy making; and to remedy the relative lack of attention by scholars to examination of the Japanese women's movement and gender policy.

A leading book comparing institutions and policy making in the West and Japan examines only environmental policies (Vogel, 1993). Other related scholarly treatments focus primarily on aspects of policy change in either Japan or the United States, such as policy toward the elderly or childcare, but do not really compare the systems and outcomes in both countries (Campbell, 1992; Goodman, 2000).[1]

In addition, few studies of comparative politics consider comparing women's movements or policies (Beckwith, 2000, 457). Analysis of comparative women's movements and impact is "marginalized" both in comparative politics and social movement scholarship (ibid.). This neglect is particularly significant with regard to Japanese feminism, on its own terms and in comparison with other national movements. There have been no book-length discussions of the impact of the feminist movement on Japanese policy published in English. Nor, in fact, have Japanese scholars devoted much serious attention to the topic: "Japanese literature on women, politics and policy making lacks a focused study of the role that political institutions play as causes for gender bias in policy making, or as reflections of gender inequality in society" (Mikanagi, 2001, 211). One reason for Japanese gender studies' neglect of political institutions is "simply because there are so few female Japanese political scientists" (ibid.). In addition, Japanese feminism originated in the radical sector of the movement and consequently de-emphasized the role of the state and political institutions as worthy subjects for investigation (ibid.).

The policy-related efforts and achievements of American feminists since the 1960s in a variety of areas have been subject to far more intensive analysis than their Japanese counterparts. Hence, although the framework employed in this study is comparative, in order to fill the gaps in knowledge related to Japan the approach employed, and the presentation, lean toward greater in-depth analysis of gender and policy in Japan.

Numerous scholars have called for more studies of gendered political change in advanced industrial societies in order to assess policy access and influence, and the nature of the state's response (Siim; Mazur, 2002; Stetson and Mazur; and O'Connor, Orloff and Shaver, among others). To date, most comparative studies have dealt with intra-European or United States-European comparisons and neglected the important insights that may be revealed by studying a non-western industrialized nation. The U.S.–Japan comparative analysis reveals distinctive patterns in each that may go unnoticed when studying states sharing a common historical background (Gottfried and Reese, 2003).

Most observers believe that Japanese women are at least "a half step behind" their Western and American counterparts. There is no question that the Japanese political system has been slow, indeed extremely reluctant, to recognize women's interest intermediation, efforts to affect policy and desire to increase representation. However, while many westerners assume that the United States is automatically ahead of Japan, particularly on some issues related to women, the comparison provides some surprises. For example, abortion policy in Japan has been remarkably free of the confrontation and division related to moral and religious differences that characterize the American system. With regard to policies that help to support working women, such as childcare and parental leave, the Japanese system appears more advanced than that in the United States. Because the Japanese system has been so closed to women's demands, comparative analysis will help to assess how trends toward transnational feminism, or political globalization, affect women in that nation in particular, mediated by national approaches to gender-related policy making (ibid.). The view expressed at the end of the 1980s that in Japan "large groups of women have not made great strides through the political process" may no longer be as valid in the present period. The post-millennium era has seen the realization of a "pluralist society and democratic polity," now with a salient public ideology legitimizing greater equality and pluralism (Ishida and Krauss, 1989, 333). The comparative framework employed in this book may help to determine whether the accomplishments of American feminists are the results of the more open and permeable political system and the continuing, effective mobilization of women's groups, which have continued to gain momentum.

Feminist students of gender and public policy call for in-depth comparative analysis of women's "agency," examining the significance of women's increased participation and representation. They urge evaluations of the "political meaning of gender in different political cultures": making a difference in the political arena "through advocacy, activities, participation and power" (ibid., 5). Feminist scholars call for a cross-national examination of the relationship between the state and feminism as well as for the examination of case studies with a view to cross-national comparisons and assessments of causal factors in cross-national variation utilizing common frames of analysis (Stetson and Mazur, 1995, 11; Mazur, 2001, 316). Gendered political opportunities may be structured by a variety of factors including increased group access, changing political alignments and a decline in the state's willingness or ability to suppress dissent (Beckwith, 2000, 447). As is true for other movements, women's movements seek to take advantage of political changes which may prove advantageous and adapt accordingly. There has been increased attention as well to the idea of "gendering" political opportunities for women's movements: conditions under which states are likely to "invite women's rebellion" or turn to women's movements for political support (ibid., 454).

The benefits of building a body of expanded knowledge, developing new indicators and honing recommendations for women's movements are substantial. These efforts help to assess the efficacy of the women's movement in each nation and the response of the state to the feminist agenda (ibid., 457). Under what conditions can feminist movements influence policy making in conjunction with the election and appointment of feminist representatives, lobbying efforts and reshaping of the political discourse (Gottfried and Reese, 2003)?

Comparing Policies and Politics: The Politics of Insularity v. Externality

The case studies examined here reveal that gender-related policy in Japan developed in part through what I deem "externality," and in the United States such policy came about through what I label as "insularity." Japanese feminists, admittedly in a position of greater weakness politically, have utilized the phenomenon of "political globalization" to strengthen their cause within Japan, hence externality. (See Bishop, 2002.) In the United States, once a significant global forerunner in enacting gender equity policy, the view that national policies are sufficient, without recourse to international prescriptions, prevails. This has resulted in insularity, or policy isolationism—suggesting that the United States can act *upon* other nations, but is resistant to influence *from* them.

Among the central points for comparison related to gender policy making in both nations are the presence of a "rights" discourse, the role of international gender norms and global feminism, issues of cultural "uniqueness" and the significance of increased political representation by women in conjunction with feminist mobilization. The assertion of rights by women has been better accepted in the U.S., expanding on a tradition emanating from the African American civil rights movement. However, as Eric Feldman convincingly argues, there is a different (and highly contested) but still significant role for rights assertion in Japan (Feldman, 2000). Ellis Krauss and Ishida Takeshi contend as well that the idea of "rights"—equal rights for women and other marginalized and oppressed groups—has gained currency in a Japanese culture that previously stressed only political obligation (1989, 328). This book shares the perspective "that the use of rights as symbols and resources, in both litigation and debates over public policy, makes them an important element of change in Japanese law and society" (Feldman, 2000, 42).

Emerging international norms of gender equity and transnational feminist mobilization have been used by Japanese women's groups as an additional resource for their rights-based claims, creating a unique form of *kansetsu gaiatsu* (indirect external pressure)[2] in an era of greater internationalization (*kokusaika*) with which to embarrass and challenge a reluctant Japanese government. While initially regarding the United States as the major frame of reference with regard to gender-related policy, Japanese women now look more to transnational actors such as the European Union (EU) and the United Nations (UN). By continuing to monitor policy and by accusing the government of falling short in international arenas such as the UN and others, Japanese feminists hold their government accountable for failure to comply properly with commitments Japan has made, as well as press their government to make new commitments. There have been similar, related precedents signaling the emergence of domestic rights groups empowered by their new awareness of international equity norms. Other groups have pressured the Japanese government to ratify international conventions and then to conform to the new obligations created (e.g., the Rights of the Child in the early 1990s; see Goodman, 2000, 157). The Japanese case suggests that the acceptance of even weak international norms may have an impact on gender policy adoption. However, the incorporation of international norms may represent purely symbolic adaptation that produces little actual policy change.

The United States, in many ways a "standard bearer" in the twentieth century's struggle for gender equity and an initiator of important policies for women ranging from equal opportunity to violence against women, has remained aloof from the strictures of international treaties, in the interests of national sovereignty. This analysis contends that the United States suffers from a "policy deficit" with regard to policies dealing with working women as a result of its failure to ratify international treaties such as the Convention on Elimination of Discrimination against Women (CEDAW; also known as the Women's Convention or as Women's International Bill of Rights) and to defer to other emerging international norms of gender equity.[3] As a result, the United States seems to have fallen behind other western nations in providing policy supports for working women that have been generated by transnational feminism converging with international institutions. By ignoring important social policies that support working women who must balance home and work responsibilities, U.S. policy making has neglected key dimensions of gender equity policy: "Market solutions have prevailed over social benefits to a greater extent than in most other nations" (Gottfried and Reese, 2003). Given this systemic resistance, the vigorous American feminist movement has been unable to press demands for social policies beyond their present limited stage.

The U.S. political system is reluctant to address issues related to a more generous welfare state and is not moved by any external pressure that would compel it to change. This book will consider the implications of the American failure to enter into multilateral treaties and other political arrangements and suggests this resistance may harm the cause of U.S. women in the long term. (See *Economist*, 29 June 2003, 24–5, for a discussion of American failure to join international institutional developments.) Unlike Japan, a non-western relative newcomer to international norms, the United States, a proud, self-confident hegemonic state, refuses to be "embarrassed" into signing most international treaties, including those related to emerging norms of gender equity. Some possible explanations: the United States may feel it already leads the world in enacting gender related policy; it is reluctant to relinquish judicial power to international courts; or American feminist advocates, expecting failure, have not aggressively pressed for treaty ratification. In addition, the United States has been reluctant to sign on to treaties because of the unpredictability of international courts and its political hostility toward supranational judicial remedies.

This study rejects the argument of Japanese cultural uniqueness, which emphasizes consensus, dependency and hierarchy as the key factors in explaining

Japanese politics and policy. Instead, I support the contention that "the institutional framework of government... decisively [shapes] the character of political competition in Japan," rather than cultural factors (Ramseyer and Rosenbluth, 1993, 4). The perspective employed here supports the notion that "scholarship on Japan is frequently... isolated and uninformed by general theoretical constructs and comparative research," perhaps perceived as too "exotic" for useful comparisons to western contexts (Haley, 1991, 4). The notion of a unique Japanese "culture" is not entirely minimized in the pages that follow; certainly the entrenched norms and values invoked by Japanese society have reinforced traditional and separate sex roles and have created major obstacles for Japanese women in the economic and political spheres. However, institutions structure the political environment to their own advantage (Ramseyer and Rosenbluth, 1993, 3). The concept of "cultural essentialism" through "traditionalism" is a way of manipulating and recombining cultural patterns, symbols and motifs to legitimate contemporary social realities through a patina of "venerable historicity." It is a common Japanese device for responding to and managing social change (Bestor, 1988, 2–10; McVeigh, 1998, 17). In this regard, "culture" is invoked to rationalize efforts to limit change-oriented policy, for example, by discouraging opportunities for litigation and emphasizing the value of consensus (Pharr, 1990; Upham, 1987).

In some ways, the case for "political exceptionalism" may be best made for the United States with its weak parties, presidential system and divided government, rather than Japan. (See Gunther and Mughan, 1993, 278; Wilson, 1998, 45.) Japan's policy-making structure, involving bureaucratic and one-party dominance as well as factional parliamentary politics, appears closer to some Latin American and European nations than does the United States. And cultural norms, in terms of values and ideology related to individualism and limited state intervention, are employed politically in the United States as well, in order to limit social expenditures and expansive social policy.

This book will demonstrate similarities and differences in the processes, approaches and outcomes in each nation and examine the kinds of policies that feminists have been most successful in advocating in each nation, as well as those that have been less successful in gaining realization. In the United States, as already suggested, the latter include policies that support working women, including childcare, paid parental leave, maternity policies and the like. In Japan, they include policies that challenge traditional patriarchal values, including the strengthening of women's position in the workforce and Civil Code reform that permits married women to retain their surnames. In both nations, policies that treat women as a "dependent" category, for example, groups who may be "treated with pity and with patronizing tools" such as aid to victims of domestic violence, might expect a more favorable hearing (Schneider and Ingram, 1993). In contrast, under some circumstances, "pro-choice" (pro-legalized abortion) groups and groups seeking to end employment discrimination in the United States and Japan may be seen as "contenders": powerful, undeserving and greedy (ibid.).

It is likely that elected and appointed feminist representatives and advocacy groups have affected the gendering of the political process in each country. Have policies toward women changed since more women have entered the political arena and gained increased legislative representation? Even when women's numbers in legislative bodies are relatively small (i.e., they do not comprise a "critical mass" of 15 to 20 percent or more), they may have an impact in reorienting policy agendas. The Congressional Caucus for Women's Issues in the United States has been an effective force for advocacy of policy reform on issues such as violence against women. Despite their relatively low but steadily increasing numbers, women in Congress have raised awareness of gender related problems, developed agendas with solutions to those problems, and persuaded male colleagues to support those agendas (Dodson, 1998). Gender differences may gain even greater significance as women approach a "critical mass" and their numbers expand; research demonstrates that women in Congress have had a unique influence on the congressional policymaking process, particularly in the area of women's issues (Swers, 2001, 175). Congresswomen use their committee positions to advocate for the incorporation of women's interests into their committee agendas and they express a commitment to represent women's interests in their legislative activities (ibid.).

In Japan, cross-party groups of women in the Diet (the elected Japanese parliament) have played an important strategic role as well in developing policy on several issues in recent years. This study will assess the significance of what appears to be a new trend in Japan: for suprapartisan or cross-party groups of women legislators to initiate policy—these are known as *giin rippo*, or Diet members' bills. Women's sponsorship has been evident in varying degrees on such issues as child pornography and child prostitution, anti-stalking policy, and most recently domestic violence legislation (DV), to be discussed in chapter three. (See Pekkanen, 2000.)

The presence of a mobilized women's movement does not always provide the catalyst for favorable gender-related policy. Title VII of the Civil Rights Act of 1964 in the United States and the Eugenic Protection Law in Japan, both of which contain elements of policy favorable to women, were passed in the absence of significant representation by women. As will be suggested below, such policies can have an important impact in helping to develop new participation and mobilization and engender new policy initiatives as a result.

Factors that affect political outcomes include the ability of the women's advocacy community to have access to the policy-making process as well as tactical options available to advocates, such as litigation, protest and elite receptivity. In addition to examining the reasons for passage of particular policies, this book also assesses how policies are enforced after passage in each country.

Herein are tested the following hypotheses related to the comparison of Japanese and American women's impact on policy making:

1. An increase in the descriptive or numerical representation of women or women office holders aids in bringing women's policy agenda issues to public attention, i.e., increases substantive representation of women's issues (see, e.g., Siim, 2000).
2. In both countries, there is evidence that cross-party agenda setting and policy sponsorship by women legislators help to create favorable conditions for the passage of legislation.

3. In both nations, varying with the policy issue, "advocacy coalitions," comprised of advocates and women in public office, join forces. These groups share perceptions, ideology and issue priorities, as well as a repertory for collective action (Lembruch, 2001, 41).[4]

4. For Japanese feminists, emerging international standards of gender equity have proven to be significant resources with which to pressure a reluctant government. The politics of externality prevails rather than the politics of insularity that characterizes U.S. gender policy.

Comparing Political Structures

A comparison of the "political opportunity structures" of Japan and the United States is essential in order to provide a context for the analysis of women's policy in each nation. Opportunity structures include alignments, ideology and institutional arrangements that affect prospects for policy making (see Gelb, 1989, 2). Institutions do matter, although their effects are contingent, mediated by other institutional and noninstitutional factors (Weaver and Rockman, 1993b, 446).

The U.S. political system is characterized by a relatively fragmented federal government and a reluctant welfare state rooted in beliefs in individualism and limited state intervention in many social policy areas. The existence of federalism and a weak and centrist two-party system create opportunities for political intervention by interest groups and social movements, which has often served groups seeking change-oriented policy well. The process has been described as pluralist, with multiple access points for well-organized groups to the political system (Casamayou, 2001, 158; Weaver and Rockman, 1993a, 26). Although it may be difficult for policy challengers to overcome numerous veto points in order to gain adoption of their preferred policies, once mobilization is under way, jurisdictional boundaries may allow many governmental actors to become involved (True, Jones and Baumgartner, 1993, 248). What has been characterized as the complex mix of governments in the federal system has often aided in the process of policy diffusion, with some issues moving from the state and local to national levels and vice versa (Baumgartner and Jones, 1993, 233). But federalism also may create problems of jurisdiction, competition and implementation, as well as conflict management (Vogel, 1993, 269; Lijphart, Rogowski and Weaver, 1993, 334). The U.S. political system may be characterized as quite decentralized and ideologically conservative in addressing policy change (*Economist*, 29 June 2002, 24). The U.S. and Japan appear to share a relatively small and "weak" state (weaker and smaller in Japan) and what has sometimes been characterized as a "residual social policy model," in which the state has a role in social provision only when the market and family fail (O'Connor, Orloff and Shaver, 43). In the United States, the powerful federal court system and often forceful chief executive—the President—have on occasion supported the goals of feminist advocates through appointments and policies on such issues as affirmative action and violence against women. However, since 1980 and the election of President Reagan, the Republican party has moved further right, and the two major parties have espoused increasingly opposite views on a number of key issues, including abortion and women's rights. The ensuing partisan polarization has affected appointments to key positions in the courts and bureaucracy and feminists' ability to impact the policymaking process. Women's groups have often been placed on the defensive during periods of Republican rule (Bashevkin, 1998).

The Japanese political system is characterized by the dominance of the Liberal Democratic Party (LDP) in the post-war period; the LDP is comprised of factions that emphasize patronage and short-term gains. These factions have been reinforced by multi-member electoral districts and a decentralized system of campaign finance. (Weaver and Rockman, 1993a, 24). The LDP policy "tribes" (*zoku*) have close financial and other arrangements with powerful interest groups. These include business and agriculture but usually not labor, whose access to state policy making has been far more limited, leading some to characterize Japan's system as "corporatism without labor" (ibid., 1993a, 28; Pempel, 1998). The LDP has shared power with coalition partners since its loss of a majority after the 1989 and 1993 elections, though it remains the dominant force in government. There is controversy among scholars over the nature and structure of the Japanese political system; in this analysis, a "new institutionalist approach" (Orren and Skowronek, 1989) stressing structure and process will emphasize the role of bureaucrats, the consultative policy making process (*shingikai*) that operates in advance of the parliamentary process, elected politicians in the Japanese parliament, the Diet; and the shifting role of interest groups and movements. It is commonly believed that the Japanese system has a weak chief executive, with the prime ministership frequently changing hands, thus relying on decision making by nonelected elites or bureaucrats to a greater degree than in the United States. Nonetheless, the need to appease political coalitions may have impelled some prime ministers in recent years to take a more proactive role on gender and other policies.

Some contend (Weaver and Rockman, 1993a, 24) that nonelected decision makers dominate the Japanese system. Bureaucrats rely on informal compromise rather than statutory rulings subject to judicial review; they avoid accountability, control access to the policy process if they can and discourage the formation of interest groups that may disrupt the political process (Schwartz, 1998, 44). Single-party dominant parliamentary systems often circulate the same elites in different positions, with the cast of players staying largely the same, and are highly resistant to short-term political pressures. (See Weaver and Rockman, 1993b, 449.) However, the lack of clear Diet involvement per se does not negate the importance of the involvement of the LDP in policy making, meaning that bureaucrats must exert influence through active engagement with politics, not apart from it (Schwartz, 23). Some have argued in recent years that the bureaucracy has become more defensive and the prime minister occasionally more "presidential" (Murumatsu, 1993, 63; Allinson, 1993, 8). A "regime shift" may have occurred in Japan by the late 1990s, although there is strong evidence as well for the continuation of "conservative governance" (e.g., a reconstituted LDP, continued power for the bureaucracy over the economy and society); "reregulation" rather than deregulation (Pempel, 1998, 137). In Japan, the judicial system, based on merit appointments, plays a far less proactive role than in the United States, with litigation tacitly discouraged.

In Japan, as elsewhere, it is often important to distinguish between *honne* (reality) and *tatemae* (outward appearance), to examine the symbolic as well as the real significance of policy change (Pempel, 1998, 137). Japanese policy is often vague and unenforceable, frustrating those who look to law and legislation in order to create change.

In this analysis, challenges to structured, "patterned pluralism" as an emerging model for Japanese policy making will be considered through the lens of women's political initiatives and gains (Murumatsu, 1993, 50–71). The term "patterned pluralism" refers to a greater role for interest groups and political parties, together with the decline of bureaucratic control. Consideration will be given to evidence that there are now greater opportunities for women's "voices" to be heard (Broadbent, 1998, 8, 344 and Richardson, 1997).[5] The political opportunity structure may have become more hospitable to social movements and pressure from change-oriented groups as disorganized or unorganized Japanese groups "have increased their ability to realize political ends" (Allinson, 1993, 6). It has been suggested that "in comparison with the United States, Japan has much lower norms of non-electoral participation and governmental accountability . . . encompassing public interest" (Vogel, 1993, 240).[6] One factor in evaluating the relevance of emerging pluralism in Japan is consideration of the relative absence of transparency and accountability, particularly among bureaucratic managers, which has historically limited the access and role of change oriented groups. In this system, those seen as *soto*—outsiders—are often treated unfairly, and their appeals for legitimacy based on universal principles through litigation or new rules are discouraged (Pharr, 1990, 216–31; Broadbent, 1998).

This volume will also contribute to the dialogue on civil society in the United States and Japan, inquiring as to the strength and impact of women's nongovernmental organizations (NGOs) as the basic foundation for a democratic polity. In this regard, it will augment the work of earlier scholars, writing with particular reference to Japan, who sought to evaluate the strength of Japanese democracy and popular participation. (See Ishida and Krauss, 1989.)

In the 1990s, the Japanese welfare state remained extremely "lean," at the bottom of OECD (Organization for Economic Co-operation and Development) nations and much lower than the U.S. (11.9 percent of GNP was expended on domestic spending compared to 21.3 percent for the United States) (Pempel, 151). In the case of Japan's "small" state, scholar Margaret McKean argues that the state follows when it can, coordinates when it must, and deregulates when it cannot coordinate (McKean, 1993, 103). How accurate is this analysis in the area of gender policy?

The Plan of the Book

After the introduction provides a framework for comparative gender policy analysis, the first chapter provides a detailed comparison of feminist movement mobilization in Japan and the United States. The rest of this volume is devoted to policy analysis. Chapter 2 deals with equal employment policy, a policy arena in which the United States has been a world pioneer and Japan a reluctant adherent. In chapter 3, domestic violence policy is analyzed, contrasting the path-breaking Violence against Women Act (VAWA) of 1994 with the more recent and modest Japanese DV law passed in 2001. Chapter 4 analyzes policies toward reproductive rights in both nations, discussing both abortion and contraception, with a focus on the conflict abortion policy has occasioned in American politics since the 1970s. The disjunction between accessible abortion policy in Japan in the post-war period and more restrictive policies toward contraception, in particular the birth control pill, is assessed as well. As a means of rounding out the comparative policy analysis, chapter 6 compares "family friendly" policy, policies that seek to harmonize work and family life for women, in both nations. It also discusses the Basic Law for a Gender Equal Society in Japan, which has no analogue in the United States. Its inclusion is intended to provide an assessment of the significance of this vague and apparently limited policy, both on its own terms and with regard to its impact on other gender-related policies including family policy. In the conclusion, a final assessment of the interface between women's policy advocacy and state incorporation of feminist demands in both countries is provided.

Studying Policy Change

Another goal of this book is to examine the relevance of theories of policy change and their applicability to comparative analysis. In large measure, these are viewed as "frameworks" rather than full-fledged theoretical precepts. The case studies will be utilized to demonstrate the applicability of U.S.–based theories to the Japanese as well as American policy processes. The assumption to be tested is that different issues in each country will be brought to the political table in different ways so that one explanatory theory may not be sufficient: "each policy change . . . [is] . . . a story in itself" (Campbell, 1992, 5).

What factors contribute to the placement of issues on the policy agenda and aid the process of agenda setting for policy change? Among the frameworks to be examined will be the "advocacy coalition" theory of Paul Sabatier and Hank C. Jenkins-Smith. This perspective, which is similar to analysis of "policy networks" and "subsystems" as well as "policy communities," stresses the significance of relationships between different policy participants who share similar policy beliefs; state and societal policy actors who group around a given policy (Mazur, 2001, 36; Sabatier, 1999, 9). They may include activists, elected policy makers and "femocrats" or bureaucratic appointees who hold feminist values (Mazur, 2001, 23). Advocacy coalitions or policy subsystems, however differently structured in each nation, may play a key role in bringing new political values based in new conceptualizations and policies to the policy agenda. (Sabatier and Jenkins-Smith, 1999, 137). Sometimes such coalitions do not emanate from the national government level but rather from sub-national (state and local) or supranational—or the international—levels of politics (ibid., 119). Domestic violence policy may be a product of the role of sub-national systems in both nations, while transnational inputs from the international arena seem relevant in Japan in examining policy change for many of the issues discussed in this book.

Policy or issue networks involving women in and outside of government have been strengthened over the past three decades: advocates have been effective both in pressing new legislation and monitoring policy thereafter in order to assure that change is secured. To some extent American women advocates have benefited from a more open and pluralistic system in which they have been able to press their claims on the political system, as well as following the model developed by civil rights groups who preceded them. The "multiple venues" of politics in the United States, enhanced by federalism, can provide numerous opportunities for change unavailable in unitary political systems (Baumgartner and Jones, 1993, 240). But the case of reproductive rights, involving conflict between two highly mobilized opposing groups also utilizing pluralistic opportunities, suggests a different and more negative scenario. In Japan, the last decade has seen an increase in women's activism, relying primarily on resources created by *kansetsu gaiatsu* (indirect external pressure), a wish to meet emerging standards of gender equality in order to maintain "place" among first-rung nations, and a newly resonant discourse on "rights." This process appears to have accelerated in recent years, perhaps partially due to increased numbers of women holding public office.

Other theories of change include John Kingdon's "policy streams," a theory that stresses the convergence of problems, policies and politics (1994). These streams normally operate independently of one another, except for those occasions when a "window of opportunity" opens, often under the influence of a "policy entrepreneur" or "sponsor," to permit policy change. "Policy windows" may have opened with regard to gender policy innovation in Japan and the United States, each building on prior change incrementally to some extent (Zahariadis, 1999, 86).

The concept of policy cycles or "secular trends," "continuous high energy activity during...clearly bounded eras..." (ibid., 244–45), seems to be worth examining as well, particularly in the context of contemporary Japanese policy making related to women. More enduring "policy cycles" may challenge the idea that policy change simply represents discrete "blips" or changes on a screen, as Baumgartner and Jones have argued in their theory of "punctuated equilibrium" (1993, 1–25; Baumgartner, 1999, 111). Cyclical theory combines the idea of expanding political opportunities, new and old organizational resources and organization of collective action around "master frames" or new ideas such as rights (McAdam, Tarrow and Tilly, 66). Issue expansion and diffusion has occurred on all of the policy issues under consideration in each nation, sometimes leading to a reevaluation of gender policy in general. In the case of Japan in particular, transnational feminism, operationalized through international meetings and treaties, may play the crucial role of "triggering" or "focusing" events that act as catalysts for policy change (Baumgartner and Jones, 1993, 10).

Policy entrepreneurs or "sponsors" may be active in promoting legislative change, as they apparently have been with regard to domestic violence on both sides of the Pacific. The term "sponsor" suggests a variety of possible actors—with skills, resources and drive—which may include bureaucratic agencies as well as individuals, such as legislators, prime ministers or even the media. (See Campbell, 1992, 47, 377, for similar suggestions.) Their role is to rally public opinion (through surveys which build evidence of support in Japan, a common technique) or bring other participants into new coalitions (ibid.). Policy enactment itself tends to create new possibilities for additional action in an issue area, even if (as was the case with Title VII of the Civil Rights Act of 1964 in the United States and the Eugenic Protection Law in Japan) the initial law-making process had little to do with advancing women's concerns. As policies are redefined and expanded, they may find new and receptive institutional venues (Baumgartner and Jones, 1993, 239). "Institutions are the legacies of agenda access"; together with new policies, they structure further participation and mobilization (ibid., 238–9). Programs that are put into place generate new interests themselves, as affected constituencies, service providers and others enter into established relationships with government officials, creating a "feedback effect" (Baumgartner, 2002, 11).

Policy communities pursue "insider" or "outsider" strategies, or a combination of both. Movement organizations gain access to decision makers, educate the public and mobilize their constituents. They may bring more radical structurally transformative ideas "inside" the policy agenda, permitting feminists to gain greater legitimacy, enter the public discourse and alter policies. (See Spalter Roth and Scheiber 1995, 107, for a discussion of the "insider/outsider" concept.) In the case of equal employment, while activists in both nations were clearly outside the system, in the United States they were able to gain access to subsequent policy development over time, in part through insider/outsider strategies, and have sometimes had significant impact on policy outcomes. Social movements endowed with staff and resources to monitor and affect public policy and its implementation are key elements in changing a policy agenda (Baumgartner, 2002, 18). In Japan, such connections between mobilized groups and elected and agency officials may be in a more nascent stage; "outsiders" have participated in prodding the system to adopt policy change although they have not always had a decisive role. In both countries, to varying degrees, domestic violence policy has involved "outsider" mobilization. In other instances, agenda change follows more of an "insider" strategy; as in the case of bureaucratic changes regarding abortion access in Japan and the adoption of the Law on Gender Equal Society. What role does what Campbell calls "cognitive" policy development play—a connection between national goals and efforts to solve policy problems with solutions (1992, 356)? In Japan, "cognitive" policy development may include reproductive policies first to address overpopulation and then a declining birth rate, as well as family-friendly and some employment-related policies as well, intended to affect the birth rate as well as to meet new labor supply needs.

Although the "stages heuristic" model (which posits the significance of viewing policy in orderly stages, from initiation to formulation and adoption to implementation, evaluation and feedback) may be too deterministic, it still provides a foundation for comprehending other theories of policy change. Some political scientists stress the limits of policy change. The incrementalism of

Lindblom—and the idea of "path dependency" or a historicized approach to policy building on earlier, more entrenched, initiatives—may provide guidance for policy analysis (Streeck, 2001, 9; Reed and Thies, 2001, 380–403; Gottfried and Reese, 2003).

In a period of rapid policy change with regard to gender in Japan, what factors explain the shift and how enduring are they likely to be? While employment-related policy change and civil code reform that involves retention of women's premarital surnames remain controversial and challenging to policy elites, other policies seem to have gained greater systemic support.

In both nations, women legislators appear to feel a special obligation to represent the views of their women constituents (Carroll, 2002) and are increasingly able to advocate on behalf of these interests. "The validating presence of other women legislators is an important precondition for women to act on parts of their agendas that differ from those of their male colleagues (Schroedel and Mazumdar, 1998, 209). Growing institutional influence has aided in bringing these agendas to the fore.

Office Holding by Women in Japan and the United States

American women's movements have been characterized by a considerable national presence since the emergence of "second wave" feminism in the 1970s. Women in the United States have increased their representation in elective and appointive office (particularly the latter) but lag behind other (Nordic) nations with regard to national legislative position. They are also represented politically through interest groups and social movements, in addition to legislative politics. In both countries, women's national representation has increased: first in Japan, during the "Madonna boom" in 1989, and in the United States, in 1992, "The Year of the Woman." These were monikers given by the media to depict the increase of elected female representatives in each nation; in each instance they reflected unusual political circumstances. In Japan, under the leadership of Doi Takako, the female head of the Japanese Socialist Party, there was an effort to capitalize on women's "outsider" status and to clean up "dirty politics" symbolized by corruption and the prime minister's adulterous affair (Ogai, 2001, 209). In addition, opposing a newly imposed consumption tax, a record number of female candidates (twenty-two) won seats in the Upper House in 1989. In the United States in 1991, anger over the all-male Senate Judiciary Committee hearing allegations of sexual harassment from attorney Anita Hill (opposing Supreme Court nominee Clarence Thomas) led to a huge increase in female candidacies with many being victorious. Aided by congressional retirements, the number of female senators tripled (from 2 to 6) and members of Congress almost doubled (from 28 to 47). (Flammang, 1997, 232). Since 1992, the Democratic Party has nominated twice as many women to the House as have the Republicans (Fox, 2000, 231).

At present, women comprise some 13.6 percent of national U.S. elective offices and a far higher number of bureaucratic and judicial appointees. Former

President Clinton appointed women to a record-breaking 27 percent of top executive positions and 41 percent of all non-career executive jobs in his first administration as well as an unprecedented 20 percent of judicial appointments (Darcy, Welch and Clark, 1995; Costello and Stone, 2002, 301). Many of these appointments were made with recommendations of feminist groups. Initial appointments by President George W. Bush suggest a similar, though reduced, pattern of female appointees. Less responsive to pressure from feminist groups, Bush has appointed women to 26 percent of administrative appointments as opposed to 37 percent under Clinton's administration (Tessier, 2002, 1). In the United States, women have far higher legislative representation at the state and local level (about 22.6 percent at the state level and presently six governorships), in contrast to Japanese women, whose local representation, particularly in rural areas, is much lower (Center for American Women in Politics, 2003).

A Congressional Caucus for Women's Issues, established in 1977 by fifteen of the eighteen women then in Congress, represented bipartisan advocacy for women and helped to focus attention on women's issues. Although the caucus was officially abolished in 1994, it continues to operate informally to make policy. As women gain positions of seniority after decades in which they lacked it, they are able to have more of a voice on key committees and in other corridors of power (Norton, 2002). In 1991, Patty Murray (D-WA) and Nita Lowey (D-NY) became the first women to head the Senate and House campaign committees, respectively. Nancy Pelosi (D-CA) became the first woman Minority Whip in the House in 2001 and Minority Leader in 2002, the highest-ranking positions held by a woman in Congress to date. Only two women have ever chaired full Senate committees; the first was Hattie Wyatt Caraway (D-AK) in the 1930s; the second was Nancy Kassebaum (R-IL) who chaired the Committee on Labor and Human Resources from 1995 to 1997. Only ten women have ever chaired full House committees (Foerstel, 1999). There continues to be incremental improvement in women's access to national legislative office, as well as a record of policy impact and some evolution in leadership roles.

Since 1992, women have held more critical institutional positions of special interest to women, which have now permitted them to shape legislative outcomes to a greater extent, including membership on the all-important conference committees (ibid.). Congressional women have often appeared to be subject to fewer constraints and cross-pressures in advancing feminist legislation than in some parliamentary systems, in the absence of strong party directives and pressures to conform.

Women legislators appear to have had an impact on a number of policies, including women's health, abortion and welfare. In 1992, after the dramatic increase in representation cited above, for example, the twenty-four women newly elected to Congress held a press conference to announce their commitment to passage of four policy priorities: fully funded Head Start for all eligible children, family and medical leave legislation, the Freedom of Choice Act and policy addressing workplace sexual harassment (Schroedel and Mazumnar, 1998, 207). Unity on some women-related issues may have abated since, as increasingly right-wing Republican women elected to the House have opposed abortion and espoused policies championed by the religious right. Ninety-seven percent of female Democratic representatives and 75 percent of Republican women voted for the Freedom of Access (to Abortion) Clinic Entrances Act (FACE) ; the male totals were 80 percent and 19 percent respectively (McGlen and O'Connor, 91). Sixty-two percent of Congresswomen were sponsors of the 1992 Freedom of Choice Act compared to 27 percent of Congressmen (ibid.). When they have served on key committees, including the Labor Health and Human Services subcommittee of Appropriations, Ways and Means, Education and Labor committees, women have been able to affect policy change related to women's health and reproductive issues (ibid., 141). Their positions on key committees helped, for example, in the passage of FACE to end violence related to abortion clinic access in the 103rd Congress (discussed in chapter 4) (ibid., 375). As women in Congress have gained seniority and experience, their ability to work on legislation important to women has increased (Norton, 2002). In the reproductive policy area, in the 104th and 105th Congress, from 1995 to 1998, Democrats Rosa Di Lauro (D-CT), Nita Lowey and Eleanor Holmes Norton (D-DC) offered 65 percent of all reproductive rights amendments. Women legislators from both parties offered amendments to seek to moderate the impact of the welfare reform legislation of 1996.

In Japan, women now comprise 7.5 percent of the House of Representatives, the more powerful Lower House, and 15.4 percent of the Upper House (a decrease from the high point to date of over 17 percent in 2000). Women's electoral opportunities have been enhanced by proportional representation for a portion of seats in the Upper House; efforts by the LDP to balance single member and proportional seats to its own advantage resulted in the slight decline in 2001–2002. A new trend toward cross-partisan legislative sponsorship by Diet women will be discussed below, primarily in chapter 3 (on domestic violence) and in the conclusion. Less formal than the U.S. Congressional Caucus for Women's Issues, the trend toward interparty cooperation is nonetheless an important indication of the significance of increased female representation.

As of June 2003, four women are governors and fourteen women are mayors of cities, towns and villages. About twenty percent of advisory council members are women. One contrast with the United States is the low representation of women in local assemblies, although there has been a steady increase of women elected at the local and national levels of government (Gender Equality Bureau, 2001). Fifty-six percent of village assemblies and three prefectural assemblies had no female representation at all.

In addition to increased political representation, American feminists have a significant lobbying presence in Washington, D.C. and in the corridors of state government. They also utilize a variety of strategies to impact policy, from litigation to sophisticated campaign finance Political Action Committees (PACs). However, they have been disadvantaged by the increased polarization of American politics due to the growing conservatism of the Republican Party, which in a break with historic tradition after 1980, now is firmly opposed to abortion rights and other feminist goals. Feminist activists have been active in political party organizing, primarily in the Democratic Party in recent years, given the hostility of Republicans, for reasons outlined above. The weakness of American parties, coupled with the transparency of the political system, creates strong incentives for feminist organizations to engage in the electoral arena and to influence policy outcomes through election of supportive legislators (Young, 2000, 185).

In Japan, previous tendencies toward fragmentation and localism in women's movements may currently be offset by overlap and coordination among feminist groups. This trend, together with the use of international equity standards and increased policy advocacy, sometimes in conjunction with elected representatives across party lines, may suggest new possibilities for Japanese women's role in politics.

This volume will hypothesize that policy-making capabilities and outcomes will vary substantially across policy areas, within the same political system and across systems. (See Weaver and Rockman, 447.) We should then expect to see different participants, stages of policy development, and outcomes among the policies analyzed here both within and between Japan and the United States. The task before us is to explain why such differences occur and how such differences affect policy success. The differences may relate to the open or closed character of the political system, opportunities for feminist participation in policy making and implementation as well as the use and success of particular strategies including litigation and lobbying. Scholars, activists, and politicians may learn from the approaches utilized and the gains and losses experienced by feminists in each nation revealed by the comparative study of gender policy.

Chapter 1

Comparing Women's Movements in Japan and the United States: Trends and Transformations

Introduction

This chapter will compare women's movements in Japan and the United States in the contemporary period, from the 1980s to the new millennium, analyzing the structure of the movements in each country and relations with other organizations, including political parties, and the state. Social movements in general and feminist movements in particular are engaged in changing societal structures and attempts to reallocate their rewards and benefits. Social movements operate within *political opportunity* structures, which may limit their range of possibilities, as well as *collective action frames* including cultural constraints that orient participants and aid them in creating identity. They develop *mobilizing structures*, involving formal movement groups and more informal social networks; and finally *repertoires of contention*, or approaches to political claim making (McAdam, Tarrow and Tilly, 2001, 14–15). How can success in movement mobilization be measured? Success may involve short-term or minor adjustments or more long-term fundamental change. A useful framework for analysis of gains achieved suggests three important dimensions of change: policy change, organizational survival and cultural or discursive change (Ferree and Hess, 2000, 200). In the case of Japan, the role of international feminism in creating a basis for assertion of rights through *kansetsu gaiatsu*, indirect foreign pressure through transnational actors, will be considered as a crucial resource for women's groups as they seek to change and influence Japanese policy making related to gender.[1] In the United States, the feminist movement continues to diversify and expand, developing into what may be called "sustained mobilization" (Gelb and Hart, 1999). In each nation, by the end of the twentieth century women's movements had experienced considerable change and transformation. To what extent have feminist organizations in each nation been able to reframe the policy process from a more gendered perspective?

A Note on Comparing Political Systems and Opportunity Structures

American women's movements are characterized by a considerable national presence—as interest groups and social movements, as well as with increasing representation in policy-making elites such as the bureaucracy and the courts. Women's movements also have numerous strategies available for pressuring the American national government and the states as well in the federal system, from the litigation undertaken by the women's legal specialists to such campaign finance groups as EMILY's List, a Political Action Committee (PAC) founded in 1985 to support pro-choice candidates and others. One question to examine is the extent to which U.S. feminism has become more professionalized and bureaucratized, leaving behind grassroots community activity, and what this means for the future of feminist activism. Another factor to consider is the growing conservatism of the Republican Party. What has been the impact of several decades of right-wing rule and virulent opposition to women's rights and the feminist movement from anti-abortion and anti-feminist groups now politically institutionalized in a major political party? During this same period of growing Republican conservatism, from 1980 to the present, the Democratic Party has become an (sometimes reluctant) ally of organized feminism. The pro-Democratic Party "gender gap," meaning that a disproportionate number of women, as opposed to men, support Democratic Party candidates, has reinforced this tendency (Young, 2000; Freeman, 2000). How has the increased polarization of American politics affected women's political options? The American feminist movement has achieved significant policy goals; is the momentum continuing or slowed?

Until recently, the Japanese system has been perceived as providing little space and opportunity for women's advocacy groups to operate effectively within it. However, there has been evidence of increased representation for women in government as suggested in chapter one; both in the Koizumi led Liberal Democratic Party (LDP) cabinet with four female members out of seventeen in August 2003 and increased representation in the Diet. In particular, in the less powerful Upper House, Sangiin, women comprised over 17 percent in 2000, decreased to just over fifteen percent in 2001,[2] and they held 7.8 percent of the seats in the Lower House, the House of Representatives (Ichikawa Fusae, 1 September 2001, 2). Women's electability has been enhanced in the House of Councilors because a portion of seats are chosen through proportional representation. The introduction of a mixed member majoritarian (MMM) system in 1994 replacing the single nontransferable vote, proved to be more favorable to women's electoral opportunities (Weaver, 2002, 121). Women leaders have headed the Japanese Socialist Party and two other opposition parties—the New Sakigake[3] (somewhat to the left of the LDP) and New Conservative parties—in recent years as well. What role do women, sometimes operating in a nonpartisan fashion in the Diet, play in advocating for women's policies? Who really controls Japanese policy making and what impact can feminists hope to have?

There is considerable evidence for the persistence of traditional roles and values in Japanese society, which constrain women's opportunities for choice in occupation and political advocacy. Women's lives are traditionally defined by childcare, housework and care of the elderly (Liddle and Nakajima, 2000, 312). Work outside the home and political participation have until recently been dominated by the gendered division of labor, in which men dominate economic life. A widespread view has been that "female emancipation is only partial . . . most Japanese females are not interested in politics. They make no effort through the ballot box to change Japan's male oriented society, nor are they much concerned by the discrimination (illegal) which they suffer at work" (ibid., 320). However, others suggest that it was the women's vote in part that ended the dominance of the LDP in Japanese politics, in 1989. The "Madonna boom" was a term popularized by Doi Takako's emergence in politics in 1987 as the first head of the Japanese Socialist party; the idea disseminated by the Social Democratic Party was that nonunion-based women candidates would bring a new and purer element into politics (Iwamoto, 2001, 225–6).[4] The "boom" peaked in 1989 when a combination of circumstances and increased women's candidacies led to an unprecedented number of women elected to office (ibid.). Joanna Liddle and Sachiko Nakajima contend that, at least for middle-class women, the process of legitimating women's rights is underway, with women creating new feminine identities, diversifying and transforming (ibid., 324). Which view represents present-day political reality for women in Japan? What are the implications for movement activism in the present era? To what extent have Japanese women's movements, utilizing rights-based claims that draw support from emerging international standards of gender equity, been effective in entering the policy process?

Until recently, women's movements in Japan have been characterized by decentralization, fragmentation and a single issue focus (e.g., abortion, equal employment, etc.), partially as a result of the lack of receptivity in the national political system (Yayoi interview in Buckley, 1997, 14). Ueno Chizuko, a leading Japanese feminist, has preferred to think of this more positively as "diversification" (ibid., 275).[5] In the present era, there are some indications of increased networking and greater feminist presence at the national level, which will be explored.

This chapter will emphasize several different aspects and dimensions of Japanese women's movements: feminist groups advocating for policy change, working women's groups who have mobilized against discriminatory practices and housewives who often are active in local politics. What policies have been successfully addressed by women activists and why have some others, such as equal employment opportunity and civil-code reform permitting retention of women's premarital surnames, been more difficult to achieve?

Feminist Movements in the United States: The Myth of Post-Feminism

"The story of the women's movement in the U.S. is one of transformation, expansion and diversification" (Wolfe and Tucker, 1995, 436). In a similar vein, it has been suggested that "the women's movement [is] among the most successful in American social history, effecting—among other things—a profound shift in political culture" (Tarrow, 1994, 184). Sidney Tarrow points to a rich and varied repertoire, a network structure embedded in society as well as institutions and electoral advantage, in explaining what he perceives as extraordinary success. U.S. feminist movements have been characterized by increasingly well-established and professional networks of national organizations, coordinating a national network of groups concerned with mainstream reform as well as goals of liberal equality (Gelb and Hart, 1999, 151). The movement has also contained vigorous, though less visible, grassroots movements including "women's liberation groups" that initiated alternative publications, and has created hundreds of self-help and direct action groups. Among these were rape crisis centers, shelters for battered women, legal collectives and health projects that challenged male-dominated medical practice and provided primary care (Ferree and Hess, 2000, 102–8). Today, given the need for resources to survive, many rely on external support from government and/or foundations, and increasingly combine service delivery and advocacy roles. Increasingly, early dichotomies between radical and reformist feminists, "older" and "younger" branches and collectivist and grassroots versus more national and bureaucratic forms have been left behind (ibid., 2000, 5) as the movements have become defined by coexistence between groups with sometimes differing goals and strategies that are all united in their commitment to feminism (Disney and Gelb, 2000). Networks and coalition building have been emphasized across ideological and issue lines. At their most effective, as a result, feminists have been able to adapt with flexibility to changing conditions, pursuing varying goals and strategies. Among the issues on which formerly dissimilar groups have united are the support of efforts to end violence against women, the defense of abortion rights, the expansion of women's rights and resistance to efforts to restrict the feminist agenda (Ferree and Hess, 2000, 184).

Scholars writing about the women's movement in the United States since the second wave of feminism in the 1960s have emphasized the significance, political impact and proliferation of feminist groups through at least the 1980s (Costain, 1992; Ferree and Hess, 2000; Gelb, 1989, 1996; Minkoff, 1992). Writing in 1988, Mayer Zald wrote that "of all the social movements on the current scene... because of its specialized organizations and constituencies... the feminist movement appears to have the best chance for high levels of mobilization and activity" (Zald, 1988, 19). Addressing issues of movement change but emphasizing that change does not imply decline, Nancy Whittier suggests that in the 1980s individual feminists searched for new ways to be activists in the face of mounting opposition, financial difficulty and their own aging. She found that women's movement has not only survived but begun grow again in important ways in the 1990s with new generational membership, renewed community presence and also increased access to the political system (1995, 3). However, others, writing from a different perspective, view the current role of American feminism more skeptically. Anne Costain has contended that the "peak period" for feminist organization has passed, political opportunities have narrowed, consciousness has diminished and organizations are preoccupied with just maintaining themselves (1992, 141). From an even more critical perspective, Martha Burk and Heidi Hartmann argued that in a period of twenty years, women's organizations have lost "political power and came to be perceived as irrelevant (or even hostile) to the common woman" (19). Barbara Nelson and Katherine Carver contend that "women's organizing"—especially feminist organizing—had many voices but few vehicles for translating demand into sustained action, in the absence of strong party commitment to its goals (1994, 739). This analysis, critical of feminist organizing, may be more a reflection of the limitations of the American political system related to policy adoption and implementation, than a true indictment of feminists. According to a listing of national lobbyists in the nation's capitol, although the feminist presence decreased in the early 1990s it began to grow again later in the decade. From 1982 to 1997, the number of such lobbying groups increased from 75 to 140 (Washington Representatives, 1995). Feminist representation in Washington politics has also been on the rise, now to about 13.6 percent of Congress (Center for American Women in Politics, 2003) and higher numbers in judicial and bureaucratic appointments, partially attributable to feminist organizing and campaign efforts. As many as forty two PACs advocate for women's interests in supporting increased electoral representation (Brenner, 1996, 69). In contrast to Japan, elected women have much higher representation at U.S. state and local levels, rather than nationally, as will be discussed below. Jennifer Leigh Disney and Joyce Gelb (2000, 40) document the continued vitality of feminist movements in the United States, partially attributable to "institutionalization" as national level lobbyists. At the same time, the range of groups described by Gelb and Marian Palley in 1996 continues to flourish and grow—ranging from single issue, staff-run groups to policy think tanks, including the Center for Women Policy Studies and Institute for Women's Policy Research, litigation groups such as the National Organization for Women Legal Defense and Education Fund (NOW LDEF) and the National Women's Law Center (NWLC), large scale membership groups such as the National Organization for Women (NOW) and National Women's Political Caucus (NWPC), as well as pro-choice groups such as the National Abortion Reproductive Rights Action League. These have been joined in recent years by the successful campaign related groups/PACs that support women candidates such as EMILY's List, Republican "Wish List" and Voters for Choice (Gelb and Palley, 1996, xvi–xx). "Submovements" have proliferated under the larger feminist umbrella, focusing on pro-choice, anti-rape, domestic violence, and women's health issues, and specialized concerns such as women in the military (Ferree and Hess, 2000, 183). Women's coalitions also continue to grow and develop, with tendencies toward fragmentation offset in part by such groups as the 100-member Council of Presidents, which coordinates activity among Washington-based women's rights groups. Other, more issue-focused coalitions reflecting specialization include the Coalition on Women and Job Training, Women's Health Action Mobilization and National Network to End Domestic Violence (Disney and Gelb, 2000, 53). In addition, feminist activists are active in political party organizing, primarily in the Democratic Party in recent years, given the hostility of Republicans and partisan polarization. There are strong connections between the women's movement and Democratic Party politics (Freeman, 2000; Young, 2000). The Congressional Caucus for Women's Issues, though "defunded" by Congress after 1994, continues to be a force for developing women's agendas in government. It aids in developing alliances between women inside government and movement activists outside. Over forty percent of all elected women belong to women's groups, according to one study, meaning that large numbers of female representatives have been inculcated with feminist values related to agenda priorities (Darcy, Welch and Clark, 1995, 37). Such linkages are firmly developed and expanding in the United States: elected women received more support from NOW and the NWPC in 2001 (about one quarter in each case) than in earlier years. And, a larger percentage of women demonstrate strong connections to feminist groups—thirty four percent are members of the NWPC and twenty six percent members of NOW—far higher percentages than at the time of an earlier, 1988 survey (Center for Women Policy Studies, 2001, 5–6). There has been some concern among feminist scholars and activists about "deradicalization" and the decline of grassroots feminism, as well as the transformation of advocacy into service provision groups. Clearly the demands of funding and survival dictate new organizational choices for many groups, and may result in structural accommodations that depart from early feminist models. However, Claire Reinelt (1995) and others have presented data to show that, while some feminist organizations have become more professionalized and bureaucratized, they have brought their values into state institutions as well, negotiating between movement ideology and institutional constraints. Locally based feminist activism continues to flourish and now includes women's community-based foundations supporting local women's groups' activities (Gelb and Hart, 1999, 154). Many groups have been able to combine advocacy and service in creative ways: groups such as Women Work! undertake both advocacy to change policy and also provide technical assistance and training for out of work women (Disney and Gelb, 2000, 70–1). Others provide health care, battered women shelters and services, rape counseling and legal services. Change is clearly in evidence, as an aging movement cannot remain static. Far from being dead, the feminist movement has become more diffuse, organizing everywhere, often unobtrusively (Katzenstein, 1995; Wolfe and Tucker, 1998).

New venues for feminist activism include the military, professional organizations, corporations and the like, mobilizing through other institutions to diffuse movement ideology and practice. Women's organizing includes the Coalition of Labor Union Women (CLUW) in the labor movement and the National Council of Neighborhood Women, energized by the language of empowerment (Gelb and Hart, 2000, 155). It is true that membership in feminist organizations tends to rise in periods of perceived crisis (e.g., anti-abortion court rulings, election of conservative presidents) and that many movement groups rely on "conscience constituencies" that provide resources, rather than active membership. Another cautionary note regarding American feminism relates to the significance of anti-feminist political backlash, with "New Right" presidents occupying the White House for twelve years at the end of the twentieth century, and again after 2000. Right wingers also dominated both houses of Congress for six years during the during the 1990's and again after 2002. As Sylvia Bashevkin has suggested, the virulence of the anti feminist movement institutionalized in the Republican Party after 1980 has no counterpart, probably anywhere in the democratic world (1998, 70). This has resulted in the need for defensive adaptation and an emphasis on survival rather than growth in terms of new policy initiatives.

A major concern for American feminism in the future is how to move from this type of reactive stance to a more proactive vision of the future (Ferree and Hess, 2000, 182). One response has been to turn to state politics where, among the fifty states, some have been more receptive to policy change than others. In the case of domestic violence, during the 1980s and early 1990s, all of the fifty states passed far-reaching legislation to implement new policy. In another policy area, however, only fifteen states currently provide Medicaid-funded abortions to poor women. Nonetheless, even under "New Right" preeminence in politics, feminists have been able to achieve some positive change such as the Family and Medical Leave Act (FMLA) of 1993, discussed in chapter six, and the Violence against Women Act (VAWA) of 1994 to be discussed in chapter four, which provides support for shelters, as well as for reformed police, prosecutorial and judicial processes to deal with victims of violence.

Fueled in part by women's studies programs and campus-based activism, younger women have organized as well. Groups such as Women's Action Coalition (WAC), Women's Health Action Mobilization (WHAM) and Third Wave are comprised of twenty- and thirty-year-olds, who are not afraid to use dramatic confrontational tactics, including protest and demonstrations protesting treatment of rape victims and harassment as abortion clinics, to dramatize their grievances regarding the system's inadequacies (Ferree and Hess, 2000, 192). "Take Back the Night" marches to protest sexual assault against women are now regularly held on numerous college campuses.

The myth of a "post-feminist" generation is challenged by what is clearly a mature but ever dynamic U.S. movement.

Policy change and continued activism. Movement success may be measured in several ways: through the continuation of movement mobilization, cultural change or through change in collective consciousness and discursive politics that may create resources for further mobilization and change, as well as levels of policy impact. Measured by the latter, in the policy sphere, a major contribution of American feminist movements has been to reform local, state and federal policy through legislative and judicial decisions. Feminist advocates have achieved recognition as major participants in decision making at all levels of government.

Initial success for American feminists arose as a consequence of implementation of Title VII of the 1964 Civil Rights Act, which though not the result of feminist advocacy, created major educational and occupational advances via continued litigation and lobbying. The Civil Rights Act was enhanced by Title IX of the Education Amendments of 1972, which barred sex discrimination in education and led to gains in professional careers for women as well as to vast increases of women in competitive sports. American feminists have relied extensively on the judicial process as a way of insuring compliance and implementation. Class action suits have used a group approach to gain individual benefits. Civil rights law, stressing individual rights for redress of grievances, has been a unique approach employed by American feminists, although increasingly their counterparts in Europe and Japan have utilized the model of litigation as well. See the next chapter for a further discussion of the impact of equal employment policy.

Feminists have also achieved significant success in policy areas related to violence against women, including domestic violence, at the state and national levels. In part through the efforts of the National Coalition Against Domestic Violence (NCADV) and Task Force and the Violence Against Women Task Force organized in 1976, under the leadership of the NOW LDEF, feminists were successful in passing the VAWA, part of an omnibus crime bill in 1994—four years after it was initially proposed (Daniels, 1997). Each of the fifty states and most municipalities also have passed laws on domestic violence, in many instances mandating state intervention and providing for mandatory arrest of suspects (Schneider, 2000, 186–7). At each level of government, support is provided for training of police and judicial personnel, increased attention given to protection for abused women and some additional support provided for shelters. The national legislation has provided unprecedented monetary support for this struggle. See chapter four for further discussion of these policy initiatives. Feminists have also been active in supporting efforts to end sexual harassment and other "women specific" policies. In the case of rape, both increased public consciousness and new options for victims—including rape crisis centers and self-help strategies—have been the legacy of the anti-rape movement (Bevaqua, 2000, 194). In addition, rape shield laws, the need for corroboration of a complainant's story and abandonment of the "rule of resistance" have been enacted in most state and local areas (Schneider, 2000, 189).

Women's policy advocacy in the United States has been less effective in at least two other areas. With regard to abortion and reproductive freedom of choice, the context has been highly contentious and politicized since the 1973 Supreme Court decision in *Roe v. Wade.* (See chapter four.) The impact of a hostile environment continues to have a profound effect on limiting progress and furthering the feminist agenda. Angered by the *Roe v. Wade* decision, anti-choice groups coalesced against the decision and seized the initiative, mobilizing effectively in the fifty states, at the national legislative level and in the courts. They have organized campaign-related strategies and have probably gained their greatest legitimacy through their alliance with the Republican Party beginning in 1980. They have mobilized protests at abortion clinics and conducted violent, even murderous attacks against abortion providers. The scope of conflict between the contending forces has been fierce. The pro-choice movement survives through such organizations as the National Abortion Rights Action League (NARAL), Pro-Choice America and Planned Parenthood, as significant membership and protest figures suggest, but it has come at a cost. Much energy has been consumed in trying to defend reproductive rights; a necessary battle, but one that sometimes has limited the movement's ability to be more proactive on other important issues.

Another area that has proven more difficult for American feminists has been that of combining work and family life/motherhood. Increasingly, European and other democratic nations have moved to provide working women with new concepts of "social citizenship" to augment political gains. These include special benefits, such as paid parental leave, state-supported childcare and the like. In the United States, however, a reluctant welfare state, which does not adhere to international equity standards, has not moved in this direction. Feminists did press for the adoption of the gender neutral FMLA, which provides that either men or women can take leave in order to care for children or elderly parents, signed into law by former President Clinton in 1993 after two vetoes by his predecessor, President George Bush. But it is unpaid. Other supports for working women have been ignored by the individualistic model employed by U.S. policy makers, who view "equality" solely in terms of access to work opportunities. So-called family-friendly policy is discussed in chapter six. A regressive policy, the Personal Responsibility and Work Opportunity Reconciliation Law, passed in 1996, creates punitive circumstances for poor women dependent on public support for their livelihood. It ends the federal entitlement to support aid to families with dependent children, provides for time-limited aid to poor mothers and their children and includes forced work requirements in order for aid to be available. This type of legislation has no parallel in other democratic nations. The result has been to exacerbate the differences between poor women and others; feminist activism has been unable to effectively address such fundamental barriers to equality for working women and poor women (Ferree and Hess, 2000, 207).

On the brighter side, other measures of policy success are to be found in organizational survival as well as cultural change, perhaps the most enduring forms of transformation (Staggenborg, 1991). In addition to the coalitions and networks discussed earlier and the staying power they represent at the national and state level, the ability of the movement to mass hundreds of thousands in support of reproductive access is indicative of significant vigor. Women's policy networks are an enduring part of the American political landscape. The ongoing presence of a group such as the NCADV, with fifty two state organizations and hundred of local groups and networks that still adhere to a (modified) collectivist "consensus" structure attests to this. It continually renegotiates issues of diversity and rejects financial support "with strings attached"—a testament to the continued commitment of movement organizations to their original goals, as well as adapting and surviving (Disney and Gelb, 2000, 73; Ferree and Hess, 2000, 209).

Regarding cultural and consciousness change, opinion surveys find high levels of support for the feminist movement and its goals; 77 percent of women favored "most efforts to strengthen and change women's status in society" in 1990—up from 40 percent in 1970. Eighty-two percent of women felt that the movement was still "improving the lives of women" and 53 percent that the movement accurately "reflects the views of most women" (Ferree and Hess, 2000, 88). The cultural transformation that has occurred, though incomplete, is "truly remarkable" (ibid., 216). Diffusion of much of the message of movement has occurred through "unobstrusive mobilization" within other institutions, including religious, professional and union organizations (Katzenstein, 1998, 186).

Japanese Women's Movements

Introduction. The Japanese women's movement had its origins before the turn of the twentieth century, with women seeking the suffrage, equality, socialist feminist goals and reproductive freedom, most importantly through the upper-class feminist Bluestockings and their journal *Seito* (Liddle and Nakajima, 2000, 14–15). After a period of repression before and during the Second World War, women's activism, though not necessarily feminist, resumed. Japanese women's movements, while active in many places in Japanese society, have tended to be localized, single-issue oriented and fragmented. Sandra Buckley views this as a strength of Japanese feminism, as this structure has aided in resisting government cooptation (1994, 158; see also Allinson, 1993, who sees it as a disadvantage, 37). Nonetheless, there are several large-scale membership groups which represent women's interests, including Chifuren (the League of Women's Regional Organizations) and Shufuren, the Housewives Association. Both have been involved in campaigns for consumer issues, often with considerable impact (Mackie, 1995, 267–8).[6] Their actions should not be isolated from the history of Japanese feminism; they work in conjunction with local groups and help to check industry and government power, in a political context in which effective opposition is often difficult to achieve (Buckley, 1994, 160). Local women often organized as housewives in their communities and pressed for consumer and environmental rights, for peace, and against nuclear power (Matsui, 1995; McKean, 1993). Some have characterized this tendency as "housewife feminism" (Matsui, 1995, 443–4; Liddle and Nakajima, 2000, 10–11). As in the United States, where women were active in civil rights, anti-war and environmental groups, women joined social movements related to other issues initially and women's movements often emanated from larger movements espousing goals involving social change.

As a result of the U.S. occupation after World War II, women gained the vote and right to run for office, and also new constitutional guarantees. Among them was Article 14, which promised equality in the family, education, employment, education and political representation (Liddle and Nakajima, 2000, 152). Civil Code reform removed the legal basis for women's subordination in the family, including the right to own family property, and equality in marriage and divorce. Because many of the guarantees proved to have only symbolic as opposed to real meaning, a "second wave" of feminism emerged in the early 1970s among women who had been active in student peace movements. Beginning in 1960, university women, together with union, student and leftist organizations, campaigned against U.S. bases in Japan, the Japan–U.S. Security Treaty, the revival of Japanese militarism and the Vietnam War (Mackie, 1995). As in the United States, and in other cause-related movements everywhere, women had been treated as sex objects and rebelled, organizing around such issues as rape and sexuality and defense of abortion rights (Mackie, 1995). As the twentieth century drew to a close, several other strands of feminism emerged in Japan, including efforts to increase women's numbers in politics, especially in terms of national representation, and also rights for working women. A source of major impact on Japanese women in general and feminists in particular has been international feminism. Beginning with the 1975 International Women's Year (IWY), which encouraged women to go out of the home and "join society" (Ling and Matsuno, 1992, 57), and through the end of the twentieth century when Japanese women comprised the largest delegation at the Fourth World Women's Conference in Beijing (together with the United States and China) as well at the Beijing + Five meeting in New York in 2000, activists have participated in international arenas, seeking to pressure a reluctant Japanese government into making policy changes. *Kansetsu gaiatsu*, the impact of international human and women's rights movements on Japanese policy and mobilization, cannot be overestimated (Fujieda and Fujimura-Fanselow, 1995, 158). Some of the disparate elements of feminism and women's movements have joined forces on issues such as abortion and labor force discrimination, creating a potentially greater force on the political scene, as will be demonstrated in the chapters on equal employment, domestic violence, and reproductive rights in particular. The activism of Japanese women challenges the accuracy of the contention that "while unemployed married women's grassroots groups are widespread, women's movements influenced by the second wave of Western feminism—which focused on securing equal rights and opportunities for women—have been less prevalent in Japan than in North America and Europe" (Eto, 2001, 243). Women in the Japanese feminist movement have developed some unique agenda issues in comparison with some of their U.S. counterparts. These include efforts to challenge offensive male Japanese sexual practices including sex tourism and pornography.

Feminism in Japan. The present feminist movement in Japan originated in the 1970s. As in the United States and other nations, it was motivated in part by disillusionment with the New Left and its sexist practices and post-war socialist feminism (Tanaka, 1995, 345). Feminist movements were motivated by goals of "sexual liberation" and against dominant Japanese cultural values; *Uman ribu* (women's lib) groups attempted to establish collectives and protested for their rights, for example, against the proposed revision of the Eugenic Protection law, which provided easy access to abortion for women. Women's groups organized effective coalitions in the 1970s and 1980s to oppose abortion restrictions. An enduring women's activist group was the International Women's Year Liaison Group (Kokusai Fujinnen Renrakukai) founded in 1975 at the initiative of Diet members Ichikawa Fusae and Tanaka Sumiko, other Diet members and feminists. Rather than making consciousness raising key, they worked on issues such as education, employment and representation (ibid., 348). This "umbrella" organization came to comprise 48 and then 51 groups. (See Mackie, 1995, 271.) It was this group that framed a set of demands in the 1980's for legislative change in the nationality law, permitting foreign children to gain citizenship through mothers and fathers (previously only through fathers), as well as for passage of an equal employment law. The group pressed the Japanese government to sign the Convention on Elimination of Discrimination Against Women (CEDAW), partially by threatening international embarrassment if ratification did not occur (Buckley, 1994, 163, 324).[7]

Among the groups that have endured in the Japanese women's activist movement is Agora. Founded in the 1960s by Saito Chiyo, Agora helped to create childcare facilities and provide opportunities for women to use their skills in the public sphere. Agora ultimately became a resource and training center for women, like many others in Japan, with centers evolving to meet the needs of local women

(Mackie, 1995, 269). It began to publish a journal, *Agora*, in 1972, now the longest running feminist journal in Japan (Buckley, 1994, 157). The multi-issue Women's Action Group attacks widespread pornography in Japan, protesting "Rush Hour as Porno Hour" (referring to men reading *manga*, or pornographic comics) and male-biased school curricula.

Sexual harassment was first raised as a public issue through a widely publicized "poll of 10,000" conducted by suburban feminists in 1989 as well as efforts to publicize the term *sekuhara* (sexual harassment) a word imported from the United States and initially regarded with media derision. Public attention to sexual harassment was enhanced as well by a Tokyo Bar Association hotline established in 1989 that received numerous calls.[8] A lawsuit in the Shizuoka district court, found for the plaintiff that a male supervisor had engaged in "wrongful conduct" in December 1990. A second successful law suit against a publishing company in Fukuoka, Japan in 1992 found that there was a "hostile working environment" and awarded the plaintiff $15,000 in damages (Hada, 1995, 266). Attention to harassment has advanced through litigation and the 1997 amendments to the Equal Employment Law, discussed below. Women labor lawyers have been potent advocates on behalf of these and other feminist issues.

As in other nations, domestic violence has been the subject of feminist organizing as well. (See chapter four for a discussion of the adoption of a national law in 2001.) In the 1970s, the Kakekomidera Shelter for women founded under the leadership of Bunka Kai, a group formed in the advent of the International Women's Year, 1975, and the Ribu Shinjyuku Center in Tokyo also provided emergency shelter and a hotline, with government support (Kaino, 2001, chapter 5). In that year, feminists founded a domestic violence action and research group. Among the NGO-operated shelters in Japan (now close to about 40 in all) are Help in Emergency and of Love and Peace (HELP) and an Asian Women's shelter founded by the Japanese Christian Temperance Union in 1986 (Buckley, 1997, 328). As in the United States and elsewhere, problems with bureaucratic management under government control ensued and the initial organizing groups dissolved by the mid-1980s. A "second" DV movement was established in 1992 under the auspices of the DV Survey Research Group. The first, and so far the only, rape crisis center operated by feminists was opened in 1983 in Tokyo (Hada, 1995, 265).

Japanese women are particularly active in movements to end male sexual exploitation and also to retain Japan's nonmilitary role. Matsui Yayori, leading journalist for the newspaper *Asahi Shinbun* and later founder of the Asia-Japan Women's Resource Center in 1995, helped to found the Asian Women's Association in the 1970s, to campaign against sex tourism and exploitation of women. This group also advocated for the revision of the nationality law, to remove sexist conditions for citizenship through fathers only (Buckley, 1994, 133). The Asian Women's Association has called attention to Japan's role in creating a forced group of "comfort women" or military prostitutes to service their armed forces. Although thus far they have not been able to press the Japanese government to provide compensation to the victims, such movements link Japanese women with their sisters in other Asian nations.

As in other nations, women in Japan have also been active in larger political movements, particularly those emphasizing peace and anti-military activism, protesting the AMPO (the Japanese name for the Japan–United States security treaty) in 1960 through the Women's Congress and other groups (Buckley, 1994, 169). Many Japanese women are firmly opposed to military intervention of any kind (Morely, 1999, 136). Since 1962, the Japan Women's Council has advocated a pro-peace position and has opposed any change in Article 9 of the Constitution, which would reactivate the military. Since World War II, The Women's Democratic Club, founded by Sata Ineko, has opposed nuclear weapons and power and promoted conservation of environmental resources (ibid., 140). Its publication, the *Women's Democratic Journal*, has 60,000 subscribers.

A unique form of communication for Japanese women is through *minikomi* (newsletters) and other written commentaries (many handwritten, mimeographed and relating individual stories and local news) (Buckley, 1997, 253) that provide alternatives to the bland mainstream national press. These informal networks of women's communication have allowed the many and diverse feminist groups throughout the country to stay in close contact while remaining autonomous from one another. These publications numbered about 40,000 by the end of the 1960s (Buckley, 1994, 158). While *minikomi* still link women activists, they have been augmented by the Internet which provides additional means of networking and communication though many continue to lack home and institutional access (ibid., 14). The use of the Internet to create networks for women includes Women On Line Media and many other sites that collect information related to women (Morely, 1999, 187).

In the 1990s, Japanese feminism was characterized by some as localized, fragmented and loosely organized (Liddle and Nakajima). Unlike in the United States, there have been no nationally based umbrella organizations in Japan. However, there are may be some countertendencies in the more recent period, as discussed in the other chapters of this book. In fact, a number of efforts, such as those to block change in abortion laws, gain free access to contraception and amend equal employment policy, have demonstrated that seemingly disparate groups can be linked in a coherent way to affect Japanese institutions and policies (Mackie, 1995, 278). Reproductive rights groups also fought successfully to rename the Eugenic Protection Law and at present seek to decriminalize abortion.

Newer groups such as Beijing Joint Accountability Committee (known popularly as Peking JAC), seeking to lobby government officials on such issues as domestic violence, have sought to develop a national presence, with the establishment of a center in Tokyo, though JAC is primarily a coalition of loosely structured groups with a "nonconcrete" structure located in regional caucuses (Nagai interview). It has employed a flatter, less hierarchical and more spontaneous structure than some of its older counterparts and favors more direct contacts with policy makers (Osawa interview). Some observers note the continuity of feminism, similar to the U.S. Third Wave, as young women continue to gather around the Asian Women's Association and Association for Japanese Women's Studies (Hashimoto, e-mail, 23 January 2002).

Political participation and representation. Some analysts have argued for the notion of women's continued exclusion from politics in Japan, well into the twentieth century: "women do not participate as men do because women were legally prevented from participating for so long, and because a privatizing ideology that discourages the involvement of women outside the home still lingers" (Pharr, 1981). The approach utilized here emphasizes a more transitional view, understanding obstacles but also noting the considerable distance women in public life have come.

In addition to their growing numbers in national elective and appointive positions, women comprise 6.2 percent of prefectural and local assemblies (International Labor Organization, 2001) with the highest percentages represented in urban areas, such as Tokyo (19.8 percent). Many rural town and village assemblies have no female representation at all. After Doi Takako's assumption of the leadership of the Japan Socialist Party, which she has chaired, with some interruptions, since 1989, the number of women candidates increased (many campaigning as "ordinary housewives") and record numbers of women came out in large numbers to hear her speak (Morely, 1999, 136). There has also been an increase in women mayors and governors, though their numbers are still small: there are now four female governors, including Domoto Akiko, a former Diet member and environmental and reproductive rights advocate, who campaigned in Chiba prefecture as an independent and defeated major party candidates in an upset victory.

The presence of Doi Takako, a former law professor, helped to galvanize women's greater interest in running for office. Doi helped to campaign for women candidates, in conjunction with networks of local feminists, even for nonmembers of the Socialist Party (Ling and Matsuno, 1992, 62). In recent years, WIN WIN, modeled after the U.S.-based EMILY's List, has provided support to women candidates, including Domoto in her campaign for the governorship of Chiba prefecture. The group charges membership dues equivalent to $100 to a present membership of 300, and attempts to support candidates who have political experience and gender equality agendas (Akamatsu interview). In 1989, women voted to oust Prime Minister Uno Sosuke, due to a sex scandal and also as a protest against the newly adopted consumption tax, as well as to elect twenty female candidates to the Upper House, the largest number up to that time since 1946 (Buckley, 1997, 334). In 1989 Prime Minister Kaifu Toshiki appointed two women to his cabinet, in order to appeal to women voters who had demonstrated clout at the ballot box, and designated Moriyama Mayumi (a career bureaucrat with a history of commitment to gender equality issues) as cabinet secretary. As of the beginning of the twenty-first century, women's interests have been institutionalized to some extent in government, first in the Ministry of Labor Women's Bureau and now in the Council and Bureau for Gender Equality in the prime minister's office (viewed as the creation of "national machinery" in accordance with UN directives). The newly merged Ministry for Labor, Health and Welfare has a Bureau for Equal Employment, Children and Families. Women now comprise an unprecedented four members of the seventeen-person cabinet, occupying nontraditional roles, as has become more common in the U.S. as well (down from five in the first Koizumi cabinet); Moriyama is now Justice Minister. The controversial Foreign Minister Tanaka Makiko was dismissed on January 30, 2002, but replaced by another woman, Kawaguchi Yoriko, leaving a total of four female cabinet members as of 2003.

As in the United States, several efforts have been undertaken to augment women's electoral representation through training and other means in Japan. The Alliance of Feminist Representatives (AFER) was founded by Mitsui Mariko, a former Socialist party representative in the Tokyo Metropolitan Assembly, who sought to increase women's numbers in government to 30 percent (Morely, 1999, 139). It has 250 members: 190 representing local assembly members, 20 national representatives, 40 activists (some former elected officials) and 10 male members, and meets annually to exchange information and ideas (Kubo, e-mail, 25 January 2002). Other efforts to increase women's elective representation include those of the Ichikawa Fusae Memorial Association (FIMA), named for the feminist activist and late Diet member. This group conducts *seiji* (political) schools to train women for political office and other workshops, and supports efforts by other women's groups through small grants.

While the short-lived New Japan Party in the 1990s offered a one year political school to interested women, few Japanese parties have made concerted efforts to appear to women voters by increasing women's representation through quotas or mandatory nominations, despite the volatility of the electoral system during the past decade. Rather they have advocated more moderate approaches: some, including the Socialist Party, have sought increased women's nominations and candidacies through numerical targets. The opposition Democratic Party, Minshuto, makes some special attempts to train and recruit women to run for office, through stipends and expanded calls for candidates. WIN WIN, mentioned above, is making efforts to raise money for female candidates. In the Diet, female representatives have sometimes functioned as a non-partisan bloc to support policies favorable to women's interests.

While a "gender gap" between male and female voters is not as visible in Japan as in the United States, as suggested above, in 1989 Japanese women angered by sex scandals, corruption and an increased consumption tax, helped to engineer a stunning defeat to the dominant LDP and increase the number of elected women representatives (Ling and Matsuno, 1992, 58). Recent evidence suggests that Japanese women do display distinct partisan and issue differences and also vote in higher numbers than men (Patterson and Nishikawa, 2002). The post-millennium era may represent a break with what has been described as the "fragmented sporadic quality of their political behavior, [which] served in the end to minimize the importance of women's issues on the national political agenda and to preserve the formal arena of politics as a nearly male bastion" (Allinson, 1993, 37).

Housewife activists. For many women, conditions for men in the workplace are so difficult due to its onerously long work day and work week as well as being subject to employers' strictures, that they have no wish to enter. Their marginal workplace status is reinforced by tax laws, which provide an incentive to work part time, tax-free (if they earn below 1.2 million yen per year). These factors, together with the persistence of traditional roles, have meant that many women in Japan, particularly those who are highly educated, resist full time employment and see their main role as being mothers and wives—although for some, more private roles have been transformed into "housewife activism" (Fujimura-Fanselow, 1995, xxviii). Middle-class, well-educated, relatively high-economic status, and urban/suburban, local female activists "have excelled at organization and lobbying" (Ueno, in Buckley, 1997, 275). Women have been the core of voluntarism, in consumer, anti-nuclear, peace and anti-pollution, as well as cooperative, movements, beginning with their leadership of the anti-Minamata disease campaign during the 1960s which opposed toxic water pollution (Morely, 1999, 122; Ling and Matsuno, 1992, 56). Women are also active in self-study groups and use local women's centers and adult education centers for political activity. In addition to the National Women's Education Center (NWEC), founded in the 1970s by Ministry of Education, Science and Culture (Morely, 1999, 123), which provides meeting space and resources, women's centers (josei senta) are government supported in prefectures, cities and local communities. Among the most active have been the Yokahama and Kita Kyushu Women's forums and the Dawn Center in Osaka, Wings/Kyoto and the Tokyo Women's Plaza. (The latter was defunded by the Tokyo metropolitan government in 2002.) All provide meeting space, workshops and training of various kinds, and provide resource materials—the "space" needed by groups to create co-optable networks through which to form a collective identity (Fujieda and Fujimura-Fanselow, 1995, 176; Ferree and Hess, 2000, 28). Sandra Buckley points to the support of local and prefectural governments into women's resource and community centers; suggesting that the "politics of these centers has been renegotiated," leading to more radical outcomes than initially intended by the funders (1994, 180).

The vigor of activism is impressive, given the pervasiveness of sex-based stereotypes that continue to prevail in Japan (Morely, 1999, 141). Working and nonworking women participate in local community activities, and as is true elsewhere, women gain citizenship and access to politics in a manner different from men (Le Blanc, 1999, 123). They may represent a new kind of citizen's movement in local Japanese politics, marking the ascendancy of NGOs or third-sector groups.

Initially, many women became active in "soap movements"—purchasing cooperatives. They embraced activism decrying the evil effects of synthetic products and pollution and lobbied for waste disposal, clean water and other environmental and consumer issues. They founded recycling clubs and mounted campaigns to get signatures to protest the side effects of Japan's rapid industrialization. Among the numerous cooperative groups in any given locale, Seikatsu (or daily life) Clubs founded in 1965, are one of the most interesting. Its members are comprised almost entirely of women, have a huge membership in Kanagawa, Tokyo and elsewhere (47,000 in Kanagawa alone in 1997) and a total membership nationally of almost 250,000 (Peng, 1999, 114; Morely, 1999, 129; Sato, 1999, 367). In addition to supervision and management of welfare activities, and the development of economic enterprises through workers' collectives, they have also entered political office through the network part of the movement. While the group has run only women candidates for office, it has been orchestrated and headed by left-wing men, with a two term limit (representatives are viewed as accountable *dairinin* (delegates) rather than elected officials (Sasakura, 1995, 383; Peng, 1999, 113). The networks have been surprisingly successful in electing women to local office (Ling and Matsuno, 1992, 60). In the early 1990s, they proved their ability to get voter support, making particular strides in large cities like Yokohama and Kawasaki, as well as Tokyo. By 1995, they had doubled their female representation in office: women were 11 of 18 local Assembly women in Yokohama and 40 of 106 in Kanagawa prefecture (Gelb and Estevez Abe, 1998, 270). As of the end of October, 2001, there were 61 women serving in Tokyo area town and city assemblies: 151 members have been elected all over Japan (out of 3,940 women in all of Japan's local assemblies) (Ogai, e-mail, 15 November 2001) Of the 9.4 percent of women who are local assembly representatives, network members comprise 3.8 percent. (Ogai, e-mail, 1 February 2001). The Seikatsu networks are among the few independent political groups to gain any foothold in local Japanese politics. Although in many ways the women involved fill traditional gender roles, there has been a degree of transformation as well. (See Le Blanc, 1999, 1620.)

Working women's groups. At workplaces in Japan, women's roles have tended to be limited to clerical and low-level jobs. (See the following chapter.) Even in the early 1990s, the traditional function of female tea pouring was in practice in almost all companies, with over 90 percent reporting that only women poured tea! (Morely, 1999, 74).

A little studied phenomenon in Japan, at least in English language publications, has been the emergence of working women's advocacy groups in the late 1990s and into the second millennium. Some of these groups were motivated to mobilize by their attendance at international women's forums such as the Fourth UN Women's Conference in Beijing in 1995. The Equal Employment Opportunity Law (EEOL), passed in 1985, discussed in the next chapter, may have raised expectations and consciousness related to workplace opportunities and led to more activism when these were disappointed. Three types of women's social movement groups have been identified: (1) working women's advocacy groups protesting discriminatory policies by employers, related to unequal pay, failure to promote women and the institutionalization of gender-biased two track employment systems; (2) support groups for plaintiffs in sex discrimination litigation; and (3) women's unions, which represent a new approach seeking resolution of work-related disputes specific to women's workplace issues. While many NGOs in Japan have been small and localized, working women's advocacy may be developing a more national presence with a potentially larger policy impact. One such group, the Equal Treatment Campaign 2000, united scholars, lawyers and political activists, as well as parliamentary members, and sought to advance the rights of part-time and temporary workers. Their struggle is an uphill one in terms of successfully impacting policy. Women's groups advocating for changes in their workplace and other employment-related status are important contributors to the civil society networks that are emerging in Japan, increasingly demanding scholarly and other attention.

Women's unions. Women's unions represent a new development in Japan: combining "new social movements" linked to feminism with labor union organizing and established in opposition to male-dominated, hierarchical, enterprise-based organizations that have been disinterested in supporting women (Kotani, 1999, 4). Such unions represent full- and part-time workers and both represent individual workers and engage in efforts to improve conditions for working women as a whole (Gottfried, 2002, 5–6). There are presently seven women's unions in Japan: three in Osaka, and one each in Niigata, Sendai, Kanagawa, Sapporo and Tokyo—the first was founded in Osaka in 1987 (Kotani, 1).

In the Tokyo area, women wanted to create something different from the largely unsympathetic male-dominated company unions: a women's or Josei Union, which, unlike its male counterparts, recognizes the individual membership of women (Kotani, 1999, 2). The Tokyo Josei Union, established in 1995, has been acting as an intermediary, and essentially representing women, in collective bargaining proceedings. With a volunteer membership of about 250, the group attempts to recruit former complainants to assist others who need help. Volunteers take phone calls, help to consult and provide vigorous *genki* (high energy) power (Kotani interview). Lawyers who specialize in labor cases are affiliated with the group.

From March to September 1999, there were 3,385 calls to the Josei Union (ibid.). However, of all the callers, only one or two will start company-based proceedings. If the caller really wants to press the issue, the union will create a "team," sending an official document to the company on her behalf and indicating that she would like to enter a collective bargaining procedure. If the dispute resolution process does not proceed in a satisfactory way, the union asks the Tokyo Labor Committee for mediation and action. If that process is unsuccessful, they may proceed to legal action, although at present very few have done so (Ito interview).

In all, there have been about 200 complaints processed. They deal with such issues as unwanted dismissal (forced early retirement, "restructuring"), sexual harassment and bullying, as well as overwork. In 63 percent of the cases undertaken, total resolution has been achieved—either through continued employment or financial restitution (Kotani, 1999, 11). In addition to acting as negotiators on behalf of the female complainants, the union has used other tactics such as picketing if companies are recalcitrant (Ito interview). The group also distributes newsletters and other informational resources related to working women.

A second group, the Tokyo Union, established in 1979, organizes temporary and part-time workers who are primarily female in order to attempt to gain new legislation to protect such workers and to notify international organizations such as the International Labour Organization (ILO) of treaty infringements as well as supporting litigants in court (Sakai interview). This group's efforts were galvanized by the epoch-making *Maruko* decision in 1993, which raised the consciousness of female part-time workers. The *Maruko* case, begun in 1993 and finally settled in

1999, found that lower wages for part-time workers were discriminatory. Suggesting that the principle of equal treatment should be taken into account, it recommended that an 80 percent differential between full- and part-time workers would be appropriate (Osawa, 2001, 193). The Tokyo Union now has over 900 members and responds to 2,000 inquiries per year (Gottfried, 2002, 3). Part of the agenda of this grassroots movement is to pressure to amend the 1993 Part Timers Law, which they view as ineffective.

Women fighting corporate discrimination. In what is often a protracted and unsatisfying struggle, women in corporate employment in Japan have utilized pressure within and outside companies to fight endemic discrimination in job classifications, wages and promotion.

Female-based pressure has occurred in numerous leading financial institutions and companies, including the Dai Ichi Kangyo and Daiwa Banks, and Nippon Trust as well as Nomura Securities, Nissan and Hitachi ("EW = EW Tokyo" Circle 1995; Nozaki interview). In Nomura, women have been fighting for nineteen years to get long-overdue promotions, first suing in court in 1993. Their group, Equal Rights in Nomura, represents about 400 members from within and outside the company, from whom dues of 4,000 yen (about 40 dollars) are collected annually (Tanao Setsuko interview).

Other groups active in the struggle for working women include plaintiffs and their supporters. They represent women who have had their own personal experience of discrimination and support the efforts of others to end practices involving discriminatory employment practices; including gender-based two track systems with women in the lower, clerical track; inequitable promotion and salary patterns and indirect discrimination.

Perhaps the most successful of these is the Working Women's International Network (WWIN), with 800 dues-paying members. This group has litigated test cases in the courts, particularly in the Sumitomo cases (in four lawsuits against the Metals, Chemical, Electrical and Life Insurance companies) rejecting unsatisfactory rulings from the bureaucratic process and has both recruited and supported the plaintiffs in these cases. The group seeks to "pack" the courtroom with supporters—Japanese and foreign—and holds rallies and protests when adverse decisions, primarily in Osaka, are handed down. After an unfavorable ruling in 2000, the group mounted a "Human Chain" demonstration with over 200 participants to protest the Osaka District Court decision and set the stage for their appeal. Each case is continually evaluated and other legal and policy developments, nationally and internationally, constantly assessed. WWIN conducts research and gathers data on discriminatory practices in order to publicize the plight of working women. The group has developed good media access and, win or lose in the courts, is usually assured of a hearing and publicity in the press. Is also seeks to change public opinion through the dissemination and sale of booklets and informational pamphlets. WWIN also holds at least four public lectures a year, as well as workshops and solicits contributions from dues-paying members of 2,000 yen per year. The group attempts to negotiate with the Japanese government and seek to bring pressure to bear on it through international testimony at the ILO, Commission on the Status of Women (CSW) at the UN, and CEDAW. WWIN and other efforts such as the Women's Labor Issue Research Group provide examples of new alliances among feminists from different backgrounds including scholars, workers, lawyers and researchers.

Policy impact. The impact of the numerous activities undertaken by elected representatives and women in social movements in Japan has produced some policy change. Access to international feminism and activism has called attention to discriminatory practices in employment and lack of political representation (Morely, 1999, 177). Policy change has tended to rely on "insider/outsider" tactics—appeals to a politics of "externality," invoking new global standards to support domestic activism. (See Norgren, 2001, 77, for a similar point; and Spalter-Roth and Scheiber, 1995.)

Women continue to lobby for more changes in the still weak EEOL, including serious attention to issues of part-time work and indirect discrimination. Women's groups have been active in protecting the right of easy access to abortion, although the right was not gained through women's activism. Twice, in 1973 when right-wing groups sought to tighten the Eugenic Protection Law, and again in 1983, they mounted a broad coalition to defend existing law. They were unable to stop bureaucratic efforts in 1989 to cut back the access to abortion from twenty-four to twenty-two weeks, although protest did occur after this decision (Buckley, 1997, 335). They successfully attained their goal of changing the name of the Eugenic Protection law to the Maternal Protection Law (botai hogo ho) in 1996, and finally gained for legalization of low-dose birth control pills in 1999, after the rapid approval of Viagra (Norgren, 130). Groups representing women's interests gained a larger "voice" in reproductive policy making as the twentieth century drew to a close (ibid., 137).

Women's groups have also lobbied the Japanese government for improved access to childcare facilities and laws to provide for childcare and parental leave, as well as aid to part-time workers (Buckley, 1994, 165; Peng, 2001). Childcare facilities, while inadequate in terms of hours and with large waiting lists for admission, are in the process of expansion. Partially paid parental leave is available, as well as improved maternity benefits.

One of the most interesting trends in Japanese policy making relates to the role of the increased number of female Diet representatives. A cross party group was crucial in the passage of domestic violence law in 2001, long a demand of feminist activists. They have also sponsored other legislation dealing with efforts to end stalking and child pornography and prostitution as well as the Basic Law on Gender Equal Society, passed in 1999. They have pressed for laws to permit women to retain their surnames after marriage, decriminalize abortion and equalization and individualize pensions. Increasingly, women's movements have played a key role in defining and advocating for rights and new policies. To some extent, in both nations, women have succeeded as well in creating enduring organizations, although those in the United States are far more professionalized, nationally as well as locally focused and coalition oriented. There are no Japanese counterparts to U.S. mass membership organizations such as NOW and the NWPC, though groups such as the International Women's Year (IWY) Liaison Group endures as an umbrella organization, now joined by newer advocacy groups such as Peking JAC. The Japanese women's movement appears to have overcome some of the tendencies noted by earlier scholars toward fragmentation and has demonstrated some ability to prod an often reluctant government into making policy related to women. Networks have fostered greater communication and resource sharing by women's groups, although their ability to affect policy change is still far more limited in most instances than is true in the United States.

Another dimension of movement success relates to cultural or discursive change. This includes strengthened identity and solidarity and shifts in public attitudes, among other factors (Giugni, 1999, xxiii). The reframing of women's experience has occurred in both nations. A discourse framed around women's "rights," which originated in the United States and other Western nations as part of "second wave" feminism, has informed most of the activism examined in recent years in Japan. This discourse, stressing appeals to women's rights as human rights, in turn, has utilized *kansetsu gaiatsu*, which has articulated new norms of gender equity and rights. As noted, activists have used these tactics not only to gain the adoption of legislation but also, once adopted, to monitor policy through the agency of international organizations seeking to embarrass the recalcitrant Japanese government into greater compliance with its commitments. The policy chapters that follow will suggest the extent to which new political "space" has been opened as a result, as a major goal has been to try to gain access to government circles which have frequently excluded women's voices. Japanese women have sought to organize where they are located, in their local communities or in the workplace, as well as to lobby for single issues. Activism by working women through their own organizations, is particularly noteworthy, in part because it is not union based and has virtually no counterpart in other nations including the United States. The distance Japanese feminists need to travel in order to influence policy remains a huge obstacle. Only in recent Japanese politics has more attention been paid to feminist issues, although it must be cautioned that there is often a gap between rhetoric and reality, as the controversy over the EEOL to be discussed in chapter three suggests. Despite a "reality gap" between women's promised and actual participation in politics and workforce gains, incremental progress has been made in recent years on issues from domestic violence to equal employment as the subsequent chapters will demonstrate (Buckley, 1994, 347–72). However, the degree of "transformation, expansion and diversification," as well as diffusion, that characterizes the American movement still remains elusive for Japanese feminists (Wolfe and Tucker, 1995)

In the United States, the continued vigor of the American feminist movements continues to be impressive, though frequently constrained by the need to adapt to hostile political environments. The accomplishment of the VAWA as well as the effort to continually redefine Title VII of the Civil Rights Act of 1964 have borne testimony to the persistent advocacy efforts of American feminists. The range of strategies open to U.S. women appears greater than that in Japan, in part due to the existence of states in the federal system, or sub-governments, though the latter can be a force for retarding as well as promoting experimentation and progress in gender-related policy (e.g., access to abortion). The system of separation of powers with its multiple entry and veto points also permits more opportunities for policy intervention, as does the fact that the bureaucracy is more open and permeable than its Japanese counterpart. While their claims are often controversial and, as noted, besieged by effective counter-mobilization, American feminists have achieved a degree of legitimacy in political decision making perhaps still far off for Japanese feminists in a system which has, in the main, not been receptive to change-oriented groups.

Policy success and failure are two extreme poles that do not reveal the range of possibilities and outcomes that may be achieved by movement activists interacting with the state. The ensuing chapters will trace the relationships between feminist advocacy and policy change within a comparative U.S.–Japan context.

Chapter 2

Equal Employment Opportunity Policy in the United States and Japan

Introduction

This chapter will compare and contrast policy seeking to provide equal opportunity (EO) in the workplace in the United States and Japan. The U.S. policy-making process was among the first, and to date, most successful efforts to create mobility for women seeking higher-level positions largely through the unexpected vehicle of the Civil Rights Act of 1964. We will explore the strategies and tactics that helped to lead to change. In Japan, the process has been much less effective in providing access to the labor market for women, despite the passage of EO legislation in 1985 and subsequent amendments in 1997. Utilizing the resources provided by the convergence of international agencies, treaties and conferences with global feminist movements, Japanese women have pressed their government to conform to new gender equity standards through *kansetsu gaiatsu*, or indirect external pressure, leading to the enunciation of new rights. The EO law, passed in 1985 in response to international standard setting, was weak, intended to be largely symbolic; but even symbolic law can have an impact on prospects for change in a political context resistant to improvement of women's labor force options. While employment opportunities for women have not been expanded in most instances, the law's impact includes changed consciousness of gender inequity, increased recourse to litigation and continuing and expanded mobilization by Japanese women (Gelb, 2000, 386).

Equal Employment Policy in the United States

The implementation of Title VII of the 1964 Civil Rights Act, via continued litigation and lobbying, created major educational and occupational advances for American women. Although the initial inclusion of "sex" in the act was intended to weaken its impact, instead feminist groups seized upon it to as a base for further advocacy and change related policy. Private litigation and government enforcement have been utilized to attack discriminatory practices.

In the United States, several factors may account for more effective enforcement of sex discrimination laws than in Japan. They include litigation, close monitoring of government agencies, professional lobbying undertaken by a strong movement and the existence of a clear statutory and administrative basis for implementation (Burstein, 1991, 1222). Specifically, feminist advocacy has been enhanced by: (1) use of the executive, judicial and legislative process to produce gains in the area of sex discrimination including numerous policy enactments, from 1964 on; (2) litigation in the federal courts. Sex discrimination cases have increased dramatically: by the early 1990s, they comprised as many appellate cases as those based on race[1]; (3) sanctions against violators of sex discrimination laws in which possibly harsh penalties are imposed on discriminators: they may involve enforcement of changed practices and compensation to aggrieved employees (ibid., 1221); and (4) intervention and monitoring by feminist groups to secure vigorous enforcement. American women have been aided in their anti-discrimination efforts by the concept of "indirect discrimination" (seemingly neutral policy that negatively impacts women), the ability to bring class action suits, which minimize individual costs and provide relief to large numbers of plaintiffs, a professional feminist litigation sector and continual feminist lobbying and networking, in a system more accessible to intervention in "multiple venues" than is true in Japan.

Title VII and the policy process. In the United States, activity related to equal employment policy began formally with the 1964 Civil Rights Act, which prohibited employment discrimination based on sex as well as other categories. Popular lore holds that sex was added to the title of the bill as something of a joke, and in order to help defeat it (Kessler Harris, 2001, 239). In 1967, sex was added to the requirements for affirmative action by contractors with the federal government, under an executive order by former President Johnson (Reskin, 9). Such contractors account for about one-fifth of the nation's labor force (ibid., 11). A 1972 Equal Employment Opportunity Act reaffirmed and strengthened nondiscrimination in federal employment by amending Title VII and making it applicable to small firms, and state and local agencies as well as permitting the Equal Employment Opportunity Commission (EEOC) to bring suit on behalf of individuals (Conway, Ahern and Steuernagel, 1999, 75). This act was enhanced by Title IX of the Education Amendments of 1972, which barred sex discrimination in education and led to gains in professional careers for women. Feminist advocates also lobbied for the passage of the Pregnancy Discrimination Act of 1978, that reversed a 1976 Supreme Court ruling that denial of benefits for pregnant women was not sex discrimination (Gelb and Palley, 1996, 165). The 1978 law prohibits discrimination against pregnant women in any area of employment, including hiring, promotion, seniority and job security. Employers who offer health insurance for temporary disability must include coverage for pregnancy, childbirth and related medical conditions. (Conway, Ahern and Steuernagel, 1999, 78). Women's groups vigorously advocated on behalf of the passage of the Civil Rights Act of 1991, which expanded the range and recovery of Title VII claims, which had been limited by the federal courts under conservative Reagan and Bush appointees. Among the gains made through this legislation were the right to a jury trial and the recovery of compensatory and punitive damages, as well as back and front pay, in cases of intentional discrimination or "disparate treatment," capped at $50,000 to $300,000 depending on the size of the company. The act promoted affirmative action and adopted the idea that a practice with disparate impact (on each gender) not justified by business necessity is illegal (Blumrosen, 1993, 3).

Equal-rights advocates in the United States have benefited from the existence of well-organized policy networks, which operate with greatest impact in a receptive political climate. They also relied on the model employed by the African American civil rights groups that preceded them into the political arena, which helped lay the groundwork for the political strategy that created new meanings for the struggle against sex discrimination (Kessler Harris, 2001, 241). The impact of the Civil Rights Act and subsequent placement of equal rights for women on the policy agenda cannot be overestimated: its new attention to issues of equality aided greatly in the development of the women's movement (ibid., 246). The importance of this legislative enactment appears to support Frank Baumgartner's view that new policies and institutions create new opportunities for mobilization leading to additional policy developments, the "feedback" effect (2002).

The feminist movement was active in advocating for legal reform at the outset: in 1966, the National Organization for Women (NOW) was formed to bring public pressure on the administrative agency, the EEOC, responsible for enforcement of Title VII's prohibition against sex discrimination in employment (Schultz, 1998, 1697). Other feminists launched their own Title VII lawsuits challenging sex segregation in the workplace (ibid.). During the 1970s and 1980s, women were more likely than racial minorities to make use of the powers of the EEOC and courts to enforce nondiscrimination (Kirp, Yudof, Strong and Franks, 1986, 144). Without the continuing involvement in equal employment opportunity (EEO) litigation of legal organizations related to the women's (and civil rights) movements, it is unlikely that women would have gained as much from the enforcement of these laws (Burstein, 1991, 171). As early as the first year of the EEOC's existence in 1965, 37 percent of the complainants protested sex discrimination (Kessler Harris, 2001, 246). In the United States, the feminist movement has relied on judicial decisions in addition to legislation to strengthen laws related to equal opportunity, as well as insuring compliance and effective implementation. Class action suits have been used effectively to press individual claims through a larger group effort.

The policy making structure. Policy making has been fragmented, between the EEOC, the Office of Federal Contract Compliance Programs (OFCCP) and the state level Fair Employment Practices Commissions, as the U.S. government has been unwilling to commit to the establishment of full-scale national machinery dealing with women's issues, as exists in some other Western nations and recently in Japan as well. Most states and localities in the federal system have adopted their own equal opportunity laws.

Anti-discrimination efforts are enforced by several different agencies. The OFCCP oversees contractor compliance with the presidential executive orders, with the ultimate sanction of contract cancellation and exclusion from future government contracts, for companies with over 50 employees with contracts of over $50,000 (Conway, Ahern and Steuernagel, 1999, 79).[2] They can process complaints and also undertake compliance reviews, similar to the EEOC, discussed below. Their efforts have produced some positive changes for women; for example, after a review of banking practices in 1978, women's representation as managers and officials climbed 20 percent (ibid., 51). Similar progress was seen in recruitment of female police officers who went from 2,000 to 20,000 from 1970 to 1990, from 2 to 9 percent (but still a long way from parity) (ibid., 52). Unfortunately, however, this agency "is understaffed, has few effective ways of encouraging compliance, lacks vigor and has . . . been poorly managed." (Bergmann, 1997, 53). Economist Barbara Bergmann views it as lacking resources for aggressive advocacy, although she feels that this agency has probably been more effective in altering corporate practices than others.

The EEOC is responsible for enforcing equal employment policy, managing the 70,000 to 80,000 cases that come before it annually, in multiple areas of discrimination, bringing suit on behalf of discrimination victims, and working with state and local affiliates. Its powers have expanded in part due to pressure from feminist groups. In addition to investigating individual complaints, the EEOC can investigate and conciliate complaints, and grant complainants the right to seek remedies in court. It can bring class action suits and file *amicus curiae* (or friend of the court) briefs. Individuals may file complaints with the commission and, if the dispute is not resolved through conciliation, take the case to court. The EEOC may also conduct "pattern or practice" investigations involving industry or company-wide discrimination, seek resolution, and, if the outcome is unsuccessful, sue in court as well. A landmark victory came via the 1974 consent decree with AT & T that resulted in a $40 million in salary adjustments paid to female and minority employees and new policies adopted related to recruitment, transfer and promotion.

The EEOC was in part a victim of its own success: the number of complaints (9,000 in the first year) far outnumbered those expected (2,000) between 1975 and 1977, the number of charges awaiting agency action more than doubled (See Casellas, 1998). Although established in 1965, the EEOC did not pursue an aggressive legal mandate until 1977 when it came under the leadership of Carter appointee Eleanor Holmes Norton (McCann, 1994, 52). At that time she improved the agency's investigative and litigative capacities, recruited hosts of feminist lawyers and consultants, and began the practice of filing *amicus curiae* briefs in wage discrimination suits, including a major suit against Westinghouse (ibid.). At present, the EEOC has a continuing case load of about 25,000 cases a year related to sex under Title VII. It brings suit in about 500 cases a year in court (Bergmann, 1997, 171). The EEOC finds no reasonable cause for action in about 60 percent of the complaints received; in about 11 percent of the cases, the charging parties receive some form of relief (EEOC, 1999B). In recent years almost half the complaints filed have been related to sexual harassment; for example, in 1998 a $34 million settlement was obtained against Mitsubishi Motor Manufacturing and $10 million settlement against Astra, a Massachusetts pharmaceutical company.

These were the largest sexual harassment settlements on record and also resulted in Mitsubishi's adoption of new sexual harassment and complaint procedures, as well as Astra's formal apology to the women discriminated against (EEOC, 1999A). In 2001, the EEOC spearheaded a "patterns and practices" lawsuit against Morgan Stanley, alleging discrimination against one hundred women (McGeehan, 2001). Its major power is to debar corporations from federal contracting; it has done this forty one times since 1972 (Bergmann, 1997, 54). While the threat of debarment, if discriminatory practices are found, rarely has been invoked, it is a credible threat that has helped to insure compliance. Under the conservative Reagan administration, sanctions were not supported and the impact of equality policy was also weakened by hostile appointments and lessened compliance reviews, which audit employer practices and investigate personnel procedures—apart from specific complaints (ibid., 68). Such reviews and "patterns and practices" charges and investigations, have often proven to be even more effective in ending discriminatory practices than responses to individual complaints.

At their most effective, actions taken by agencies such as the EEOC have resulted in massive changes in women's representation in managerial and non-traditional jobs (Bashevkin, 1998, 67; Kirp et al., 1986, 162). The EEOC has issued guidelines and advanced the gender equality agenda on such issues as affirmative action, pregnancy discrimination, insurance reform and sexual harassment. On the negative side, the commitment of such agencies has varied greatly, with the commitment of successive presidents and their appointees. Burstein describes federal enforcement efforts as erratic, disorganized and underfunded, and points to the long years often required to resolve cases, as well as vast expenditures of time and effort. During the Reagan years, in particular, efforts to curtail employer discrimination were sidelined by leadership that opposed government intervention and civil rights enforcement and cut resources and staff for the agency. But during other periods as well, the backlog of cases has been almost insurmountable (73,000 in the early 1990s; Reskin, 1998, 25), although recent data suggests it has been improved under more assertive leadership. Some feel that in recent years leadership has been strengthened, more efforts have been made at creative mediation and attention to clearing the backlog has been made a priority (Goodman, Outten interviews). The EEOC does offer complainants free legal assistance and, often, resolution of their complaints (Williams interview).

Ultimately, the significance of much of equal employment policy making relies on court decisions: under the influence of Reagan and Bush appointments (both father and son), to be discussed further in the next section, there has been pressure to reduce enforcement activities and restrict criteria used in fair employment practices, including affirmative action. (Even former President Clinton was ambivalent about the latter, saying "mend it but don't end it") (Conway, Ahern and Steuernagel, 1999, 80).

The future of equal opportunity policy in the United States. As of the twenty-first century, the most common sex discrimination cases appear to center on "glass ceiling" issues and particularly relate to high-level professionals in the financial industry (Outten, Goodman interviews; *Economist*, March 2, 2002, 60). High-profile cases have recently been settled against such leading financial institutions as American Express, Merrill Lynch and Solomon Smith Barney, while one has been pending against Morgan Stanley since 2001 (ibid.). Other recent cases involve prejudicial treatment of pregnant women or women with children ("sex plus") where mothers are treated with subtle discrimination regarding careers (Clark interview). Women's litigation has also challenged the practice of compulsory arbitration of employment discrimination claims, limiting access to the courts, with the Supreme Court ruling in *Circuit City Stores v. Adams*, in 2001 (532 US 105; 16 EDR 451) that such contracts may not be enforceable. They remanded the case to the Ninth Circuit which found the arbitration agreement "unconscionable" (279F3; 889 FEP-1609; 18 EDR 166).

However, the ability to win equal opportunity lawsuits in court may decline over time, as easy access cases may have been resolved early on, succeeded by subtler discrimination that is more difficult to prove. "First generation" employment cases shared characteristics of "clarity, uniformity and simplicity," violating norms of fairness and formal equality and deliberate exclusion or subordination based on race or gender (Sturm, 2001; Schultz, 1998). Challenges to fundamental patterns of exclusion, job segregation and bias that frequently emerge from such more subtle, interactive and structural dynamics may be more difficult to sustain (Sturm, 1998, 640). According to law professor Susan Sturm, (2001, 459) "second generation" employment discrimination may result from unconscious bias rather than deliberate, intentional exclusion"; may involve social practices and patterns of interaction that are difficult to trace to intentional actions, and may only be visible in the aggregate. They are "structural, relational and situational," and may be less amenable to court based solutions (ibid., 462–3). The present standard of "disparate treatment" related to blatant practices that are based on discriminatory intent appears more difficult to prove than earlier approaches. Cases that rely on the "disparate impact" standard, seemingly neutral policies that impact more negatively on one group, are also difficult to prove and many present cases represent individual litigants rather than systemic patterns of group bias (Williams interview). Employers' practices may have become increasingly subtle and less amenable to legal remedies.

Changes in the political system also affect the rights-oriented sympathies of federal agencies and the courts (Burstein, 1991, 1214). The Supreme Court never extended standards of "strict scrutiny" to cases involving women or viewed sex-based classifications as inherently "suspect" under the Fourteenth Amendment's Equal Protection clause, unlike those based on race. This means that to date in sex-related cases, treated as a "quasi suspect" classification, the Supreme Court has demanded that the state must show a "legitimate interest" in justifying a challenged law (Koppelman, 1996, 18). The court and other federal institutions have been ambivalent—"not friendly"—on affirmative action and other sex discrimination issues in the 1990s, in the aftermath of more conservative appointments by the Reagan/Bush administrations (Williams interview). Only once, in *Johnson v. Santa Clara Transportation Agency*, 480 IS 6166 631 (1987), did the Supreme Court permit a public body to choose a female candidate for a position in accordance with an affirmative action plan, despite the candidacies of other qualified males who would ordinarily have been chosen. The court has often recognized the need for race- and sex-based remedies to alter patterns of occupational segregation, although in recent years its rulings have made affirmative action more difficult to sustain (Bergmann, 92). Even though most attacks on affirmative action have been directed at racial minorities, the decisions affect women by inference as well. As in Japan, court cases can drag on for decades, making the process frustrating; in one case begun in 1973, a group of women sued the U.S. Navy, alleging wage and promotion discrimination due to sex. It took eight years before a judgment was rendered, then another five for additional issues to be resolved, then another five for damages to be determined. Even then, the matter was not resolved as it was appealed to a higher court (Bergmann, 1997, 170).

Access to the courts has been increasingly limited over time, through tightening of standards related to class action suits, and rulings on such issues as "mandatory arbitration," which contractually require employees to renounce recourse to law suits at the time of hiring (Williams interview). Class actions, which permit multiple plaintiffs to pool resources and engage in collective action (Sturm, 2001, 1215), often helping to produce legal victory (ibid., 1221), have been on the decline as the courts have gradually tightened criteria for bringing such suits. The court has also made it more difficult for employees to establish their burden of proof to demonstrate discrimination. The burden of proof is generally on the plaintiff, although a recent Supreme Court ruling voted unanimously to make it easier for employees who do not have direct evidence of discrimination at the time they file a lawsuit to bring a complaint against their employers (*Akos Swierkiewicz v. Sorema* NA 00–1853, 2002 US Lexis 1734; *Economist*, "Women in Suits," 2 March 2002, 61).

There are two major types of discrimination cases that the courts have addressed. "Disparate treatment" cases, the first category recognized by the courts, deal with employment practices that treat one gender or group less well than the other, based on a discriminatory motive. Such practices may affect an individual or group. Defenses by employers may involve evidence of non-discriminatory reasons for the disparity in employment outcomes (*Robinson et al. v. Metro North Commuter RR CO*) (U.S. Court of Appeals, 2nd Circuit, 00–9417) (267 F3rd 147). "Disparate impact" cases rely on neutral policies that impact more adversely on one gender (or other group) than the other; they focus on the result rather than the intent of employment policies. For example, an employment criterion for a police officer requiring a mile to be run in five minutes may affect women more adversely than men. Even if such a facially neutral practice has a disparate impact, an employer may attempt to defend it by showing a business necessity. If the employer alleges a "business necessity" justification for the policy that has a disparate impact, the burden shifts back to the plaintiff, to show how the disparate effect might be lessened through other policies.

Women's litigation groups rarely provide direct legal assistance in sex discrimination cases today (with the possible exceptions of the California-based Equal Rights Advocates and the Philadelphia-based Women's Law Project) (Schneider interview), which have now become a province of the private bar, though they continue to act as *amici curiae*. It has been suggested that foundation support is no longer as forthcoming for these frustrating, difficult to prove, time-consuming lawsuits (Williams interview). Nonetheless, despite the difficulties, as of the mid-1980s Burstein found that women in sex discrimination cases won more than half the time, though women in professional and higher-level jobs were less likely to do so. Most victories led to compensation rather than changed practices (1989, 660). Still, as of 2002, one in five civil lawsuits deals with harassment or discrimination, as opposed to one in twenty a decade ago (*Economist*, "Women in Suits" 2 March 2002, 61), supporting the view that women as individuals and groups have mobilized effectively to litigate on sex discrimination issues, sometimes with government support.

Gains for women. The most obvious change for American women has been their movement into managerial positions; they now occupy a much larger percentage of high-level administrative and managerial positions than ever before. Women's representation increased from 19 percent in 1970, to a overwhelming 46 percent of women in management and professional careers, the largest such group in the world (ILO Bureau of Labor Statistics; 44% according to the Unifem *Progress of World Women*, 2000; the next highest percentage of women in such positions in developed nations was found in Canada with 36%).

The comparisons with Japan are clear; the latter has the smallest number of highly placed women in any developed nation (9% in 2000, though up from 7% in 1980) (Spain and Bianchi, 1996; 91; Brown et al., 1997, 129; *Progress of World Women*, 2000, table 4.3). The impact of equal employment policy has also led to increased labor force participation and the possibility of increased earnings in the future (Burstein, 1991, 151). Nonetheless, despite major increases in group share, and particular gains for well-educated white and non-white women, women's incomes still remain far behind those of men (77.1% in 2003 compared to 61% in 1960) and occupational segregation persists (ibid.; Spain and Bianchi, 1996, 96; Leonhardt, 2003). In both instances, however, there has been a significant and continuing decline in gender based differences and segregation, particularly in comparison with Japan (Brown et al., 1997, 99, 129). Women tend to be employed in middle- rather than top-management positions in service industries, working in administrative or support jobs (National Women's Law Center [NWLC], 2000, 43) and the "glass ceiling" prevents them from rising to the top where they are employed (General Accounting Office, 2002). In 1999, women comprised just 11.9 percent of corporate officers in America's 500 largest companies, and only 5.1 percent of highest ranking officers. (NWLC, 2000, 38). Only 1.2 percent of Fortune 500 CEOs were women in 2002, in contrast to one-fifth of college presidents, judges, doctors and state legislators (Stanley, 2002, 10).

Title VII as interpreted and advocated for by feminist activists has proven to be a potent tool for American women in the labor force to date. It is possible that its future applicability may be limited by the idea that protected groups such as women should be treated the same as the normative group, white men (Abrams,

1994), as well as the increased difficulties of legal access and interpretation discussed above. As analysis in chapter five will suggest, regarding provisions supporting working women, without recourse to external pressures to provide more benefits and leaves, the United States appears to be falling behind other democratic nations.

Equal Employment Policy in Japan

Increased access to international feminism and changing international standards of gender equity have been utilized by Japanese feminists to call attention to discriminatory practices in employment in Japan and other policy concerns (Morely, 1999, 177). Activist women have utilized the discourse of human and women's rights to pressure the Japanese government to change and strengthen employment-related policy, with mixed results. The effort to pass an Equal Employment Opportunity Law (EEOL) in Japan was one of the first instances in which *kansetsu gaiatsu* was used to invoke emerging international standards. Women's groups, although weak politically in the mid-1980s, were nonetheless able to "shame" the Japanese government into action, first into signing the Convention on Elimination of Discrimination Against Women (CEDAW) and then into writing a (largely symbolic) law to comply with the treaty. Finally, activism propelled by the first round of legislative change aided in efforts to amend and strengthen the EEOL in 1997.

Unlike the changes in domestic violence policy to be discussed below, the process leading to the EEOL was bureaucratically driven through the vehicle of the *shingikai* (advisory council), which makes policy in advance of its submission to the Diet. This process involves a kind of neo-pluralist representation by interest groups in a structured fashion; while bureaucrats play a central role, ministries are constrained by politicians and their own clienteles (Schwartz, 1998, 284). In 1985, the process was dominated by (primarily female) bureaucrats at the Ministry of Labor Women's Bureau, female and other union leaders and male leaders of Nikkeiren, the peak business association (Kobayashi, 2002b). The International Women's Year Liaison Group of 48 women's organizations helped to press for change as well. Dissatisfied with weak enforcement provisions, women activists who had pressed for the passage of the EEOL in 1985 helped to gain amendments to the law in 1997. By 1997, while the process remained similar in structure, there appears to have been an enlarged group of participants.

The EEOL in Japan was passed in 1985 and implemented in 1986. In contrast to Title VII of the Civil Rights Act of 1964, which provides for an enforcement agency and process as well as sanctions against recalcitrant employers, the EEOL relies upon a process of prefecturally based mediation and weak, indeed, virtually nonexistent enforcement mechanisms. Unlike the U.S. law, particularly as it developed over time, the EEOL emphasized voluntary compliance by employers, imposing few obligations upon them (Gelb, 2000, 385–6).

In a 1980 meeting of the Cabinet, it was decided that Japan would ratify the Women's Convention by July 1985 (Kamiya, 1995, 40), in the final year of the UN

Decade for Women (1976–85). The Japanese government began to review its statutes in terms of the convention to reconcile its demands for gender equality, seeking a balance with national customs and law.

Japan's decision to participate formally with respect to the newly developing international norms related to gender equality seems to have been at least partially due to a desire to be considered a "modern" nation, worthy of prestige and accept-ance. The activism of Japanese feminist groups also "embarrassed" the Japanese government into signing the treaty, as they sought to prod the government into action through expanding norms of gender equity. Seen from this perspective, Japan's perception of international pressures crystallized during the UN Decade for Women as Japan wished to take its place among other nations seeking to uphold new norms of gender equality: journalists, female Diet members and activist groups mobilized pressure to sign the international CEDAW as did the female bureaucrats in the Ministry of Labor Women's Bureau. A significant role was also played by the International Women's Year Liaison Group (Kobayashi, 2002; Higuchi, 1984, 312). CEDAW, adopted by the UN in 1979, was the most comprehensive code of women's rights in international law, applying to all aspects of women's social and economic life. In 1989, Akamatsu Reiko, former head of the Ministry of Labor's Women's Bureau, and a continued advocate on behalf of women's rights issues, declared that "without this international convention" the enactment of the EEOL "would not have been born." "There is no international treaty that imparts as much influence on our lives as CEDAW" (Yamashita, 1993, 77–8).

From the outset, the law was controversial. The advisory council that consid-ered the legislation prior to its enactment failed to reach consensus during a period of seven years. After Japan signed the treaty, its ratification depended on the adoption of suitable legislation. This process was overseen by the ministry in which the legislation and oversight process fell; the Ministry of Labor Women's and Minors Bureau, as it was then known.[3] In the absence of strong internal pres-sure to draft a bill with powerful enforcement mechanisms, other than the International Women's Year Liaison Group and relatively weak voices from oppo-sition parties and unions, a weak, voluntary and gradualist law was passed, which largely left the issue of workplace discrimination to employers' discretion: "The deliberations on the bill went on amidst great confusion and bewilderment; heated opposition from both labor and management resulted in a law 'with its teeth taken out of it' " (Imada, 1996, 2). While women's groups favored passage of an EO law, many were opposed to the final outcome, largely related to abolition of protective measures, as were working women's groups and trade unionists, a split reminiscent of debates within the U.S. women's movement earlier in the twentieth century. The law ceded control over workplace conditions to employers, who created a two-track system that subverted the intent of equal rights, and exacted another policy change, amendments to the Labor Standards Act of 1947, which abolished most protective policies for professional women (such as night and overtime work). Unlike in many Western nations, the women's movement was divided on the concept of total "equality" with many Japanese feminists opposed to abolition of protections, fearing that, in the unique conditions of

Japanese employment, these changes would lead to a worsening of working conditions without any gain (See Gelb, 1991, 86). In large measure, the traditional male-dominated corporate culture of Japanese companies, which is deeply entrenched in Japan's political, educational and bureaucratic systems, emerged victorious in the compromise policy that was adopted (Hanami, 2000, 6).

Policy change. The noncoercive, weak EO law that was adopted left essentially unchallenged the male-dominated, seniority-based system, replete with gender distinctions based on unequal treatment for women. Despite its name, "The EEOL was never meant to be effectively enforced" (Hanami, 2000, 2): it may have been intended as an 'ornament' to make Japan look respectable in western eyes (Bergeson and Yamamoto, cited in Liu and Boyle, 2001, 393). Despite its name, the EEOL was not really an equal opportunity law because it dealt only with discrimination against women, as compared to men, and not vice versa (ibid.). The EEOL did not regulate wages, but left that function to Article 4 of the Labor Standards Law, dating back to 1947, which specified that wage discrimination based on sex was discriminatory (Nakajima, 1997, 30). The 1985 law prohibited employers from discriminating against women in education, training and benefits and with regard to mandatory retirement based on marriage, childbirth or age. Weaker provisions sought only "good faith" efforts for recruitment, hiring, job assignments and promotion. Reflecting a purported predilection for conflict resolution as opposed to litigation as a means of settling disputes, rather than enforcing legal norms in a universalistic way (Hanami, 2000, 6), arbitration was chosen as the favored means for resolving complaints. A prefectural mediation process was put in place to resolve complaints but as the approval of both employee and employer were required (before the 1997 amendments), the process proved difficult to implement. The prefectural Women's and Minors offices (later renamed Women's Bureaus; now renamed again and called the Equal Opportunity, Children and Families Bureau in the combined Bureau of Labor, Health and Welfare), then empowered to provide administrative guidance for the law, lacked the power to investigate complaints, summon witnesses or demand documentation (Kamiya, 79). It was a weak agency with limited authority, although occasional directors of the Women's Bureau played a more proactive role with regard to discrimination against women. Nor could the Ministry of Labor (MOL) or the equal opportunity mediators initiate proceedings or act on behalf of the complainants in court actions (Lam, 1992, 104). The Equal Opportunity Mediation Commission could only recommend and encourage resolution of complaints; the parties were under no legal obligation to follow its advice. In the majority of cases the prefectural Director of the Women's and Minor's Bureaus denied mediation requests (Hayashi, 1995, 43).

The failure of the mediation process to provide an avenue for the redress of grievances, together with decreasing job opportunities for young female college graduates led to increased disillusionment with the EEOL and this mechanism for resolving complaints of discriminatory behavior (Lam, 1992, 106). Only one mediation was accepted at the prefectural level prior to the 1997 amendments, due to the requirement that both parties agree to the process in order that it go forward. The outcome in this 1994 mediation, dealing with the Sumitomo Metals company, disappointed the women complainants because it lacked concrete remedies. The sense that this process "was a door that did not open" and was not effective as a mechanism for dealing with discrimination, led to increased reliance on litigation (Koedo interview). Lawsuits against Sumitomo Metals and other Sumitomo companies continue to be litigated, on appeal. However, despite the failure of the mediation process to produce concrete gains for working women, the prefectural agencies did provide for consultations regarding female reemployment issues, and such efforts resulted in a huge response, in the range of 10,000 requests each year. Since female college students have also been seeking advice, the number after 1994 increased to close to 20,000 per year. In 1994 and 1995, about one-half of the complaints related to recruitment and hiring, as the economic situation had worsened and many firms stopped hiring women (Rodosho, 1995, 1).

After the adoption of the EEOL, most large companies instituted a two-track system, *kosu betsu*, dividing the work force into two largely gendered, functional streams—the managerial, *sogo shoku*, and the general/clerical, *ippan shoku*. The managerial track generally involves complex judgment, involuntary rotation and transfers and unlimited access to promotion. The clerical track is less pressured, though full time; employment involves limited responsibility, exemption from transfers, and shorter hours—a kind of "mommy track." This system circumvents the intent of the law, while appearing to comply with its spirit. Few women have been able to enter the management track; they are fewer than 10 percent of those recruited for executive positions (Molony, 1995, 292). In 1991, women comprised only 3.7 percent of *sogo shoku* (men were automatically placed in this category), while they were still 99 percent of *ippan shoku* employees. In 2001, only 2.2 percent of senior management workers were women (Ichikawa Fusae, March 1, 2002, 3). Although there has been incremental change, women today comprise only 2.1 percent of the higher-level department heads or chiefs and 3.4 percent of division heads. The most significant increase has been at the lower section head level, where they now comprise some 8 percent (up from 2.6% in 1979). (Japan Institute of Women's Employment, 1995; Japan Trade Union Confederation (JTUC-RENGO), 2000–2001, 46; Gender Equality Bureau, 2002, 8; Ministry of Health Education and Welfare, 2001). As of July 2002, the Asahi Bank announced the abolition of the two-track system, the first major bank to do so, permitting women to compete for promotions on the same basis as men under a new employment system (*Asahi Shinbun*, 2002, 21), although the future of such policy remains unclear.

Now popularly dubbed the "Ice Age," the dire employment picture for women (Fukuzawa, 1995, 155), was revealed by a 1994 Ministry of Labor Survey which found that only 56 percent of women found jobs in comparison to male students (ibid., 156). By 1995, male college graduates were twice as likely to find jobs as female graduates (*Chronicle of Higher Education*, 1995, A43; *Wall Street Journal*, 1995, B1 reported that there were 45 jobs for every 100 women graduates; 133 for male graduates). Female unemployment rose from 3.5 percent in 1992 for 20- to 29-year-old women to a record unemployment rate of 5.3 percent among women as of May 2002 (*Nikkei Weekly*, 2002, 4). An increasing number of women are employed in part-time positions, beyond the scope of the EEOL or other laws; 38.1 percent of female employees work in part-time, temporary or piece work jobs, marginal to the work force and with no benefits or security (Ueno, 1997, 3; Fukuzawa, 1995, 156 also points to the decline in full-time, permanent jobs and the adverse impact on women's employment). As suggested above, due to the problems encountered specifically by female graduates, the Ministry of Labor opened special consultation offices at the prefectural level, resulting in close to 5,000 complaints per month (Kamiya, 1995).

As of 1997, Japanese women earned only 58 percent of male salaries (UN Department of Economic and Social Affairs, 2000, table 5G) suggesting that the concept of equal pay for work of equal value, although accepted through treaty ratification, is a long way off in reality (Hayashi, 1995b, 40; Japan Institute of Women's Employment, 1995).

Efforts to improve the EEOL: international and legal

International efforts. Participation in international meetings and forums has increased women's litigation and activism related to the EEOL in Japan as well as other activities. Women have sought to use international treaties, such as CEDAW, to impact national changes (Liu and Boyle, 2001, 398). The international system, though lacking formal sanctions, can provide normative and structural resources that impact local changes in important and concrete ways (ibid., 399). Other groups in Japan have utilized this approach as well, related to reform of legislation dealing with children's rights (Goodman, 2000). The individual has emerged as an object of international law and institutions, permitting women to make claims with reference to transnational treaties and international conferences (Sassen, 1996, 41). Japanese women's groups at the UN (CEDAW) have vigorously challenged the government's view that the role of Japanese working women has improved since the law's passage utilizing the new opportunities presented for assertion of global rights (Knapp, 1995, 36). The Working Women's International Network (WWIN), based in Osaka, has brought consistent complaints regarding the ineffectiveness of the EEOL before the ILO and CEDAW, as well as the UN Human Rights Committee, in an effort to gain media and public attention to embarrass the Japanese government and force greater compliance (Buckley, 1995, 68). The Women's Circle and other groups (such as Shosha ni hataraku josei no kai—Working Women in the Shosha Trading Companies) issue reports critical of the Japanese government's view that much positive change has occurred under the EEOL at annual meetings of the Commission on the Status of Women (CSW) (under the Women's Convention, CEDAW), held at the UN. The 1992 report of the Shosha women contended that equal employment is not a reality, but instead the EEOL had "worsened the circumstances surrounding women's labor and even made their work more difficult" (Knapp, 1995, 110). In 1994, a letter from the Japanese Women's Circle issued a Counter Report to the Japanese Government's Second Report to CEDAW. Osaka working women gave talks to the International Women's Rights Action Watch (IWRAW), and through WWIN, attended the CEDAW convention and ILO meetings and lobbied UN delegates. In 2001,

WWIN submitted a "Counter Report" to the UN Committee on Economic Social and Cultural Rights of the UN. They also sponsored a nongovernmental workshop at Beijing and Beijing + Five in New York City, 2000; at the latter, the Japan NGO Report Preparatory Committee issued an alternative report to the UN General Assembly. These numerous efforts to rally international support have produced critiques of Japanese policy by international bodies. A 1995 report issued by the CEDAW committee found that the policies of the Japanese government "demonstrated the state's indifference to integrating women fully in the economic development process," calling for attention to indirect discrimination and increased dialogue with Japanese women's organizations (UN, 1995, 221). The UN Economic and Social Council (Concluding Observations, 2001) reported concern with Japan's continued gender inequality as well as the two-track system, and, while applauding initiatives related to violence against women and children and gender equality (See chapter 6), and urged strengthening of anti-discrimination policy. The critical responses by respected international bodies suggest that the efforts of various women's groups to embarrass the Japanese government through *kansetsu gaiatsu* are producing some, albeit limited, gains by highlighting the contradictions between international human rights strictures and domestic policy. Such efforts may have led to the willingness of the government to revise the EEOL in 1997 through amendments.

Women's international efforts were galvanized as well by the attendance of 6,000 Japanese women at the 1995 Fourth International World Women's Conference in Beijing. This experience and those at other conferences helped to convince other groups to gain support from outside international institutions. Those who have done so also include plaintiffs in suits against major Japanese companies, part-time workers, unions and their allies, a group of Japanese female labor attorneys (Japan (NGO), 1999; Kawashima et al., 2001; WWIN, Counter Report, 2001, 2003). WWIN has also collected petition signatures from overseas and at home to support plaintiffs suing their employers from scholars and others. Many publications decrying working conditions are written in English in order to try to reach a more international audience (e.g., "EW = EW Tokyo" Women's Circle, 1995 and the WWIN newsletter). Although the odds against significant change remain formidable, WWIN and other women's groups continue to believe that *gaiatsu* is important as a resource in appealing to a global standard of women's rights (Bishop, 2000, 232).

Litigation.   Litigation has helped to keep issues of gender discrimination and harassment in the public arena, as women have brought a number of lawsuits in normally nonlitigious Japan. In the general unions, which tend to be company based, have provided limited or no assistance to their female employees' lawsuits ("EW = EW Tokyo" Circle, 1995, 32). Because of the costs and time involved in bringing lawsuits, particularly in absence of third-party support, the litigation efforts undertaken by Japanese women are particularly impressive.

The analysis presented here, following law professor Eric Feldman, rejects what is sometimes perceived as a sharp disjunction between rights advocacy in Japan and the United States (2000, 9). As in the United States, the invocation of rights in Japan by aggrieved populations can be and has been used to mobilize group supporters, publicize concerns and seek policy change (ibid.). By extending the notion of discrimination, Japanese activists who have operated outside of the traditional spheres of policy making have condemned indirect discrimination through lawsuits emphasizing the collective rather than individual nature of the process (ibid., 400). Global standards of gender equity are invoked by plaintiff's attorneys to attempt to sway the judges (Kuroiwa interview). These rights claims continue to gain force despite efforts by bureaucrats to constrain rights assertion and difficulty in accessing the courts due to statutes (such as the EEOL) that require conciliation and reliance on "administrative guidance" rather than enforcement of the law (Feldman, 2000, 11). Viewed in this manner, rights are symbols and resources, and litigation a means of articulating public policy, as they are in the United States, which have an important role in fashioning the discourse related to policy change (ibid., 10). After the passage of the EEOL in 1986, and through 2001, about 59 cases dealing with discrimination, promotion, wage differentials, forced retirements and part-timers have been filed in the courts (Asakura and Konno, 1997). A number of additional cases may have been settled and numerous sexual harassment (*seku hara*) suits have been brought as well, beginning with a 1989 case in the Fukuoka District Court. Such cases may be more successful in court because they appear to have a lesser impact on society and are not expandable to other issues, while challenges to institutionalized sex discrimination would have profound reverberations and potentially lead to massive change if broadly applied (Kuroiwa interview). However, these numbers should be measured against the total number of labor-related cases per year: the number of labor-related cases has been rising (from 662 in 1991 to over 2,000 in 2001)— although many deal with limited issues (data supplied by Kuroiwa Yoko and Hayashi Hiroko), of which only a small percentage are related to sex discrimination. In contrast to 45 sexual harassment cases filed at the district level in 2001, the Supreme Court did not accept any new cases in that area or in the sex discrimination area in general (Kuroiwa, e-mail, May 2, 2002)—there were only 1 or 2 of the latter at lower court levels. As of 2000, there were 60 sex discrimination cases before the courts; 18 dealing with dismissal and 10 with wage differentials; just 3 with promotion (Tokyo Metropolitan Government, 2001). There are a large number of sexual harassment cases being filed: 33 in 1999 and 62 in the most recent period. Requests for consultations on sexual harassment have increased by ten times during the past six years (Cabinet Office, 2001).

Japanese courts have proved to be reluctant allies in the struggle against employer-based sex discrimination practices. While some monetary compensation has been provided to plaintiffs, there have been only limited remedies, at best, for the practices involved. In most cases, defendants have been ordered to pay 3 to 8 million yen (as much as 58 million in the Sharp Electronics case; see Tokyo Metropolitan Government, 2000). The Sharp Electronics case decided in 2000 was considered a milestone because it awarded the largest sexual discrimination judgment to date (French, 2000). While in a number of cases (e.g., perhaps up to 80% in recent years according to labor expert Asakura Mitsuko) women have been awarded monetary compensation for discrimination in promotion and salaries (companies are required to pay only two years of compensation): given women's low salaries this amounts to very little money (Ohmori interview). However, in this case, the court did not find that there was sex discrimination related to the promotion of men and women in the company and therefore no order to the company to pay the balance of wages or promote the woman was issued (*WWIN Newsletter*, 2000, no. 8). Japanese courts have been loath to rule that placing women in subsidiary positions without access to promotion and higher pay is discriminatory, finding in recent Sumitomo rulings that such practices are "not against public order and standards of decency," because in the 1960s when the plaintiffs were hired, the practices were not illegal. Employers do not have to rectify current gender wage-based discrimination arising from past hiring discrimination before the passage of the EEOL (Kawashima et al., 2001, 4). While these lawsuits have not been successful in attaining all of their goals, they have been significant in that they document discrimination against married women, and also hold the state as well as the company responsible for such practices (*WWIN Network Newsletter*, 2001, 10, 1; Japan (NGO) Report, 1999, 55). The unfavorable judgments were protested by sympathizers abroad and in Japan attempting to mobilize international support, as noted above (*WWIN Newsletter*, 2001, 10). The plaintiffs utilized novel (for Japan) legal tactics by suing not only the companies but the government as well, alleging that the government is in violation of its CEDAW commitments (ibid.). In only one of the four cases did the Osaka court find (27 June 2001) that a Sumitomo company, Sumitomo Life Insurance, was guilty of discrimination based on promotion and pay due to marital status, but the court rejected the idea that the state was responsible as well (*Voices from Japan*, Autumn 2000; *Mainichi Daily News*, June 27, 2000). Twelve plaintiffs, married women employees who had been victims of promotion and salary discrimination, finally won a settlement in the Osaka High Court on December 16, 2002 (*Asahi Shinbun*, 2002).

Documentation of discrimination is often more difficult in Japan than elsewhere, because rules related to "discovery" in legal proceedings differ, although they have been modified slightly during the last several years. There is no published job evaluation system and it is much more difficult to obtain records and accountability related to company practices. While courts can order lists of wages, they cannot examine employee lists in order to ascertain patterns of discrimination (Kawashima et al., 2001; Kuroiwa interview). It is difficult to prove gender discrimination given the need to demonstrate that men and women have the same abilities and personalities, necessitating identical work assignments (ibid.). Nor are successful lawsuits precedent setting. It may be easier to address equal pay issues than equal job assignments, according to one labor law expert (Asakura interview).

A key test of judicial willingness to rule more broadly and demonstrate greater sensitivity to gender discrimination issues was provided in the encouraging outcome of the *Shiba Shinyo Credit* case, in which a settlement was reached on October 24, 2002 after pending for fifteen years. In the Shiba Shinyo Credit company, men received seniority-based promotions and raises without regard to jobs performed; while only one woman succeeded to the managerial level. The company has maintained that women do not qualify to pass the promotion

examinations (Takayama, 1996, 22). Upholding lower court rulings, the settlement in this case ordered promotion and damages in part due to an employment
contract specifying that there should be no gender-based discrimination under
Article 3 (equal treatment of workers) and Article 4 (same wages for men and
women) under the 1947 Labor Standards Act. However, while a positive ruling
orders promotion to a specific rank, *sikaku*, which corresponds to a defined wage,
it does not specify a mandated or specific position for the women in question
(e.g., *shokui* or particular status such as section head under Articles 93 and 13 of
the Civil Code) (Kuroiwa interview). The court ordered compensation to the
women plaintiffs, who succeeded in winning almost all of their claims of 223 million yen (about $200,000), which included compensation, unpaid salary and
attorney's fees (*Mainichi Interactive News*, 2002).[4] This decision related to unfair
labor practices, the first sex discrimination case to be decided after the passage of
the revised EEOL, has been viewed as having broad applicability beyond the single ruling, sending a message to other employers as well.

As suggested above, Japanese law has less substantive power to nullify company
policies that discriminate and lacks the basis in equity and common law that
makes U.S. law powerful; there is no notion of indirect discrimination, burden of
proof or unfair labor practices (Asakura, 2001; meeting *Shiba Shinyo Credit* case,
Diet, 2001). An example is the Tokyo District Court decision in the *Nomura
Shoken* case on February 20, 2002. This was the first case to be decided under the
amended EEOL of 1997 and found that the two-track (*kosu betsu*) system adopted
before the amendments was legal (Kuroiwa interview). The result typified the
limited approach employed in Japanese discrimination related jurisprudence,
providing compensation but no requirement for promotion or rank adjustment
(ibid., Asakura interview).

Even more than in the United States, sex discrimination is increasingly invisi-
ble and difficult to prove than ever, calling into question the future efficacy of
litigation. Many companies have not just a two-track system in place but many
variations involving categories that are less obvious (Kuroiwa interview). The
depressed economy creates increased obstacles to expanding litigation efforts.
There is no "powerful legal framework" through which to successfully prosecute
outcomes and even so called favorable decisions fall far short of providing meaningful remedies. Cases take many years to wend their way through the tri-level
appeals process, discouraging many would-be litigants.

Groups such as WWIN and lawyers groups including Action 2003 (with 700
members), Lawyers for Working Women and others have been active in approaching litigation as a group-based process, joining individual lawsuits in the absence
of options for class actions, seeking a variety of compensatory damages, using
both administrative appeals and the courts if necessary, and utilizing the media,
public hearings and other mechanisms to publicize their complaints. As Feldman
notes, rights are means as well as ends; they represent strategies as well as goals.
The task is complicated by the obstacles the legal system embodies including
lack of transparency about administrative processes and a Freedom of
Information Act that provides little access to information (Ohmori interview).
Litigation has a consciousness-raising function, win or lose, in that plaintiffs may

get media coverage, embarrass the government and "gain self respect and aware-ness" (Nozaki interview), as well as helping to mobilize support for their cause within and outside the company.

In both the United States and Japan, disadvantages of utilizing the legal process include high "participation" costs, limited access and the time consuming nature of litigation. (Komesar, 1994). In both countries, the advantages may include per-ceived evenhandedness and autonomy from the political process, although this may put too favorable a "spin" on rulings in Japan. (Ibid., See Ramseyer and Rosenbluth for the view that the Japanese judiciary is not really autonomous). But there appear to be few alternatives for Japanese women experiencing work place discrimination.

The 1997 amendments to the EEOL. In June 1995, the Labor Ministry issued a White Paper in which it concluded that "discrimination in hiring, placement, and treatment of female workers has disappeared from systems, but remain[s] in practice" (*Japan Times*, 1995). In July 1996, some ten years after the enactment of the EEOL, the interim report of the Advisory Committee on Women's and Minors Problems was issued. Dismayed by what were viewed as weak recommendations for change, Japanese women voiced their disapproval through protest and com-ments and sought to monitor the final result through intervention in the process. The level of concern was demonstrated by the 20,888 opinions the interim report of the advisory committee received concerning the proposed revisions (*joho kokai*); a large number from employers who sought to limit the proposed changes and a large number from individual women and women's groups as well as unions (Nakanishi interview). Most opinions favored strengthening the law, and called for sanctions against lawbreakers as well as the establishment of an independent equality commission (Women's Bureau, Ministry of Labor, 1996). The Japanese response to the desire for new international stature (as well as domestic pressure from women's rights groups) has been to adopt the trappings, if not the reality, of new standards and regulation related to gender issues. National policy making, still reliant on business, the Liberal Democratic Party (LDP) and bureaucrats, has tended to invoke the symbols of gender equality with limited attention to serious implementation of change. Yet, changed expectations among women and the nation's continued, expanded exposure to the international community created a momentum that has resulted in some modifications to prior practice. The increased reliance on international standards helps to maintain pressure for more regulation of practices related to gender inequity. Continued concern for "losing face" due to adverse publicity generated by women's rights advocates has imposed new, albeit limited, costs on government and employers. One result has been the 1997 enactment of amendments to the EEOL that became effective in April 1999.

By 1997, the media were more attentive to the issues related to EEOL, which has received considerable public attention during the intervening years, and women's groups gained more publicity and more "space" for active participation. Attorney Tsunoda Yukiko contends that while in 1985, when the EEOL was passed, women's voices were not heard, in 1996 and 1997, they were 12.

As suggested above, the number and scope of women's lobbying groups has grown in response to evidence of the law's inadequacy and increasing work-related problems. Shortly after the EEOL was passed, disappointing many advocates of legal reform in this area, women began asking the government to eliminate its many defects. In addition, institutionalization of the "public comment" system alluded to above (*joho kokai*) by the MOL, opened more opportunities for women's and working women's groups to gain a voice, although many were in fact mobilized by labor unions (Ueno and Osawa, 2001). Female bureaucrats continued to be dominant actors, but there were more participants in the decision-making process. Groups like Peking JAC advocated new, more direct contacts with bureaucrats and LDP members. The labor union Rengo sponsored the Kinto ho Forum or Equality forum, a symbol of changing and somewhat more inclusive attitudes, which created a "space" through which women's groups might press their claims (Asakura interview).

There was considerable disagreement among the three groups participating in the *shingikai* that negotiated the 1997 amendments: labor, employers and public members. Although women as a discrete group lacked representation, they were represented through the Kinto Ho Forum of the Women's Bureau of the Japanese Trade Union Federation, RENGO, which had been organized in the early 1990s and helped to coordinate efforts of the Women's Bureau of the MOL, labor attorneys and feminist scholars who were consulted about the content of the amendments. There is some sense that during the negotiations, again bureaucratically driven during the period of consideration of the amendments, the scope of participation increased significantly, now including more input from the labor side and other groups (Asakura interview; Kobayashi, 2002b). Areas of disagreement included the degree of prohibition of discriminatory behavior, indirect discrimination, positive action, the creation of new administrative machinery, the ability to begin mediation upon the consent of one party only, publicizing names of offending companies, increased maternity protection, treatment of part-time workers and sexual harassment. Rengo played an active role in the process and called for the scrapping of the provisions of the Labor Standards Act which prohibited overtime and late-night work by women (*Japan Times*, May 27–June 2, 1996). Rengo recommended that part-time work be utilized for both male and female workers, rather than for women only. The proposal was viewed by some as a way of trading a concession for the strengthening of the "prohibition" requirements in the proposed bill (Owaki interview). These efforts may have helped pressure the Japanese government into revising the EEOL through amendments effective April 1999, that, in contrast to the 1985 law mandate equal opportunity in recruitment, hiring, assignments, training and promotion, excluding on-the-job training (Gelb, 2001, 58).

The amendments also permit mediation to go forward with a request from only one side, and names of recalcitrant employers are to be publicized. All remaining overtime protections of the Labor Standards Act were repealed at the same time as the EEOL revision was adopted. The changes do not create an independent agency, or provide more enforcement powers. Furthermore, there is no consideration of indirect discrimination, penalties for infringements of the law, requirements for positive action, consideration of mediation based on positive action or sexual harassment or attack on the "two-track system." Nor does the legislation affect part-time workers, who, as noted below, are predominantly women. The amendments do require increased "consultation" regarding positive action and sexual harassment; subsequent MOL guidelines stress prevention of verbal or physical harassment, including a broad definition of "workplace" that encompasses after-hours activity (MOL announcement, no. 20, 1998, 1–2).

In the period since the passage of the amendments, through 2001, there were some 34 cases filed for mediation primarily involving job assignments, promotion and on-the-job training (Women's Labor Association, Josei Rodo Kyokai, 2001). However, the hearings are held behind closed doors, results are not made public and the process still is deemed ineffective for women with problems of discrimination (Ohmori interview). The first case to be mediated, brought by Japan Airline (JAL) employees, ended with unwillingness by mediators to demand an end to company discrimination and by the withdrawal of the JAL complainants from the mediation process (Nozaki interview). The complainants reported that the committee said "it could do nothing about" the ambiguous criteria for promotion and rejected any discussion of the two-track system (*Voices from Japan*, 2000, 21–3). Observers decried the "opaqueness" and unsatisfying nature of the process (Nozaki interview). Mediations at the prefectural level are conducted at present by EO committees of the Labor Ministry (*kikai kinto choutei iinkai*). Despite the ineffectiveness of this process, there has been an increase in mediation requests; 57 were agreed to in 2001 and 164 in 2002. However, there has been only one decision made, in 2001 (Ministry of Welfare Labor and Health, 2002). Individual Trouble Coordination Committees (*kobetsu funsou chosei iinkai*) were established by the MOL at the prefectural level to deal with complaints related to sexual harassment, maternity, childcare and other issues related to women and work that do not involve sex discrimination concerns, but, rather other violations of the EEOL and other gender-related laws (Asakura interview). This process has elicited a large number of complaints, indicative of the dire labor situation in which Japanese women find themselves. The vast majority of the complaints to both of these mediation bodies are from working women (ibid.). However, in 2002 the number of sexual harassment and labor-related cases declined (ibid.). But, the number of complaints from female workers is increasing in contrast to a declining number from employers, as table 2.1 suggests. (The latter usually increase when new law or system starts, and then decrease gradually.)

The scope of cases brought by women now includes sexual harassment. Sexual harassment policy has been more positively affected by the EEOL amendments, and the number of successfully prosecuted cases dealing with this behavior has risen significantly.[5] In 1992, the first lawsuit was decided that found on behalf of the plaintiff and provided compensation. The publishing company involved in harassment was held liable, found to have created a "hostile working environment," and the plaintiff was awarded the equivalent of $15,000. In Osaka in 1995, a company president was ordered to pay $15,000 in damages to a nineteen-year-old female employee whom he had pestered for sexual favors: the first time a sexual harassment case did not involve touching or defamation. Sexual harassment has

Table 2.1

Fiscal Year	Total Number of Complaints	Number of Complaints from Female Workers
1999	9,451	4,882
2000	8,614	5,883
2001	7,633	5,925

Data supplied by Muraki Atsuko, Ministry of Health, Labor and Welfare.

been interpreted broadly in the guidelines issued pursuant to the 1997 amendments, so that "workplace" harassment includes after-hours contact. Indicative of increased awareness of sexual harassment, perhaps in response to the heightened attention provided in the revisions to the EEOL, is a huge increase in complaints brought to prefectural-level employment equality offices, from 850 in 1994 to almost 9,500 in 1999 (Cabinet Office, 2001, 19). Through a policy called Opportunity Now, the Japanese government, though still recalcitrant in punishing noncompliant employers, now is rewarding those who do have favorable EO policies with some cash incentives. (Nichirei, a food company and Daimaru, a department store, received such awards in 2002.)

A final issue to consider related to the implementation of equal employment law relates to the consequences of elimination of the Women's Bureau of the MOL due to administrative reorganization. The Women's Bureau and its director were intermittently, though rarely, strong advocates on behalf of women's work opportunities in the past. The merger of the MOL with the Ministry of Health and Welfare (to form the new Ministry of Labor Health and Welfare) has now resulted in the creation of a new agency to replace the former Women's Bureau: the Equal Employment, Children and Families Bureau. It now has multiple missions that include family policy and has scarcely added any additional personnel, so that its policy position may be weakened even further (Muraki interview).

Women workers in nonregular employment. One of the consequences of the EEOL has been a huge increase in "nonstandard" or atypical work among women workers; ninety percent of part-time workers of prime working age are women (Kezuka, 2000, 39, 6). Part-time employment has increased both for men and women, but for women, full-time employment has increased only slightly. The major difference between full-time and part-time workers is the gap in terms of employment and working conditions. (Other non regular employment includes contract workers [*arubaito*], dispatch workers [*shokutaku*] and the like.) Employers set the classifications for part-time work, which may often not accurately reflect the worker's status (e.g., in fact part-time workers may work for roughly the same hours as full-time employees but are paid by the hour; *giji paato*). Part-time workers (*paato taimu*) lack insurance, pensions and other benefits. As of 2002, 9.8 million women were engaged in part-time work, in comparison to 10.6 million with full-time jobs, making this issue one of crucial significance (*Nikkei Weekly*, 2002, 3).

A 1993 part-time work law required that employers "endeavor" to provide hiring notification to part-time workers and includes a guideline saying that part-time workers employed continuously for one year should be given advance notice of contract termination. As is true of the EEOL, this law has no legal impact on firms that violate the directives (Kezuka, 2000). In the context of part-time work, the 1999 Maruko Alarm case has been potentially significant. Twenty-eight married women alleged that the wage difference between full-time and part-time workers was a violation of the Labor Standards Act and Principle of Equal Wages for Work of Equal Value. The court found that as a "universal principle of civil law" individuals should be paid equally for work of equal value. However, not all wage differentials were deemed to be unlawful, and a wage difference of 80 percent between full-time and part-time employees was viewed as permissible. The practical impact of this ruling remains unclear. A 1999 revision of the part-time work law requires only one recommendation of the Study Group established by the MOL in 1996: "a clear statement of working conditions apart from wages." Otherwise, issues related to gender were tabled (Gottfried, 2002).

Activists fear that the economic downturn may have a depressing effect on future litigation. Nonetheless, women continue to lobby for more changes in the still weak EEOL, including serious attention to issues of indirect discrimination.

Conclusion

In both the United States and Japan, equal employment policy may initially have been intended to be largely symbolic and anti-discrimination policy was passed in the absence of women's voices. However, whether Title VII of the Civil Rights Act of 1964 was intended to be symbolic or not, feminist advocates soon redefined it to have more practical meaning and they have continued to do so during the intervening years. In the United States, policy networks comprised of women activists mobilized around symbolic policies to put them to work (Mazur, 2002, 252). The effectiveness of women's lobbying, through mobilization by women's groups and a more penetrable state in the United States helped to further the cause of equal opportunity. The presence of a national enforcement agency, the EEOC, and sanctions for nonenforcement have also been significant factors in creating almost unequalled opportunities for women in the professions and managerial ranks. Litigation has proven to be a crucial tool for American feminists, sometimes supported by government efforts through the EEOC and other agencies. The cause of equal employment was aided by the ability of the EEOC to prosecute discrimination cases and act as a repository for complaints (ibid., 253–4). There have been thousands of cases litigated in the U.S. courts since 1964, in comparison to fewer than one hundred in Japan since 1985. In the United States, when outcomes have been most helpful to working women policy communities have brought together bureaucrats ("femocrats") and feminist advocates, as well as members of Congress, to support legislation to strengthen civil rights.

Although used more widely in Japan than some believe to advocate for women's rights, the results of litigation have had far less effect in changing embedded practices of gender discrimination than in the United States. The concept of indirect discrimination has not yet entered the Japanese legal system.

The weakness of the enforcement process of the EEOL, perhaps occasioned in part by the ineffective authority of the MOL Women's Bureau, together with the reluctance of employers to initiate more than superficial change, has created limited progress in this area of potential social change. The narrowness of the law and its interpretations by the bureaucracy have permitted employers to modify their surface policies, while continuing to exploit women and perpetuate traditional approaches based on gender bias. However, while employment opportunities have scarcely improved at all for most Japanese women, consciousness and activism were mobilized in part by the expectations created through the EEOL.

In Japan, where traditional norms are ingrained and powerful governmental and societal actors wish to block, halt or limit equality policy, the activism of feminist litigants, lawyers and advocates has kept the issue of sex discrimination in the forefront. Women have resisted the notion that they are passive recipients of policy through continued advocacy. Their efforts resulted in a stronger role in the negotiations related to the 1997 amendments, although the results were only an incremental step toward more vigorous legislation. Both litigation and the use of international norms have aided in the assertion of the right to equal opportunity in the labor force in a system of representation and interest group advocacy previously closed to women.

In both countries, it is difficult to litigate successfully—in the United States, the most blatant cases of discrimination have been dealt with by the courts and it is now more difficult to utilize the judicial system to press for major change. Conservative appointments to the courts and the bureaucracy may further limit future options for American feminists as well.

Chapter 3

Domestic Violence Policy in Japan and the United States

This chapter assesses the adoption of legislation related to domestic violence against women. What factors affected the passage of the path-breaking Violence Against Women Act (VAWA) in the United States in 1994, and the more recent passage in 2001 of the Law for the Prevention of Spousal Violence and the Protection of Victims (popularly known as the "DV law") in Japan with a significant but more modest agenda for change? In the case of the U.S. act, years of advocacy by feminist groups bore fruit in 1994, when the increased number of women in Congress acting collectively through the Congressional Caucus for Women's Issues and receptive male politicians were able to merge domestic violence with a larger crime bill, the Violent Crime and Law Enforcement Act of 1994 (PL-103-332). National legislation, the "DV law," was passed in Japan on April 6, 2001, led by a cross-party group comprised primarily of eleven female Diet members, in part a result of increased women's representation. The DV law was significant because of its all-party female sponsorship in Sangiin, the House of Councilors. In both countries, the use of "insider/outsider" tactics and development of advocacy coalitions proved useful as women inside and outside government supported legislative change (Spalter Roth and Scheiber, 1995).

Policy Toward Domestic Violence in the United States

The feminist movement in the United States placed the issue of domestic violence on the local and national policy agenda in the mid-1970s when, in both Britain and the United States, this became an issue of public concern. While the initial focus of the movement was on shelter provision and empowering abused women to control their own lives, national level legislative mobilization efforts began as well in the mid-1970s. The National Organization for Women (NOW) founded a Task Force on Domestic Violence in 1976. Galvanized by a White House meeting in 1977, which led to the founding of the National Coalition against Domestic Violence (NCADV), and the U.S. Commission on Civil Rights hearings in 1978, feminist groups turned their attention to the idea of national legislation. Both the NOW Task Force and the NCADV represented and included local and state organizations, making it possible to call upon grassroots support for legislative change. The landmark Violence against Women Act (VAWA) of 1994 thus reflects several decades of organizational groundwork, which helped to secure legislation with the support of sympathetic male members of Congress and the increased number of women legislators who were placed in key positions. Women in Congress, despite their relatively low, though increased, representation, have raised awareness of gender-related problems such as violence against women, developed agendas with solutions to those problems, altered the terms of debate and recruited male colleagues to support those agendas.

Despite setbacks during the 1980s from the conservative sway of the Reagan/Bush era, all fifty states and the U.S. Congress have now enacted significant legislation on domestic violence. Initially, a major focus of movement change was shelter creation. The shelter movement that was galvanized in the mid-1970s was very successful, now with over 1,200 shelters serving over 300,000 women per year. While most are non-profit, many have turned to government and foundation support in order to survive. A second focus of the movement has been to mandate police intervention in situations of domestic violence and to train police and judicial personnel (prosecutors, judges) to intervene more effectively as well. Lawsuits were undertaken in many American cities to force police departments to change their policies of non-intervention, reform their policies and improve their responses to battered women. Mandatory or "pro-arrest" policies and criminal penalties for abusers who violate protection orders have been widely enacted (Schneider, 2000, 184). In the case of domestic violence policy, the example of legislation provided by sub-national governments (e.g., the states and localities), served as key as models for the congressional policy-making effort. Initial efforts at policy change were met with hostility at the national level. During the intervening years between their efforts to gain a domestic violence law and its enactment, feminists turned their attention to the states for a more receptive response. The lessons learned at the state and local level, involving the creation of broad-based coalitions, bipartisan support and neutralization of right-wing forces, proved instructive in the 1990s when finally the opportunity to pass a federal law arose.

The capstone of U.S. anti-violence policy is the VAWA passed by Congress in 1994—almost 15 years after the first efforts at legislative reform were initiated. It proved difficult to pass an anti-violence law during the conservative Reagan/Bush years, although bills were introduced from 1978 on by (then) House member Barbara Mikulski. In 1977, after the defeat of two initial efforts to pass domestic violence legislation, former President Jimmy Carter established the Office of Domestic Violence with a budget of $900,000 (Brooks, 1997, 68). With the election of Ronald Reagan as president, the office was abolished in 1981 and opposition to domestic violence legislation increased. However, in an incremental manner, limited federal funding for domestic violence was secured even in the conservative 1980s. In 1984 a Family Violence Prevention and Service Act was attached to a Child Abuse Act, providing some support ($8 million) for shelters and other assistance including research and training, following six years of pressure by movement activists. This legislation was a monument to the "energy, hard work, increased political sophistication, alliance building and tactics of the feminist movement" (Dobash and Dobash, 144). A few months later the Victim of Crimes Act authorized the use of fines for violations of state victims' compensation programs by shelters, infusing a total of $150 million to aid victims of domestic violence and other abuse (ibid.; Brooks, 1997, 68). Amendments in 1992 and 1993 increased federal funding for shelters and provided some support for state-based coalitions. The organizing efforts around these legislative changes as well as support for state domestic violence coalitions helped to provide a foundation for what may be viewed as the most significant feminist legislation to be passed in the 1990s. Once viewed as radical and controversial, and rejected as interference in the private family, the passage of VAWA represents a triumph for grassroots feminists who sought successfully to make what was once a "personal" and private issue a "political" and public one.

The Passage of the 1994 Violence Against Women Act. The VAWA, part of the Violent Crime Control and Law Enforcement Bill of 1994, is the most significant law ever passed in this policy area, and a massive piece of legislation affecting all fifty states. The enactment of the law, four years after its introduction into Congress, relied on an insider/outsider strategy (Spalter Roth and Scheiber, 1995) and marked a triumph for groups outside the political system moving to center stage. The move toward a renewed effort at passing federal legislation gained momentum after a Washington meeting in the late 1980s of grass roots activists, largely state anti–domestic violence coalition members who were concerned about the need to enforce protection orders across state lines and the dearth of funding for shelters, as well as the need for the federal government to provide leadership. The law "resulted from the work of an extraordinary coalition of women and civil rights groups over several years," including the Center for Constitutional Rights, Center for Women Policy Studies and National Center on Women and Family Law, the National Association for the Advancement of Colored People (NAACP) and the U.S. labor movement (Schneider, 2000, 44, 188). Links between grassroots and professional women's activists and policy entrepreneurs or sponsors in Congress in an advocacy coalition appear to have been significant in gaining passage of the new VAWA. The formulation of violence as a violation of women's rights—a violation of the fundamental right to equality—has been a key element in the discourse related to this policy area (ibid. 49).

A domestic violence bill was initially introduced in 1990 by Senator Joe Biden (D-DE) who became its primary congressional advocate; after its failure to pass over the next several years, he continued to press for its passage until he finally succeeded. The 1994 law was passed due to support from important male and female politicians from both parties, especially Senator Biden, now chair of the key Senate Judiciary Committee, whose influence in the process was key throughout, although the mobilization of women's groups helped to legitimize his efforts. Orrin Hatch, a conservative Republican from Utah, also proved to be a key supporter (Brooks, 1997, 78). The legislative process was also given impetus due to political circumstances, the opening of a "policy window." The major factor affecting this "policy window" related to the significance of the "gender gap" which became evident in 1992, when women voters supported Democratic candidates more than Republicans. Member of both parties shared the perception that legislation on domestic violence would enhance support among women voters. The O. J. Simpson murder case in 1994, which involved domestic violence, functioned as something of a "focusing event," creating additional attention to this policy area (ibid.). Other factors which contributed to the convergence of the problem, politics and policy change (or "policy stream") involved the presence of record number of women legislators in Congress, many active in the Congressional Caucus for Women's Issues which came to play a key role, and a sympathetic president in the White House. The Congressional Caucus on Women's Issues Violence Against Women Task Force helped to focus attention on the issue and mobilize support. The caucus was able to move the legislation out of House sub-committee gridlock and later insure that the conference committee that resolved differences in the bill between the two houses maintained higher funding levels. It also helped to obtain support from the 225 co-sponsors in the House and the 67 in the Senate. "Insider" women legislators were key, including Barbara Boxer (D-CA), who moved from the House to the Senate during the period that the bill was under consideration. Senators Nancy Kassebaum (R-KS) and Diane Feinstein (D-CA) and Carol Moseley-Braun (D-IL), the first woman on the Senate Judiciary committee, and House members Pat Schroeder (D-CO), Connie Morella (R-MD), Susan Molinari (R-NY) and Jennifer Dunn (R-WA) occupied important committee positions as well. "Outsiders" were represented by the Violence Against Women Task Force organized by the NOW Legal Defense and Education Fund (LDEF), a task force of over 170 groups including unions and religious groups as well as a variety of women's organizations (Brooks, 1997, 71). The media were important in helping to mobilize public opinion on behalf of the law: "by the time the bill passed, VAWA had become a virtual 'sacred cow' which no one dared to question or oppose" (Carroll, 1995).[1]

As the process developed in the years from 1990 to 1994, it was slowed by shifting policy agendas among members of Congress and crowded agendas. However, the "outsider" lobbyists helped to keep the issue alive, generating external pressure for its passage (Brook, 1997, 72). In 1994, it was incorporated into the Crime Bill as one section, Title XVI. In keeping with the "rights" discourse discussed with regard to equal opportunity policy, this legislation was designed within the framework of other federal anti-discrimination laws (Goldfarb, 2000, 8), linking violence with equality (Schneider, 2000, 188). It also was placed squarely within the American federal tradition, as federal funding for state and local programs was at the core of the new law. The law created a federal civil right to redress violence and to be free from gender-related crimes, under Title VII of the Civil Rights Act of 1964, and a new federal criminal offense for interstate battery. This was an important breakthrough because it conceptualized violence from a feminist perspective seen as resulting in women's second class citizenship, as part of a broader social pattern, rather than an isolated event (Goldfarb, 2000, 509).

However, six years after VAWA's passage, the U.S. Supreme Court in *United States v. Morrison* (529 US 2000) declared unconstitutional the provision of the law that required interstate enforcement of the "civil rights remedy," permitting victims of gender-motivated violence to bring actions for damages in federal court. This decision is in keeping with other Supreme Court rulings of recent years, which uphold the role of the states, as opposed to national government in providing rights remedies; under the so-called new federalism approach. (See Goldfarb, 2000, 502.) Although this reversal strikes at a key element of the law, which Biden and women's groups avidly defended in congressional hearings, it does not influence compliance with any of the other provisions (Resnik, 2001, 626). As of 1999, over 170 prosecutions related to violation of protection orders involving crossing state lines were filed (ibid., 643). In 2000, more than 230 criminal cases were filed related to different aspects of the VAWA (ibid.). Some municipalities and states have attempted to fill the gap by after *Morrison* by enacting laws to protect women from gender-motivated violence.

The content of the 1994 Violence Against Women Act. The Violence against Women's Act's (VAWA's) success was due to feminist advocacy, key congressional support and a widespread public discourse, including attention to domestic violence from the O. J. Simpson murder trial, which contributed to a changed political environment. The law covers all forms of violence against women, from rape to domestic violence. It improves record keeping. It provides significant funding for shelters, as well as police and judicial intervention and training and aid to community projects. It subjects perpetrators of federal sex crimes to increased fines and mandatory restitution, provides grants to law enforcement, prosecution and victim services to improve state and local law enforcement and improves safety in parks and public transportation. It also requires states to give full faith and credit to protection orders issued elsewhere in the nation, provides for increased shelter funding, encourages arrests in domestic violence cases and advocates improved coordination of services for victims. The law encourages the federal government to undertake research on domestic and sexual violence. About $1.8 billion was allocated for the VAWA portion of the Crime Bill, including $325 million for shelters, $800 million in training grants for law enforcement personnel, $205 million in support for victims and $120 million to encourage mandatory arrest (Brooks, 77). A national abuse hotline was established: 800-799-SAFE, inaugurated by former president Clinton. In addition, support for educational and prevention programs, and special protections for immigrant women and children, were included. The latter provision was pressed for especially vigorously by the VAWA Task Force (ibid., 78). The law established the Violence Against Women Office (VAWO) in the Department of Justice. (The Department of Health and Human Services has a similar agency.) (See Goldfarb, 2000, 542.) In 1996, the law was amended to include stalking as an additional federal crime.

VAWA (and its reauthorization in subsequent years) has continued to promote innovative-policy making efforts at the state and local level. In the year 2000, the five-year re-authorization provided almost a doubling of funding for the anti-violence effort: $3.3 billion in grants, including $185 million a year for state programs to coordinate support for victim advocates, police and prosecutors; $175 million for shelters; $40 million for legal assistance to battered women; and

$25 million for transitional housing (Resnik, 2001, 643). In 2001, the coordinating agency, the Violence against Women Office, reported making grants of over $1 billion, with over 1250 discretionary grants and 336 services, training, officers, and prosecutors (STOP) grants to the states for training, establishment of specialized units and other programs. More than 6,500 STOP subgrants have supported community partnerships among police, prosecutors, victim advocates and others to address violence against women (VAWO press release). The Battered Immigrant Protection Act restores and enhances the protections afforded to women in this vulnerable group (Goldfarb, 2000, 542). In addition, the activist women's coalition that fought for VAWA has sought to broaden its understanding of the social factors related to spousal abuse and authorizing funding for housing services, including rental assistance (Schneider, 2000, 197). VAWA 2000 enhances protections afforded to battered immigrant women as well. The "very breadth of the VAWA" signaled a dramatic and lasting change in the way federal law approaches domestic violence (Goldfarb, 2000, 541).

Analysis. As this section has suggested, the Task Force founded by the NOW LDEF was both a progenitor and enduring legatee of the VAWA's passage after its founding in the 1970s. Now over one thousand strong, it represents a broad coalition of women's, civil rights, labor and religious groups, continuously engaged in lobbying for improved legislation and monitoring the effects of the laws passed. (See Goldfarb, 2000, 543.)

Nonetheless, despite the clearly significant achievement represented by VAWA and its successors, highlighted by the clear focus on violence against women, many feminists disliked the Crime Bill into which VAWA finally was inserted. They particularly objected to its framing as a "criminal" problem, ignoring other roots of violence (Schneider, 2000, 198; Brook, 1997, 79). Initial concerns by some feminists about engagement with the state gave way to the efforts at legislative reform described, although uneasiness remained about transforming notions of patriarchy and dependence into "crime control." (See Schneider, 2000, 182–4 for a discussion of this conflict.) However, the process of enacting legislation involves tradeoffs and compromises; the passage of VAWA marked the culmination of a near thirty-year effort by "second wave" American feminists to achieve legal reform and support for legislative change on behalf of domestic violence victims. They succeeded in placing legislation to aid victims of domestic abuse prominently on the public policy agenda. (See Goldfarb, 2000, 546.)

Domestic Violence Policy in Japan

Domestic violence (DV) policy has been the subject of mobilization and energy among women activists in Japan for many years. In Japan, the bureaucracy contributed to the process of reform as it did in the formulation of the Equal Employment Opportunity Law (EEOL), but it was not the sole architect of new policy, due to the key role played by Diet women.

The passage of DV legislation in Japan was also influenced by new attention to this issue from the international community. The 1993 UN Declaration on Elimination of Violence Against Women, the 1995 Beijing Fourth World Conference on Women with a call to eliminate violence against women, and the Beijing + Five international women's meeting in New York, all contributed to *kansetsu gaiatsu*, or indirect external pressure, which was utilized by Japanese feminist advocates. The DV legislation reflects inputs from multiple sources; nongovernmental, Diet-based and bureaucratic, making it a more pluralistic effort than many of the other policies considered in this study. This policy appears to be a victory for a specialized "policy community" and various "entrepreneurs"; bringing together advocacy groups, sympathetic Diet-based bureaucrats and female Diet members in a joint effort. It also suggests the importance of the "policy window" that opened due to a variety of factors to permit the legislation to be passed earlier than some had anticipated, as the new international standards derived from directives and treaties and domestic pressure came together in a "policy stream" connecting the problem of violence against women with politics and new policy.

Domestic Violence Policy: The Passage of Legislation

As in the United States, policy toward domestic violence seems to have been influenced by coordinated efforts between activists outside and officials inside the government structure, perhaps to a greater extent than was true in either nation with regard to equal employment policy at the time of initial passage of legislative enactment.[2] In Japan, the "Law for Prevention of Spousal Violence and the Protection of Victims" (popularly known as the DV law) was passed in April 2001 and put into effect in October of that year. Among the factors that may have contributed to the passage of the DV law, as suggested above, were international pressure and recourse to emerging norms and standards by Japanese women or "activism across borders,"[3] advocacy from women's groups and their allies and the coordinated effort of a suprapartisan group of female Diet members. One major advocate of reform (Professor Kaino Tamie) referred to the adoption of this law as an "epoch-making process" involving nongovernmental organizations (NGOs), Diet-based women, and bureaucrats as well as invocation of new international norms. The Council for Gender Equality, established in the Prime Minister's Office in 1996, played an important, though less significant role, in calling for this policy development. It is possible that enactment of the Basic Law for Gender Equal Society, in 1999, may also have helped to facilitate the passage of DV legislation (Furohashi; Kawahashi; Owaki; and Osawa interviews).

The response of the Japanese government was motivated by at least in part by interest in being considered a "leading" and "modern" nation (particularly after passage of DV legislation in other Asian nations including Taiwan and Korea) and efforts by women's groups brought pressure to bear on it, as was true for the EEOL as well both in 1985 and the 1997 amendments.[4]

Pressure for legislative reform emanated from group activism dating back to the early 1990s. Many DV activists, in addition to participating in UN conferences, have lived abroad for periods of time, (e.g., Yoshihama Mieko, who participated in the first Japanese survey [in 1992] on DV and has been a tireless advocate for reform, lives in the United States) and have studied models created in other nations (Grubel, 2002, 2). Similar to the EEOL, the energy of the Beijing women's conference and its declaration on the Termination of Violence against Women, together with the advocacy of the Japanese Domestic Violence and Research Group, founded in Tokyo in 1992, helped to galvanize support for change in the DV law. Utilizing research advocacy at the Vienna UN Human Rights conference in 1993, this group presented a report in English to show that the Japanese DV problem was identical to that elsewhere in the world (Kaino interview). The Domestic Violence and Research Group also submitted a report on DV to the Fourth World Women's Conference in Beijing on husbands' (and boyfriends') violence in Japan, which served as a basis for further discussion. This report contained key survey data which demonstrated a high incidence of DV in Japan (58.7%), challenging the view that such violence was a problem only in the West (Zwarensteyn, 2001, 91).

In 1995, prompted in part by the Beijing meeting, a research committee founded by Komiyama Yoko and Fukushima Mizuho (later Diet members active in the law's passage) determined to keep up pressure to change policy. Among the most active women's groups advocating legal change in this policy arena were the National Network of Women's Shelters and Research and Study Group on Violence against Women. As in the United States, the existence of DV was publicized by a "focusing event": a notorious case in February 1999 in which a Japanese consul general was charged with beating his wife in Vancouver, Canada (Yoshihama, 1999, 76).

Pressure to pass a law legalizing a new approach to DV began to build after this. By the late 1990s, shelter group activists and women's groups began to move from a view that women should only seek protection to perceiving a necessity for legislating reform (*Yomiuri Shinbun*, 13 July 1999). In the aftermath of the 1995 Beijing UN Conference, numerous small groups and government bodies undertook action and conducted their own surveys in such cities as Sendai, Fukuoka and Yokahama (Grubel, 2002, 2). The practice of conducting surveys to underscore the need for policy change has also been employed in other policy areas such as child abuse, increasing awareness of hidden violence, and enabling formerly private issues to enter public consciousness in significant ways (Goodman, 2000, 165). Political consciousness was raised by the collection and publication of survey data: the Tokyo Metropolitan Government, under pressure from local activists, released its own survey in 1998; one was also conducted in Osaka. The first national survey was released by the Prime Minister's Office in February 2000 (ibid.). It found that 15 percent of married women suffer abuse from their husbands; 4.6 percent reported life-threatening abuse (*Mainichi Daily News*, 27 February 2000; *Japan Times*, November 2001). National and local statistics, documenting high incidence of violence against women, lent legitimacy to reform efforts to deal with the problem. Numerous local groups, including an activist organization in Hokkaido, Women's Space (Onna no Space) contributed to expanded interest in this issue by creating and disseminating videotapes documenting abuse (Grubel, 2002). Another resource for legislation aiding battered women was the establishment of the DV Prevention Information Center in Kobe, which published a newsletter and pushed for enactment of a national law to punish domestic violence perpetrators (Grubel, 2002, 3).

After the Beijing conference the Japanese government implemented a new policy that emphasized strengthening consultation for battered women (ibid., 93) as a limited effort to provide counseling and support. Counseling centers in temporary emergency shelters to accommodate battered women with children in locally supported public short-term facilities, were established under legislation initially intended to house prostitutes, the Prostitute Prevention Law of 1956 (*fujin sodan sho*). The intent of the law was to provide aid for "women in need of protection" or to "rehabilitate" women at high risk because of activity in prostitution, and to provide counseling and guidance (Yoshihama, 2002, 544). In recent years, eligibility requirements for assistance at these centers has been broadened, as in fact women seeking refuge have often been fleeing violent spouses and the percentage of prostitutes utilizing the facilities has dropped to fewer than 10 percent (Yoshihama, 1999, 80; 2002, 549). Under this legislation, the forty-seven prefectures and some local administrations as well have aided some battered women (Kaino interview). As suggested in chapter two, there are relatively few private/NGOs operated shelters in Japan—so the need for further intervention in domestic violence cases is acute (Fukushima, Kaino interviews; *Mainichi Daily News*, 27 February 2000). None of the short-term assistance shelters have had national government assistance (though a few have had a little aid from local government); support groups for battered women have provided information and advice in a number of Japanese cities (Yoshihama, 1999, 81; Kaino interview). Under these circumstances, the need for additional legislation to address the issue of domestic violence appeared clear to many.

In the case of DV policy, following a recent trend related to legislative enactments on women's issues, a suprapartisan group of women legislators took the lead in promoting legislation, utilizing *giin rippo*, or private member's sponsorship. Female legislators worked closely with bureaucrats (the Research Committee) in the Sangiin (House of Councilors) and subsequently with bureaucrats in the relevant ministries related to the new law. Female parliamentarians consulted with women's groups, activist scholars and shelter workers throughout the process. The DV legislation proved to be far less controversial than the EEOL, which had to go through several Diet votes before final passage (both in 1985 and at the time of the 1997 amendments). In contrast, the DV law gained unanimous support and passed in just four days. It is possible that the limited monetary outlay, desire to appear to conform to newly emerging international standards, emphasis on protection of female victims and the fact that this legislation does not challenge prevailing societal mores related to women's secondary position all contributed to the law's success. Nonetheless, wishing to preserve husband's property rights, the government refused to compromise on a longer (than two week) ouster order for the abuser from his domicile (Kaino interview).

Giin Rippo (private members' bills): cross-party sponsorship by diet women.
The effort to pass national DV legislation was led by a suprapartisan group
comprised primarily of female Diet members. Initial efforts to pass a law were
initiated by Osaki Masako, a lawyer and member of the House of Councillors, as
part of the activist group called the Japan DV Prevention Information Center
(Nippon DV Boshi senta) mentioned above but they did not initially prove
successful. It took the international events, *kansetsu gaiatsu* and all-party, women's
sponsorship in the Sangiin, the House of Councilors, where women's representation was at its highest point ever, (17 %), and the political circumstances related
to coalition government to foster policy change.

The phenomenon of private members' bills, or *giin rippo*, is a relatively recent
one and the utilization of this approach, particularly in the collective manner
employed by female Diet members in the passage of the DV law, is unusual. Most
bills in Japan have historically been sponsored by the government, originating in
the bureaucracy. During the Hashimoto cabinet (1996–1998), 315 of 340 bills
were government sponsored; during the Obuchi cabinet (1998–2000) 197 of 229.
In the Koizumi cabinet before 2001, 120 of 127 bills were bureaucratic/Cabinet
submissions (Kobayashi, 2002a). Private members' bills have clearly been in the
minority; from 1987–1996, there were only 26 members' bills introduced.
However, by 1997, there were 45; 92 in 1998; 86 in 1999; 55 in 2000 and an unusu-
ally large number—126 in 2001. Although the ratio of successful bills was only ten
percent to twenty percent, this increase in private members' bills clearly appeared
to represent a challenge to bureaucratic dominance of the legislative process. One
reason for the increase in member's bills has been the successful collaboration of
Diet women, across party lines, of which the passage of DV law is a particularly
important example.

Collaborative attempts by women date back to the post-war period, and to
the activity of Ichikawa Fusae and other Diet feminists to vote in favor of certain
types of legislation; but at that time they could not prevail. The successful efforts
in the late twentieth century initiated by suprapartisan groups of women legislators were on issues concerned with bringing Japanese laws on women into
harmony with international equity standards and victim protection, included
laws combating child pornography and child abuse and stalking and, more
recently, maternity protection. A November 1999 Law for Punishing Acts Related
to Child Prostitution and Child Pornography and Protecting Children was the
first major result of this type of collective process employed by female Diet members.[5] Its passage, utilizing both *kansetsu gaiatsu* and *giin rippo*, prefigured the
adoption two years later of the DV law. Noda Seiko, a Liberal Democratic Party
(LDP) member of the House of Representatives, began to champion the causes
of anti-prostitution and anti-pornography. Although she asked the Ministry of
Welfare to revise the Law for Child Welfare to sponsor legislation, the agency was
resistant, expressing concern regarding definitions of "indecent" and "obscene"
actions, the age of a child (16 or 18) and punishment for possession of pornographic material (Moriyama, 1999). The Minister of Welfare at that time, Kan
Naoto, recommended that Noda introduce a member's bill, given this hostility.
Ms. Noda decided to recruit like-minded female Diet members to assist her cause.

A "policy window" opened, reflecting participation in an International Conference on ending Child Prostitution in 1996 held in Sweden, attended by Japanese female Diet members and bureaucrats from the Welfare Ministry. Shimizu Sumiko, a former Diet member who attended the conference, recalls that reports from the conference indicated that Japan lagged twenty years behind other countries with regard to anti-pornography and anti–child prostitution legislation (Shimizu interview). The Japanese government became even more concerned about its international image when the national media accused it of failing to punish massive wrongdoing by Japanese men, adding their voices to those at the Swedish conference. In 1997, a study group was organized by a Government Parties' Project Team comprised of members of the coalition government, the LDP, the Social Democratic Party (SDP), and the third party, Sakigake, was formed under the leadership of Moriyama Mayumi, at that time also an LDP member of the Shugiin (the Lower House). Foreshadowing the process of adoption of the DV law, a Project Team was created, consisting of women members (and one man) from Sakigake, the SDP and others. According to Shimizu, a former Diet member, study groups were also organized with interested NGOs, similar to the advocacy coalitions created between activists and Diet members in the DV legislative process (ibid.).

The bill was introduced to the Diet in March 1998 and approved in May 1999. Unlike the domestic violence bill to be discussed below, which passed almost immediately, this legislation was carried over from one session to the next, perhaps because opposition party members resisted the government's linking of this bill with another related to organized crime (Moriyama 1999). The bill ultimately succeeded because of support from the LDP and the Socialist Party, despite hostility from some opposition party members (Shimizu interview). The legislation adopted, The Law for Punishing Acts related to Child Prostitution and Child Pornography and for Protecting Children, punishes those found guilty of engaging in child prostitution (a child is defined as under 18) with three years' hard labor and a fine of one million yen (about $10,000); soliciting is subject to harsher penalties. Similar fines and penalties are stipulated for child pornography. In 2000, a new law to punish stalkers was enacted (cnn.com, 25 November 2000). Both the anti-pornography/anti–child prostitution and anti-stalking laws include criminal penalties and are being enforced (*Mainichi News*, 29 December 2000).

The passage of the anti–child pornography/prostitution law, a progenitor of the DV law to be discussed below, appears to be an example of what Robert Pekkanen describes as a new phenomenon characterized by legislative and coalition politics, made possible because the need for coalition partners helped to lead the government to a new position. Once agreement was achieved, the bill passed unanimously (Moriyama interview). In this instance, the role of *kansetsu gaiatsu* also played a major role. International criticism of Japan as the source of 80 percent of commercial child pornography available on the Internet contributed to the urgency of providing a new approach (Goodman, 2000, 169). Politicians, not bureaucrats, took the lead in proposing legislation, partially because the existence of a coalition government changed the operative political dynamic (ibid., 112, 142). The second component described by Pekkanen, extensive citizen lobbying, is more apparent in the actual case study examined here, the adoption of domestic violence legislation.

Giin Rippo **and domestic violence policy making.** Women legislators have increasingly taken on legislative sponsorship via "indispensable collaboration," often based in individual personal connections as well as assistance from the representatives from women's bureaus in each party which help to formulate bills (Yamaguchi interview). These legislative initiatives and the DV law under examination in this chapter represent examples of *giin rippo* or legislation proposed by Diet members across parties, rather than the customary bureaucratically drafted legislation adopted by parliament (Pekkanen, 2000, 112). The inclusion of members of the LDP as well as opposition parties in the legislative process aided the passage of the nongovernment-sponsored Diet member's DV bill (Kobayashi, e-mail, 10 August 2002). Unlike the U.S. Congressional Caucus for Women's issues, female-sponsored legislative initiatives have resulted from ad hoc coalitions, rather than from a formal system of interaction.[6] Informal groups of women—*josei giin kondankai*—join to support legislative initiatives. Such efforts, aimed primarily at protecting victims, may be representative of new state/civil society relationships reflecting greater importance of lobbying groups and increased power to Diet members in policy making in Japan, a topic to be further analyzed in the concluding chapter. However, it is clear that women politicians have been submitting a far higher number of bills on all issues than their male counterparts: 4.3 bills submitted in the House of Councilors before the election in 2001 to 1.7 for men, although most did not involve the collective process discussed here (Kobayashi 2002).[7]

Legislative process. Among the multiple constituencies involved in the legislative process related to the passage of the DV law were group-based advocates, bureaucrats in the Council for Gender Equality and Diet members. The Council for Gender Equality helped call attention to the need for policy change, and women in the House of Councilors ultimately implemented the policy. At both levels of government, bureaucratic and parliamentary, there was consultation with women's groups, research undertaken to support the need for law and reports issued to support legislative reform.

In the bureaucracy, one source of support for DV legislation originated with the deliberative council of the Gender Equality Office in the Prime Minister's Office in 1996. In 1996, in the aftermath of the Beijing conference, the "2000 Year Plan of Gender Equality" of the Council for Gender Equality adopted elimination of the violence against women as a major goal. In 1997, Prime Minister Hashimoto asked the council to submit its opinion of a basic plan to eliminate violence against women. The council established the Committee of Violence against Women that heard testimony from women counselors, researchers and shelter providers, and led to the publication of a report entitled "Aiming to Make A Society without Violence against Women" in May 1998 (Shiomi and Yoshioka, 2001; Takai, 1). Initially hesitant about supporting a new law, in 1999 it submitted a report on "how a society without violence against women could be realized" signaling its interest in gaining legislative reform (*Tokyo Shinbun*, 29 November 1998; Shiomi and Yoshioka, 2001). Perhaps the final impetus for legislative change came from the international arena: the pressure from the Beijing conference helped to change the minds of some reluctant Council of Gender Equality members (Shiomi and Yoshioka). In July 2000, a final report issued by the Gender Equality Council endorsed the need for legal reform related to DV.

In the Sangiin, House of Councilors, the less powerful Upper House of the Diet, a 25-person research committee (*Chosokai*) of Diet members, including 8 bureaucrats, proved to be the spearhead for DV legislation. The Research Committee on a Cooperative Way of Life helped to focus attention on this issue by investigating it from August 31, 1998 through September 1999 on as part of its mission to research *kyosei* (cooperative life),[8] in order to examine how new cooperative relationships and society might be realized. During their deliberations they determined that the legalization of DV policy should be considered as their major area of emphasis. In June 1999, the committee submitted a report to the House of Councilors Chair calling for a fact-finding inquiry and calling urgent attention to the issue (Shiomi and Yoshioka, 2001). They based their recommendations on public hearings to which they had invited academics including national and foreign experts, lawyers, shelter operators and other participants familiar with DV policy and issues. In September 1999 they sponsored a study tour abroad to England, Italy and Norway, in order to gain a deeper understanding of how this problem was being dealt with elsewhere (Yoshioka interview). Women's groups who were consulted included the Kobe Center, Peking JAC, the National Network of Women's Shelters, Onna no Space of Sapporo, the Research Group of Violence against Women, the Kansai-based DV Protection and Information Center, and others—all of whom moved toward the need for legislation. They pointed to earlier legalization of domestic violence reform in the United States and Britain, and, more recently, by Korea and Taiwan, in order to embarrass the Japanese government into awareness of how far out of line it was with some Western, and other Asian, nations on this policy (*Yomiuri Shinbun*, 13 July 1999; Goodman, 2000, 169).

Governmental agencies began to devote attention to DV as a result of increased interest. In 1999, the National Police Agency changed its official policy from one that permitted inaction to one that now required officers to intervene in domestic violence cases when requested by an abused woman, calling upon local police stations to adopt pro-intervention, pro-indictment policies (Zwarensteyn, 2001, 116; Yoshihama, 2002, 547). (In response, Kanagawa Prefecture established a support center for female victims and police stations staffed by female officers [Yoshihama, ibid.].)

The DV law's unanimous passage was spearheaded by an eleven-person project team founded in April 2000, which guided it through the process with leadership by Nohno (LDP) and Komiyama (Democratic Party) as well members of the SDP, the Communist Party, Komeito, and the Liberal Party. Participants also utilized the "plus one" idea: one member from each party on the project team plus one additional member from that party to broaden support (Nohno,

Komiyama interviews). One of the latter was a male Diet member from the LDP. The process included negotiations with bureaucrats, as well as some participation by citizen activist groups and lawyers, for a period of over two years (Kobayashi, 22 February 2002). The legislation passed both houses unanimously within four days; issues that divided the participants were hammered out in pre-Diet negotiations with the Ministry of Justice and the Cabinet Legislation Bureau led by the female Diet members who may have sought to limit discussion in order to get a bill passed [9] (Kaino interview). The one-week decision-making process was closed and criticized as lacking substantial discussion including the perspectives of shelter-based commentators by an activist attorney, Hasegawa Yoko (*Kyodo News*, 14 October 2001). Because of the pre-Diet negotiations (*nemawashi*—or prior consensus in support of policy) bureaucrats could not publicly object to the content of the bill (Owaki interview). Not all observers view the process uncritically despite the successful passage of the legislation: according to a leading attorney/activist, female politicians were ignorant of aspects of the proposed legal process, including protection orders; lacked negotiating skill; and, in their eagerness to pass a bill, left too much of the bill drafting to the Bureau of Legislation in the House of Councilors, making the final content weaker than desired (Hasegawa interview).

The content of the law. The law passed in October 2001 refers to violence as a violation of human rights and barrier to equality, suggesting that Japan is now conforming to other efforts undertaken by the international community. The preamble is stronger than the actual provisions in the text as the premise of the policy is based on assistance rather than rights (Kaino interview). Although the Japanese government has sometimes resisted suggestions that it follows international strictures, the preamble of the 2001 DV Law shows a more globally sensitive perspective: "In order to remedy these conditions and to achieve the protection of human rights and the realization of genuine equality between women and men, we must establish measures to prevent spousal violence and protect victims. Such action will be in line with the efforts taken by the international community to eradicate violence against women" (Research Committee 1999, 1; Grubel, 2002, 5). It defines violence as illegal attacks that threaten the spouse's life or physical conditions. Unlike the VAWA in the United States, it does not focus specifically on violence against women as a group (Rice, 2001). The law defines violence as pertaining only to couples living together, regardless of marital status, so divorced husbands are not covered nor is child abuse. The law permits protection orders to be issued for six months, ordering perpetrators to vacate their homes for two weeks for one time only, and provides jail terms of up to one year or one million yen in fines (about $8,000) for those who violate these conditions (Zwarensteyn, 2001). The protection orders may be issued by district courts after a petition is submitted with an affidavit and the abuse is reported to doctors, the police or a local women's center (*fujin sodan sho*—the former prostitute's centers, now known as Spousal Violence Counseling and Support Centers) to demonstrate threat of risk of life or serious physical damage. In emergencies, the court may issue an order to violent spouses without a hearing, although victims are required to submit notarized affidavits to support their claims—these may cost the equivalent of $100 (*Japan Times*, 7 April 2001). It is possible to obtain additional restraining or emergency orders after the initial six-month period is over if there is imminent danger, without a hearing (Rice, 2001, 5).

Monetary support is recommended for local shelters and women's centers; in particular, prefectural governments are encouraged to provide advice, support, encouragement and emergency protection, as well as refuge for victims and to provide trained counselors to assist victims (ibid.). They are to offer financial assistance to the existing prefectural institutions which provide abuse victims with shelter, (the former *fujin sodan sho*), although this does not involve financial aid to support the cost of running shelters (Bando interview, *Japan Times: Kyodo News*, 14 October 2001b, 3). There is no intention to establish public shelters; rather the goal is to encourage support of those that exist, at least one in each prefecture housed in the former prostitute centers (Kaino interview). As many existing private shelters in the prefectures face crises in funding and personnel, they were disappointed at the failure to expand government support. (See *Kyodo News*, 19 December 2001a.) The prefectural shelters will not provide other services such as housing, social security, or children's welfare (Kaino interview).

A survey taken by the Cabinet Office for Gender Equality of respondents in private or public shelters revealed that the police, government offices and local community have been unresponsive to women's abuse in the past, emphasizing the need for a new approach (*Japan Times*, 11 November 2001). As is true elsewhere, the police in Japan have historically been reluctant to become involved in domestic disputes (Goodman, 162). While the DV law urges that police "shall endeavor" to prevent victims from suffering harm from spousal violence; this is a recommendation, not an obligation. The law does punish violence against women as a criminal offense.

Some are concerned that only physical as opposed to psychological violence is included in the new law (*Japan Times*, 30 April 2002; Kaino interview). The legislation has also been criticized for the short two-week period during which the abuser must vacate the family domicile, as well as a cumbersome bureaucratic process to obtain an order of protection, which requires the victim to come forward after the violence has occurred and places the burden of proof on her. In addition to the need for proof, it is necessary to petition the District Court providing notarized evidence to prove a considerable threat of significant harm to life, evidence from the Spousal Violence Counseling and Support Center, police or physicians and certification of marital status (*koseki*) (Gender Equality Bureau, 2001). No coordinating agency has been established and there is no provision for training of police or judicial personnel, nor was a hotline established to report abuse. As of the fall of 2001, the equivalent of $1 million or one billion yen was allocated for this new policy, a very small sum by any measure.

However, despite the problems, early reports of compliance suggest that the law is being utilized by victims. Arrests for spousal abuse have increased, from 365 arrests four years ago to 1,097 in 2002 (Kaino interview). As of April 2002, 508 requests for protection orders had been taken to court and expulsion orders issued, as well as 1,119 prohibitions against approaching battered wives. The average length to complete the procedure is eleven days. Forty-three men have been arrested for violating protection orders, with ensuing fines and prison sentences of about eight months, though some receive probationary sentences (Kaino interview, Research Group, June 6, 2003). There has been a large number of consultations—including requests for support or protection by victims to the police—a total of 14,140 through June 2003 (ibid.). On April 2, 2002, Spousal Violence and Support Centers were opened at the prefectural and local levels, with trained councilors available in most (Rice, 2001). They have now consulted with over 30,000 women; the average length of stay for those who seek shelter has been fourteen days. The city of Tokyo has reported an average of 1,800 DV-related phone calls per month, an indication of the significant response this public policy has engendered (Makita, e-mail, 29 July 2002).

The Ministry of Justice has also reported on efforts to sensitize new public prosecutors to the needs of female victims. More female police officers have been hired (Nohno interview) and efforts have begun to train prosecutors, judges and other judicial personnel in Tokyo and other areas. Activists complain of lack of sensitivity by the police, though there are some reports from shelter staff members of changed police attitudes (Kaino interview). The National Police Agency and other government agencies have recorded dramatic increases in reports of domestic abuse, up by 50 percent, in part due to publicity related to the new law (*Mainichi Interactive*, 2001; *Kyodo News*, 14 October 2001b). However, there is concern among professionals surveyed that the public is ignorant of the law, limiting its ultimate effectiveness, and that almost 90 percent of hospitals and clinics lack measures for dealing with DV victims (*Japan Times*, 30 April–7 June 2002).

A significant first step, the DV law will be reviewed three years after the initial law's passage by statute; Diet women are already assessing ways to strengthen DV policy in the next round.

Conclusion

In both nations, the creation of national policy related to domestic violence reflects the input of "policy communities" that developed as a result of second wave feminism, as well as the input of "policy entrepreneurs" inside the government structure. In Japan, the entrepreneurs were Diet women. Suprapartisan groups of the increased number of female Diet members developed a policy agenda related to women's issues, including laws dealing with DV, anti-stalking and anti–child pornography and prostitution. In the U.S., the entrepreneurs were male and female members of Congress and the Congressional Caucus for Women's Issues, who played advocacy roles with regard to the emerging policy. The VAWA could not have been passed without the support of political "insiders," including Senator Joe Biden and other bipartisan advocates in Congress. "Outsiders" were represented by such groups at the NOW LDEF Task Force and the coalition it created who raised the issue initially and kept it on the policy agenda for decades. As in the United States, the enactment of domestic violence policy in Japan reflects the importance of women holding political office and working in conjunction with movement activists, or "policy communities." It was the synergy created between outside advocates and inside politicians that permitted policy change to occur. In the case of Japan, the process was greatly assisted by *kansetsu gaiatsu*, indirect pressure from UN directives and other Asian and Western nations, before whom Japan did not wish to appear as a backward nation. Some movement "outsiders" have been given roles in negotiating policy and in government bureaucratic processes perhaps marking the creation of a new "space" for women in the political arena.[10]

In Japan, the DV policy represents one in which the bureaucracy did not play a strong role but rather acted as an auxiliary to the Diet leadership. The enactment of this law proved far less controversial than that of the EEOL because there was less perceived opposition from business and others who felt their interests threatened.

What accounts for the popularity of legislation related to dealing with domestic violence? The male breadwinner model is more threatened by equal opportunity than the DV law, although the latter does raise issues about the male family role and right to private property which are not completely resolved in the enacted legislation. In the United States as well, the idea of protecting women victims elicited a great deal of sympathy as the testimonies of abuse in Congress and in the members' constituencies gave credence to the widespread incidence of violence. (Surveys to demonstrate widespread violence against women in Japan as well as testimony created support for policy change there as well.) The transformation of this issue in American politics from one viewed as controversial and radical in the 1980s to one that few dared oppose appears to be related both to the protection of women victims and the criminalization of violent behavior.

Advocates in both nations are pleased with the gains made through legislation but retain a critical stance regarding some aspects of new law in each instance. In the United States, some feminists express concern with the placement of the domestic violence act in a crime bill that emphasizes law and order, rather than as a separate law that would emphasize the issue from a more feminist perspective. Most, however, applaud the gendered "naming" of the law and its inclusive nature as well the continued commitment of decision makers to supporting it. In Japan the new DV law, with its extremely modest outlay of public resources, is seen as a beginning first step. Its limitations are many, including the restriction to couples living together only. The failure to support shelters and to provide for the training of police and judicial personnel means that the DV law lacks the multifaceted approach utilized in the landmark U.S. legislation.

Chapter 4

Reproductive Rights Policy in the United States and Japan

Introduction

In this chapter, the impact of the landmark abortion Supreme Court decision *Roe v. Wade* (410 US 113; 1973) on reproductive rights policy in the United States will be assessed and compared with related policy in Japan. The historic ruling, which legalized abortion nationwide in the fifty American states, had unforeseen consequences resulting in mobilization and polarization, which have persisted during the ensuing decades. In contrast to Japan, where relatively free access to abortion was a legacy of the post-war period, in the United States a reciprocal dynamic was created in which exclusive moral perspectives and identity politics prevented compromise, despite the continued activism of the feminist movement on this issue, considered "the core" concern for many (Warren, 2001).

Unlike in the United States, however, and in contrast to the case of abortion policy, the politics of contraception in Japan proved more contentious and less easy to resolve, making Japan the only nation with legal abortion but no legal contraceptive pill as late as 1990 (Gelb, 1996, 121). This situation was finally altered in 1999. In the Japanese context, it is necessary to explore the reasons for the apparent contradiction between abortion and contraceptive policies. The former has been liberal since 1948, though not without conflict, and the latter conservative, limiting access to the low-dose birth control pill.

The American women's movement has had to remain on the defensive with regard to the erosion of abortion rights, sometimes leading to neglect of other issues and constrained resources and strategies. Contending forces, the pro- and anti-choice movements, rooted in collective identities reflecting differing ideologies and cultures as well as symbolic and real issue divides, have been unable to resolve conflicting values and norms (Johnson, Larana and Gusfield, 1994, 7). This case study is instructive because it involves almost all sectors of American policy-making, as well as the impact of social movements and interest groups. Both nations share relatively high rates of abortion: 2.3 percent of Japanese women have an abortion by the age of 49 and twice as many do in the United States (Gelb, 1996, 119). In the United States teenagers are most likely to have abortions, while in Japan they have been more likely to be mothers with children, ages 30 to 39 for whom abortion is utilized as a kind of birth control (ibid., 124). In contrast to the

United States, married women get the majority of abortions in Japan; varying from about 30 percent to 40 percent during the 1960s to the 1990s (Ogino, 1994, 76).

To what extent are women's groups in general and feminists in particular accorded a voice at the decision-making table in determining reproductive rights policies in each nation? And particularly in Japan, have reproductive rights and health policies been related to state and national goals and control: are policies largely pronatalist or aimed at affecting population growth? Even though abortion policy originated in the bureaucracy in the post-war period, this chapter will emphasize the significance of women's advocacy efforts in preserving access to reproductive freedom.

The United States: Abortion Policy from *Roe* until the Present

The landmark cases *Roe v. Wade* and *Doe v. Bolton* in 1973 tested state laws prohibiting abortion, based on the right to privacy and equal protection of the laws. These abortion cases marked the first major direct national confrontation between pro- and anti-abortion forces, a harbinger of what was to become a hallmark of bitter conflict (McGlen and O'Connor, 1995, 231). Women's rights groups, including the National Organization for Women (NOW) and Planned Parenthood, were arrayed against such anti-abortion groups as Americans United for Life, Women for the Unborn and Women Concerned for the Unborn Child.

The momentous decisions handed down in January 1973 found seven justices concluding that a women's right to privacy superseded the state's right to regulate abortions. Invalidating the abortion laws of the fifty states, the Court divided pregnancy into trimesters, balancing the rights of the woman versus the state differently in each. After the first trimester, in which the pregnant woman's private right to decide whether to abort or not is paramount, the interest of the state becomes more "compelling," related to maternal health and the viability of new human life (ibid., 232; Craig and O'Brien, 1993, 29–30).

Group mobilization
Anti-choice. The abortion decisions were greeted with intense enthusiasm by women's rights groups but they also provided the catalyst for counter-mobilization by the anti-abortion movement.

In the aftermath of the abortion cases, several anti-abortion groups were formed or restructured. The pro-life movement (referred to hereinafter as anti-choice) may have succeeded initially by building grassroots strength and targeting state legislatures to change policy, while the pro-choice movement concentrated on national organizational development. In fact, both sides utilized similar organizational approaches, with varying degrees of success at different times. Movement activism on both sides has mobilized intense minorities.

Although much of the anti-choice movement originated independently of the Catholic Church, that institution provided an infrastructure, communications network, material support and people that provided the movement with a national and local presence (Ginsburg, 1998: 44). Initially, the primary opposition to abortion reform was led by the U.S. Catholic Conference, formed in 1967 in the aftermath of the *Griswold v. Connecticut* decision (381 US 479; 1965) that upheld contraceptive use through a right to privacy. Its affiliates were the National Conference of Catholic Bishops (NCCB) and the National Right to Life Committee (NRTLC), formally organized with resources and financial support after *Roe* (O'Connor, 1996, 59). The NCCB's commitment to end federal funding of abortions and mobilize all Catholic groups was underscored in the 1975 issuance of the "Pastoral Plan for Pro-Life Activities" calling on all Catholic agencies to support a comprehensive pro-life package (Craig and O'Brien 1993, 47). Part of the NCCB's strategy was to organize "right to life" groups in every state. They called for local Catholic dioceses to fund anti-abortion activities. The group also sought a constitutional amendment to give full rights of personhood to the fetus from the moment of conception and provided support for an ultimately unsuccessful National Committee for a Human Life Amendment (McGlen and O'Connor, 1995, 59). Other anti-feminist groups, such as Feminists for Life and Phyllis Schlafly's Eagle Forum effectively linked opposition to the Equal Rights Amendment (ERA) with anti-abortion sentiment. By 1980, Ronald Reagan's election as President legitimized the political role of other conservative and religious groups in the struggle. Now known collectively as the "New Right," they included the Moral Majority and the National Conservative Action Committee (NCPAC). Tensions between the two different components of the anti-choice community may have limited their impact in some instances. In the first category were groups focused on abortion among other social problems, organized at the national level favoring libertarian politics, utilizing such techniques as mass direct mail and political action committees. In the second category were single issue anti-choice groups, mobilized largely at the local level, engaged in face-to-face interaction (Ginsburg, 1998: 9).

By the mid- to late-1970s, fundamentalist, evangelical churches became key actors of the "New Right," relying on a broad social base rooted in their multifaceted attack on lifestyle issues. They proved to be an even more potent force in the Republican Party and abortion politics than the Catholic Church (O'Connor, 1996: 61). Impatient with the slowness of change within the system, groups such as Operation Rescue presaged later, more militant groups who endorsed violence against abortion clinics and providers. Some anti-choice groups, such as Americans United for Life, pursued a litigation strategy, while others within this increasingly specialized political community gathered signatures and pursued legislative and electoral strategies. With the decline of the Moral Majority in 1989 due to diminished revenues, the fundamentalist Christian Coalition quickly took its place (ibid., 132).

Pro-choice. At the time of *Roe v. Wade*, since women's rights groups were perhaps not well organized enough to launch a state-by-state assault on laws, seeking a response from the Supreme Court that would be binding on all states seemed to a more effective (short-term) approach (ibid., 1996, 32). In the aftermath of *Roe*, while women's groups continued to work through their state chapters, their major emphasis was on developing professional national organizations to lobby and mount legal efforts for abortion rights (Craig and O'Brien, 1993, 59). Pro-choice forces in the 1970s included NOW, the National Abortion Rights Action League (NARAL), and Planned Parenthood, as well as more traditional women's groups such as the Young Women's Christian Association (YWCA). The American Civil Liberties Union's Reproductive Freedom Project (RFP) was soon joined by other feminist legal groups.

Many analysts feel that the pro-choice sector was reactive for several years after *Roe*, while the opposition mobilized effectively, although the tide turned again after the *Webster* decision in 1989, discussed below (O'Connor, 1996, 78; Craig and O'Brien, 1993, 59). Pro-choice activists were short on money and numbers in the years after *Roe*. Nonetheless, the pro-choice constituency came to include a wider base, including health associations such as the Guttmacher Institute, the College of Obstetricians and Gynecologists and the American Public Health Association, and religious groups such as the Religious Coalition for Abortion Rights and most mainstream religious denominations (Craig and O'Brien, ibid.).

The fortunes of pro-choice advocates have varied with external factors. The Supreme Court's decision in *Webster v Reproductive Health Services* (492 US 490; 1989), which permitted state restrictions on abortion access, galvanized pro-choice forces in much the same manner as *Roe* did for their opponents (O'Connor, 1996, 152; Craig and O'Brien, 1993, 234; Tatalovich, 1997, 228). The unprecedented numbers of *amicus curiae* briefs in the *Webster* case and others are evidence of the persistent politicization of both sides around the issue: there were three times as many briefs as in the controversial 1978 *Bakke* affirmative action case (438 to 265), and 83 percent were pro-choice (Tatalovich 1997, 229). In congressional abortion hearings from 1973 to 1978, 67 pro-life and 139 pro-choice groups testified; during the same period in 18 Supreme Court cases there were 156 anti- and 465 pro-choice briefs filed (ibid., 229). The Supreme Court was besieged by 40,000 letters in contrast to the normal 1,000 per case (Craig and O'Brien, 1993, 62). As a result of the threat to reproductive choice posed by *Webster*, NOW increased its membership and doubled its budget; NARAL's membership more than doubled (from 150,000 to 400,000) and its budget tripled (ibid., 64). However, while Planned Parenthood also experienced a quadrupling of donations from 1980 to 1990, pro-life groups such as Operation Rescue also used *Webster* as a lightening rod and increased membership and donations as well (O'Connor, 1996, 134). The seesaw of policy and advocacy continued as 178 pro-choice organizations contested the 1992 *Casey* suit. In this case, they were opposed by Feminists for Life, the U.S. Catholic Conference and the National Right to Life Committee in a case that ultimately resulted in the replacement of the central principle of *Roe* with a lesser standard, one permitting abortion restrictions if they did not create an "undue burden" on women (O'Connor, 1996, 143–4). In the late 1990s, a new pro-choice coalition, Abortion Rights Mobilization, challenged the then current government policy of banning the drug RU 486 which produces spontaneous abortions, and continued to advocate on behalf of this issue after its legalization.

Advocacy strategies utilized by pro- and anti-choice forces. Strategies to advance policy goals in the abortion conflict have been similar to those employed by all advocacy groups. They range from litigation strategies, to legislative strategies at the state and national level, to efforts to influence electoral and party politics and public opinion, to grassroots lobbying, to demonstrations. Both sides have sought to manipulate symbols and create sympathy for their views from prospective supporters of all types. On the anti-choice side, violence directed against abortion clinics has dramatically escalated, disrupting services and gaining media attention. Extremism and the shift to violence is a consistent pattern in American history, when movements are or think they are stymied in achievement of their goals (Ginsburg, 1998, 53–4).

Legislative activity. As suggested above, immediately after the *Roe* ruling, right-to-lifers embarked on a campaign to lobby Congress for a constitutional amendment to ban abortions, to press for the Hyde amendment, which limits federal funding for Medicaid abortions and other Congressional legislation and to place restrictions and conditions on women's access to abortion through well-organized state-based activities (McGlen and O'Connor, 1995, 233). While unsuccessful in securing a constitutional amendment, anti-choice forces enjoyed more success at the state and congressional level. They sought to pass laws to try to save the life of the fetus, obtain "informed consent" and notification provisions and deny public funding and facilities for abortion-related procedures (Craig and O'Brien, 1993, 73–102). By 1989, only sixteen states did not require some form of consent or notification; only thirteen states provided unrestricted publicly funded abortions. State abortion politics have at least as many variations as there are states; the composition of the houses of the legislature, position of the governor, relative strength of pro-and anti-choice lobbies, demographics and the nature of competing issues have all influenced a state's abortion policy (ibid., 1993, 283). The *Webster* and *Casey* Supreme Court decisions, discussed below, led to renewed attention to state politics in the 1990s to make abortion laws more restrictive or legalize them further.

In Congress, by the end of 1973, the model for anti-choice activism was already set. In addition to introducing constitutional amendments, there were efforts to define the word "person" to include fetuses, to restrict federal funding of abortion services and to pass "conscience clause" legislation that would permit medical personnel to refuse to perform abortions (ibid., 103–4). As of 1976, the Hyde amendments banning federal funding for abortions were in place. In subsequent years, the debate over Hyde amendments centered on language: abortion permitted or not related to the "endangerment" of life and the health of the mother as well as to cases of rape and incest. In addition "riders" (or attachments) were added to numerous other bills, regardless of the policy area, including funding for the Defense and Education Departments, the Peace Corps, and for the District of Columbia: "All combined to place an enormous strain on the collegial decision making process of the legislative body," affecting legislative behavior and essentially placing pro-abortion forces continually on the defensive (ibid., 135, 150). The anti-choice side, while effectively restricting funding for access to abortion, was nonetheless never able to achieve its goal of passing a constitutional amendment and dismantling *Roe.*

Perhaps the major success enjoyed by the pro-choice side in Congress during the period under review came with the passage of the 1994 Federal Access to Clinic Entrances Act (FACE). Under the Democratic controlled 103rd Congress and with efforts by the Clinton administration to stop clinic violence, Congress, rather than enacting a pro-choice policy which had been sought by some supportive groups passed an anti–clinic violence bill. (O'Connor, 1996, 166). After the killing of a Florida abortion provider, Dr. Michael Gunn, Attorney General Janet Reno called for federal legislation; it was subsequently introduced in both houses of Congress. The tragic murder of Paul Hill, another abortion provider, also in Florida, produced increased support for the bill, and it passed 241 to 174 in the House and 69 to 30 in the Senate; making it a federal crime to block access to reproductive health clinics or to use violence against those seeking and providing such services (O'Connor, 1996, 167; Appelbaum interview). A number of states passed similar laws, before and after the congressional legislation.

Battle lines were drawn again when the 104th Congress passed the Partial Birth Abortion Act, a term coined by anti-choice groups to discuss a relatively rare abortion method used late in pregnancy. Despite candlelight vigils by the NRTLC and Catholic bishops, during his presidency President Clinton continued to veto this legislation. As of June 2000, the Supreme Court declared the so-called partial birth ban unconstitutional in *Stenberg v. Carhart*, although conservative Republicans continue to press for its legislative enactment.

The judicial process. Judicial decision making helped to set the stage for mobilization and counter mobilization by pro- and anti-choice groups. Since *Roe v. Wade*, there have been twenty additional Supreme Court rulings involving restrictions on abortion rights (Planned Parenthood Federation of America, 2000, 1). The strategy of using the courts as arbiter has continued to be key for both sides in the continuing struggle over abortion rights. In 1977, pro-choice forces were dealt a major blow when the Court rejected women's rights groups' challenges to the refusal of Medicaid to support publicly funded abortions (*Maher v. Roe* [432 US 464]; McGlen and O'Connor, 1995, 234). Steadily, with Reagan appointees and with the appointment of William B. Rehnquist as Chief Justice of the court, the scope of *Roe* was continually limited (ibid., 235). The *Webster v. Reproductive Health Services* (492 US 490) decision in 1989 upheld Missouri's restrictions on abortions in public hospitals and tests for fetal viability; states were invited to pass additional restrictions (ibid., 235). *Rust v. Sullivan* (500 US 1973; 1991) upheld Reagan administration regulations barring family planning clinics receiving federal funds from discussing abortion.

Efforts by women's rights groups to protest the constitutionality of a highly restrictive Pennsylvania law did not succeed. Instead, the court upheld the view that replaced the central principle of *Roe* with a lesser standard in the *Planned Parenthood of Southeast Pennsylvania v. Casey* (305 US 833) decision in 1992, permitting state laws that did not place an "undue burden" on women to stand. Nonetheless, as was the case for *Roe* some fifteen years earlier, these decisions, although "a victory of sorts for the pro-life forces," may have taken some steam out of their drive (Craig and O'Brien, 1993, 197). Reacting to the rulings, the pro-choice groups were able to fill their coffers and mount full-scale public relations efforts to gain support as well as targeting key elections and orchestrating mass rallies (ibid.).

As was true in the U.S. Congress, the issue of violence against abortion clinics produced somewhat different outcomes than that of access to abortion. The *NOW v. Scheidler* (114 US 798) decision in 1994 found the court ruling unanimously that anti-choice activity could be curtailed by recourse to the Racketeer Influenced and Corrupt Organizations Act (RICO), in order to curb clinic violence and harassment, although the law was originally designed to stop illegal business practices. In this case, "creative lawyering" was utilized to stop practices viewed as illegal but for which no statutory remedy existed (O'Connor, 1996, 159).[1] This decision, together with action in the U.S. Congress, and some state legislatures, reflected rejection of the violence and confrontations mounted by the anti-choice forces nationwide (Tatalovich, 1997, 71).

As suggested above, in June 2000, in *Stenberg v. Carhart* (530 US 938), the Supreme Court ruled that Nebraska's so-called partial birth abortion law was unconstitutional because it failed to include an exception to preserve the life of the woman. It imposed an "undue burden" on the woman's ability to obtain an abortion.

Abortion and party politics. The intense partisanship that has developed around abortion contributed to the failure to achieve political compromise on this issue (ibid., 150). The two parties' platforms have differed dramatically on support for abortion since 1980 when Reagan incorporated anti-choice views into the Republican platform (Tatalovich 1997, 155). The platform of that party ever since has called for the appointment of judges at all levels who "respect . . . the sanctity of innocent human life" and also uphold the rights of the "unborn child." In contrast, the Democrats recognize reproductive freedom as a "fundamental human right." Many political campaigns have been affected by the issue.

The weakness of American parties makes them vulnerable to infiltration by intense pressure groups; primary elections to choose party nominees are often susceptible to intervention from well-organized policy activists (ibid., 165). Political Action Committees (PACs) representing each side funnel aid directly to candidates who support their views. Campaigns and elections are therefore subject to "capture" by well-organized single-issue groups who control many votes. The polarized party system has been unable to produce compromise or moderation on abortion due to the intense politicization of this issue by pro- and anti-choice pressure groups in political campaigns through funding and endorsements.

Protest activity: legal and illegal. Because of the emotion and passion surrounding the abortion issue, demonstrations and marches have been used by both sides to seek influence over politicians and to rally the faithful. Marching on Washington has become an indispensable part of pressure politics in the United States, sending a message to opponents and supporters, and rallying membership

(Craig and O'Brien, 1993, 48). Each year since the *Roe* decision, abortion opponents convene in Washington for a "March for Life." By January 1980, their numbers ranged from between 50,000 and 100,000 participants (ibid.). During the next decade and after, annual national and state marches by both sides had become the norm. Pro-choice groups were slower to enter the process of "marching" but in 1989 demonstrations to prevent and then protest the *Webster* decision attracted between 300,000 and 500,000 participants. Additional rallies were held in the nation's capital and more than 150 cities throughout the United States in November 1989 (ibid., 307).

The Pro-life Non Violent Action Project (PNAP) was one of the first to "use nonviolent action to protect babies" (Craig and O'Brien, 1993, 57). Their activities set the stage for numerous other "rescue" activities to close abortion clinics. By 1989, Operation Rescue was organized in over 200 cities, claiming to use non-violent tactics to blockade clinics and prevent entrance. The aim was to create media attention. Violence erupted in a number of confrontations, possibly creating sympathy for those arrested, or, conversely, creating a public backlash against the perpetrators. Throughout the 1990s, fire bombings of clinics, blockading of clinics by such groups as Operation Rescue's offshoot, the Lambs of Christ, and murders of abortion providers and clinic personnel gained intensity. Primarily comprised of evangelical Protestant men, the use of terrorist tactics escalated the abortion issue and may have begun to undermine the anti-choice movement's legitimacy (Ginsburg, 1998, xii). A group that condoned the violence, the American Coalition of Life Activists, publicly declared its commitment to "justifiable homicide" and targeting of doctors who perform abortions (ibid., xiii). Presumably these acts were the work of a fanatic minority of anti-choice activists frustrated with the pace of success in their crusade. Their tactics had a two pronged impact: further reducing access to abortion services for American women as well as leading more moderate anti-choice forces to distance themselves from extremist violence.

Hospital mergers: A new phase of the abortion conflict? Hospital mergers are increasingly subject to growing media attention and discussion in the public venue, bringing the abortion conflict to a new policy venue (Bucar, 1998, 16). With increasing frequency, Catholic and non-Catholic hospitals are merging, ostensibly for cost-related reasons, resulting in decreasing availability of reproductive services.[2] There were 127 such mergers in 31 states from 1990 to 1998, as well as an increasing number of Catholic-owned managed healthcare systems (Gold, 2000, 1). Between 1990 and 1996, Catholic hospitals were involved in 40 percent of hospital mergers, new affiliations and acquisitions (Weissman et al., 1997, 11–14). In 1998 alone, 43 such mergers were completed, compared with 14 in 1997. The trend is seen by many as "stealth elimination" of reproductive services (Baumgardner, 1999, 12).

Concern occurs because Catholic hospitals and facilities follow the ethical and religious directives of the Catholic Health Care Services, which prohibit abortions, tubal ligations, vasectomies, contraceptive services and most fertility treatments (Bellandi, 1999). In half of the mergers to date, the non-Catholic hospital has agreed to terminate some or all provision of reproductive services (Ornstein, 1998).

However, in many instances, community pressure, often from the pro-choice side, has forced hospital partners to come up with "creative solutions" or to terminate the mergers if compromise is not possible. In some instances, "creative solutions" or "material cooperation" (on access other than abortion, in the main) involving continuation of some, if not all, reproductive services such as tubal ligations have been agreed upon when the Catholic hospital gains dominance. In states such as California, legislation has been adopted that provides for the state attorney general to review proposed mergers, considering their impact on the healthcare of the community (Gold, 2000).

While the anti-choice movement was able to use the infrastructure provided by religious institutions to its advantage for much of the history of this conflict, the battle over hospital mergers may present a different model. (See McCarthy, 1987, 64.) Regarding the most recent conflict related to access to reproductive rights for American women, hospital mergers under Catholic aegis, a major factor in determining policy outcomes appears to be the strength of locally based pro-choice advocacy, often operating in conjunction with professional women's groups and experts. (See Skocpol, 1999, 461–505; Putnam, 2000, 154, 165; and Zald and McCarthy, 1997, 339–42 for an opposing view.) They have mounted broad-based coalitions, reaching beyond pro-choice issues to citizens concerned about continuation of medical services and free access. Such successful efforts may be reflective of a new phase of the movement, broader and more inclusive than the original single-issue pro-choice movement, which has mobilized a new constituency and sought to develop new strategies (Zald and Useem, 1987, 249). Effective links have been developed between grassroots activists and their professional allies in the pro-choice and feminist movement.

The overview of mobilization by pro-and anti-choice groups presented here takes issue with those who have argued that an "infrastructure deficit" has impeded the role of pro-choice forces, who have relied on national, professional advocacy rather than grassroots organizing (McCarthy, 1987, 64; Putnam, 2000, 154; Staggenborg, 1991, 155). Their task, in some instances, has been eased by the dominance in this policy arena of Catholic hospital administrators and local church clergymen, rather than the fully mobilized forces of the anti-choice movement. Shifting the discourse on abortion to a new focus on economic interests and the role of community consultation regarding loss of service provision may produce support from a broader, more diverse issue constituency. In sum, mergers may be more susceptible to bargaining and compromise than identity oriented nonnegotiable abortion-related policy issues. As interest-based structures such as hospitals enter the fray, with budgets to develop and services to deliver in an environment of shrinking resources, they may prove more amenable to negotiations than the single-issue, religiously based anti-choice groups that have previously dominated the local political arena.

However, Pope John Paul II has recently warned that Catholic sponsorship of creative solutions may be lost to hospital administrators who bend church rules on reproductive services; he has also threatened increased scrutiny of compromises and intervention in some existing merger compromises (O'Donnell, 1999, 28). The National Conference of Catholic Bishops followed suit by announcing a tightening of conditions related to hospital-based sterilization. Does the future suggest a continued or abated struggle over reproductive health and rights in the United States, given some successful efforts at the community level to resolve conflict over hospital mergers?

Policy outcomes. From 1990 to 1997, the numbers of abortions performed annually has fallen from 1.429 million to 1.186 million (Planned Parenthood, 2000). As of 1995, 86 percent of U.S. counties have no known abortion provider; nor do 95 percent of women in non-metropolitan counties (Henshaw, 1998). The average cost of a first trimester abortion is about $350—limiting access for younger and low-income women (Talbot, 1999). Legal restrictions in many states mandate parental consent, waiting periods or court-imposed requirements for minors (Henshaw, 1998). Forty-two states have passed laws requiring parental consent to a minor's abortion; 31 have established judicial or other barriers (Planned Parenthood, 2001).

Mifepristone—formerly known as RU 486 (the "morning after" pill)—was approved as a medical alternative to abortion by the Food and Drug Administration (FDA) in September 2000, despite intense lobbying by anti-choice groups. These anti-abortion forces delayed the adoption of the legalization of this drug for eight years, successfully linking opposition to RU 486 to the issue of abortion in general. They sought to present the drug as an extension of the abortion process, rather than equating it with contraception (Jackman, 1997, 113). Anti-abortion forces threatened an economic boycott and violence against the designated drug manufacturer and successfully banned the drug's importation into the United States for a time. The drug manufacturer was concerned about the controversy accompanying the sale of this pill and the first Bush administration put the medication on its list of drugs banned by the FDA from U.S. importation for personal use. Framed as an extension of the abortion struggle by the opposition, pro-choice forces challenged the scientific and political underpinnings of the ban, and brought the force of media attention and constituency pressure to bear on the issue through legal tests and lobbying in the form of letters and petitions (ibid., 132). During the Clinton administration, the power of the presidency was brought to bear on the issue and the drug underwent trials for the first time and the importation ban was rescinded. Difficulties related to widespread distribution remain, due to pressure on manufacturers from some anti-choice groups not to produce this drug (Talbot, 1999). Anti-choice groups have continued to introduce legislation in Congress to prohibit testing, development or approval of the drug as well (Talbot, 1999, 39–43). This form of contraception has been available in France since 1988; in the United Kingdom since 1991 and in Sweden since 1992; as of September 2000, four years after declaring it "safe," the FDA gave final permission for Mifepristone to be marketed in the United States. However, the drug is not made available to women directly; rather, it is distributed only to physicians (Guttmacher Institute, 2000).

Efforts to bring issues of abortion into the international political arena have been undertaken by successive Republican presidential administrations (Reagan and both Bush presidencies), as they seek to exclude abortion from reproductive health services. They have banned the use of U.S. federal funds to assist international family planning groups that offer abortion or abortion counseling, with President George W. Bush reinstating the prohibition after its suspension by the Clinton administration in 1993 (Gupta, 2001).

The abortion conflict in the United States reveals the tremendous obstacles created by an effective counter mobilization, which has succeeded in dramatically affecting the discourse and outcomes of reproductive policy in the United States. The costs of defending access have been significant and have contributed to a hostile environment that permeates consideration of all women's issues.

Japan

Abortion policy making. As suggested above, the politics of abortion in Japan are among the most liberal of developed nations, dating back to 1948. In 1949, Japan became the first country to permit legal abortion and abortion via the Eugenic Protection Law, based on socioeconomic grounds, ending the principle that abortion was a serious criminal offense. In 1952, a requirement that women appear before a review committee before undertaking abortion was eliminated (Norgren, 2001, 3). Abortion has continued to be a contested policy issue but free of the confrontation that distinguishes the American case. However, there have been periodic efforts to restrict abortion access, and pressures may grow due to a steadily declining birth rate. Contraception has been the more controversial reproductive issue in Japan—it appeared highly likely that Japan would be the only nation in the UN that had not legalized the pill in the new millennium when a furor over rapid approval of Viagra for men led to vociferous protest, leading to approval of the pill in June 1999 (ibid.). The effective copper intrauterine device (IUD) (in contrast to the less effective plastic one) also gained approval only in 1999 (ibid., 6).

The effect of Japanese reproductive policies has been to increase women's reliance on abortion as well as the condom as the primary means of contraception (ibid.). What explains the discrepancy between two reproductive policies that normally operate in tandem in most nations? What is the role of the Japanese government in controlling and directing reproductive rights, and why has there been opposition to alternative methods of birth control? Where do these policies fit into a "bureaucratic" versus "advocacy coalition" model of policy making in comparison with others evaluated in this volume?

In her analysis of Japanese reproductive rights policy Norgren suggests the relevance of the idea of a "path dependent" approach or the reinforcement and magnification of policy over time without apparently rational causes (ibid., 10). This in itself, however, hardly explains the reasons for the adoption of specific policy choices made initially or for their continuation. The "feedback" effect, or emphasis on the policy process, suggests that policies produce new politics, often by resulting in the creation of groups that defend and oppose constituted policy (Baumgartner, 2002, 10–11). Seen from this perspective, group mobilization, along neopluralist lines, may be a promising means of understanding reproductive rights policies in Japan (as Norgren persuasively argues, 2001). Professional and women's interest groups, in conjunction with state actors, particularly bureaucrats and some Diet members, have been the major players in the policy debate related to reproductive issues in Japan, although their positions particularly on contraception have shifted over time. The next section will explore the mobilization of women's groups in support of policies they had little or no role in adopting, similar to the relationship of U.S.-based feminist groups to Title VII of the 1954 Civil Rights Act.

Legislative activity. The Eugenic Protection Law passed in 1948 represented the government's anti-natalist position at the time when the government was concerned with unlimited population growth in a ruined economy and a nation beset by massive destruction after World War II. The law reflected a progressive stance in that it decriminalized abortion but it did so within the framework of a regressive and outmoded eugenic ideology (ibid., 40). In addition to stating that the protection of the life and health of the mother was key, it also sought to prevent the birth of "inferior descendants" (Ogino, 1994, 72). The bill's sponsors were socialists who saw a "window of opportunity" and obstetricians/gynecologists (ob-gyns) who represented interest group activism within the Diet as opposed to bureaucrats, an early post-war example of the potential strength of Diet members. The socialists proposed a law that permitted abortion almost freely on demand as well as other forms of reproductive control, but also provided for compulsory eugenic sterilization. The bill finally passed was sponsored by an Upper House ob-gyn named Taniguchi Yasaburo. It eliminated the initial "financial hardship" grounds for abortion and added that only approved doctors could perform abortions as well as stipulating that a Eugenic Protection Committee needed to approve them. Since eight of the ten sponsors of the bill were physicians, it is widely believed that the medical professionals were the likely beneficiaries of the legislation (Ogino, 1994, 72). The law's passage may have been motivated in part by the desire of doctors (ob-gyns) to gain control over women's healthcare, wresting control from midwives and ensuring access to the lucrative abortion practice (Norgen, 2001, 42).

In 1949, the abortion law was liberalized to permit abortion if serious harm would come to the mother's health for economic or physical reasons or if rape occurred (ibid., 45). Since this revision, 99 percent of Japanese women have cited "economic reasons" when choosing to have abortions (ibid., 46). In 1952, the requirement to appear before a special committee for abortion permission was abandoned, permitting access to abortion virtually on demand (Ogino, 1994, 72). In the aftermath of the law's passage, a group called Nichibo (Association for Maternal Welfare), unofficially dedicated to defending and liberalizing the abortion law, was established. The group had ties to the powerful Japanese Medical Association which in turn had strong connections to Diet members.

The legislation served to enhance the role of Nichibo in the policy process; it became a "subsystem" with privileged access that remained relatively independent of popular control for decades (Baumgartner and Jones, 1993) seizing upon a "window of opportunity" presented in the post-war period. While the women's movement did not participate at all in this key decision affecting many women's major choices, it played an active role later, both defending abortion access and revising aspects of the law.

There have been periodic efforts to restrict abortion access in Japan, particularly among family planning advocates, some feminist Diet members who feared abortion was out of control, and the group Seicho no Ie, a movement organized by a new right-wing religion. The latter group mobilized after the mid-1960s and 1970s, when it became more actively engaged with Liberal Democratic Party (LDP) members in the Diet, many of whose re-election campaigns it had supported. It founded the League to Revise or Abolish the Eugenic Protection Law in 1967. International pressure also played a role in revisiting this issue, as Japan became concerned that it was being viewed as an "abortion haven" by other nations (ibid.). A compromise reached by Nichibo and the Seicho no Ie group would have resulted in legislation abolishing the "economic reasons" clause that promoted easy access to abortion, a plan strongly supported by the Ministry of Health and Welfare in 1973. But, before the revised law could be passed, an impressive countermobilization was mounted, comprised of feminist groups, women's groups, members of opposition parties, Diet members, representatives of the handicapped, family planning organizations, trade union members and leaders and others, contributing to the defeat of the proposed law reform (Gelb, 1996, 130). This protest even included a sit-in at the Ministry of Health and Welfare (MHW) building. Feminist and handicapped people's rights groups, from the Marxist-oriented Gurupu Tatakau Onna (Fighting Women's Group) to the nascent Ribu Shinjyuku Senta (the latter's agenda expanded to include battered women's issues as well as lectures and demonstrations on other issues) (Ogino, 1994, 66) were galvanized by this effort. Chupiren, a women's liberation group discussed in chapter two (the militant Group to Oppose Abortion Prohibition Law and Lift the Pill Ban), also opposed the proposed law reform as well as advocating contraception, unlike other Japanese feminist groups in this period. The latter emphasized an individualistic rights-oriented discourse, unusual for Japan at that time. The offensive legislation was dropped in 1974.

A second effort to limit abortion access under the Eugenic Protection Law occurred in the early 1980s. At that time, prodded again by an even more powerful Seicho no Ie, whose membership had grown from 1.5 million to 3.5 million (ibid., 72), the MHW announced plans to delete the economic reasons clause of the law. Three hundred conservative Diet members had joined the pro-revision Respect for Life League (Seiseiren kokkai giin renmei) to support this effort, in addition to successfully mobilizing local assembly efforts to pass pro-revision resolutions. Anti-revision groups saw the attempt to repeal abortion access as part of larger conservative agenda that they wished to defeat, which included remilitarization and a return to more traditional sex roles. Again, the anti-abortion groups were met with vigorous opposition, this time from feminist and traditional women's groups, family planners and doctors from the Japan Medical Association as well as Nichibo. By May 1983, almost one and one-half million signatures had been collected as opposed to one million for the pro-revision groups. Three types of women's groups were involved in the protest effort: one organized by the Family Planning Federation of Japan; a second representing more establishment kinds of women's groups such as the Japan Women's Christian Temperance Union and Japan Nurses Association; a third, more feminist "hub," which included members of the earlier 1970s pro-choice organizations (Norgren, 2001, 74). The latter included Umu, umanai wa onna ga kimeru ("Women decide to bear or not to bear") and the "[19]82 Antiabortion Law Reform coalition" or Soshiren, comprised of more than sixty groups (Ogino, 1994, 88). Finally, younger, college-age women as well as housewives and workers mobilized over 5,000 grass roots groups around the nation (Norgren, 2001, 74). Protests were also held at the Diet and in Tokyo's Yoyogi park. Groups participating in this massive effort included the Housewives Federation, Japan League of Women Voters, Japan Women Lawyers Association and countless others. Some had been galvanized by the 1975 International Women's Year (IWY), which advocated reproductive choice for women, an early use of international pressure on changing equity norms.

As a precursor of later developments on women's policies discussed in chapter three and elsewhere in this volume, a non-partisan group of twenty-five female Diet members issued a statement opposing revision (Ogino, 1994, 75). Because of the IWY, as is true for other issues discussed here, the government may have been more sensitized to the disregard of women's concerns. By the early 1980s, public discussion of reproductive access gained more visibility, as conflict around it was socialized, or made more public, than the earlier 1970s attempted abortion revision. Somewhat in contrast to the first conflict, which revolved primarily around interest groups and their political allies, in 1983 a broad-based coalition of women's based anti-revision forces resisted policy change (Norgren, 2001, 77).

In 1990, the Ministry of Health and Welfare did shorten the period during which abortion is available from twenty-four to twenty-two weeks, without consulting women's groups at all and in just a period of three hours of deliberation in the Public Health *shingikai*. Their action may have been motivated by fear of broad resistance given the election of ten new women to the Diet, including Domoto Akiko, who was committed to reproductive choice (Gelb, 1996, 130). Despite a year of protests, the revised rule went into effect in 1991 and has remained ever since.

In 1996, a revision of the Eugenic Protection Law finally succeeded; this time more in accordance with feminist demands, as the name of the law was changed to the Maternal Protection Law and eugenic provisions were dropped. Handicapped groups in particular objected to the eugenic aspects of the law as did small groups of left-wing feminists. Groups such as Josei Sogaisha Nettowaku and Soshiren had participated in international conferences including the 1994 International Conference on Population and Development in Cairo and the 1995 Beijing conference in order to call attention to the "anachronistic, discriminatory, and coercive" aspects of the law and they gained heart from the more individualistic approaches of their international sisters (Norgren, 2001, 79). These advocacy groups wanted to also highlight women's reproductive rights and health, rather than maternal protection, to eliminate the Criminal Abortion Law originally passed in 1880 and partially revised in 1907, and to make sterilization and abortion available on demand, without any restrictions at all (*Women for Alternative Legal Systems*, 2000, 1). Although there have been few prosecutions under the Criminal Law given the relative broadness of the "economic" criteria category, activists have nonetheless pressed for its elimination as violating Article 2 of the 1995 Beijing Platform for Action which opposes all national penal provisions that discriminate against women[3] (ibid. Ogino, 1994, 72). Efforts by a cross-party group of Diet women from LDP (Nohno), the Democratic Party (Komiyama), Japan Socialist Party (Fukushima and Shimizu) as well as Domoto and others to change this policy through Diet legislation have not proven successful to date (Ashino interview).

The Social Policy Committee of LDP together with bureaucrats from the MHW took a leadership role in drafting legislation and hurriedly drafted a bill in one and one-half months. The LDP threatened to withdraw support from this bill if there was reconsideration of the Criminal Abortion Law or other issues (Ashino interview). Women's groups and smaller handicapped groups were not participants in the process; rather the more established groups like Nichibo and established groups representing the handicapped were (Norgren, 2001, 80). Some view the outcome as at least a partial failure of the *gaiatsu* strategy, although in the absence of the Cairo meeting as "trigger" or focusing event, reform would not have been undertaken at all (*Women for Alternative Legal Systems*, 2000, 1). Women's groups were "disappointed" with the outcome of the legal revision for the law, in terms of the name and content, now called the Maternal Protection Law or the Law for Protection of Mother's Bodies (*botai hogo ho*) adopted in February 2000 which did eliminate the eugenic protection aspect of the law (e.g., abortion and sterilization for mentally defective persons; Ashino interview). Provisions providing for doctors and husband's approval were left in the law (ibid.).

Advocates of abortion choice remain concerned about what they view as lack of accessibility to abortion for many, despite apparently wide availability. Abortions (and birth control) in Japan are not covered by national health insurance since they are not seen as women's health issues (Ashino, 1999, 91); first trimester abortion cost about 100,000 yen (close to $1,000): for second trimester abortions the costs may increase to as much as 300,000 yen. Birth control pills (to be discussed below) may cost up to 60,000 to 70,000 yen per year, prohibitive for many. Nor are there family planning clinics or women's centers that provide assistance to women, contributing to general ignorance of reproductive issues (Ashino, 1999, 91).

Although there has been controversy regarding continued access to abortion in Japan, as in most nations, there is no major religious or moral opposition comparable to that mounted in the United States by Catholic and fundamentalist Protestant churches. Nonetheless, Buddhist temples have sought to play upon feelings of guilt by inducing women to purchase *Mizuko jizo*, or memorials to the departed souls of dead infants, erected on temple grounds. Abortion in Japan has remained a contested, but less confrontational, policy arena particularly in contrast with the United States.

Policy toward contraception. In the aftermath of World War II, abortion was largely accessible due to intervention by interest groups, but during this same period few voices spoke in favor of dissemination of birth control information. In contrast to the United States, where oral contraceptives were approved in 1960, controversy about the low-dose birth control pill dragged on for over thirty years in Japan (Ashino, 1999, 86). In June 1999, the low-dose pill was finally approved, together with a copper IUD, by the predominantly male General Pharmaceutical Council (21 men and 3 women) (ibid.). Despite concerns about overpopulation, Japanese government officials were divided on contraception[4] Concern about the impact of legalization on birth rates, public health and morals was apparently linked to the more accessible politics of abortion (Norgren, 2001, 103).

In the absence of strong interest group advocacy for pill legalization—in contrast to support for abortion access—government bureaucrats and their political allies dominated this policy arena for decades. Although Eugenic Marriage Consultation Offices were established and could have served as family planning facilities as part of the Eugenic Protection Law, they proved to be under funded and ineffective (it is not clear that they would have been used anyway). Ministry of Health and Welfare bureaucrats were determined to block access to contraception, treating it as "dangerous" (ibid., 90). A Pharmaceutical Law passed in 1949 did permit manufacture and distribution of a number of contraceptives. But cost and poor quality limited impact and contributed to the widespread view that contraceptives were unreliable and unsafe. A key player in the politics of contraception was Diet Representative Taniguch Yasaburo who unsuccessfully proposed more efforts to promote birth control (ibid., 95).

In 1954 the government created a permanent Population Problems Advisory Council, which exists today, and strove to provide contraception to poor women. The government was instrumental in encouraging the formation of a major family planning group, the Japan Family Planning Association, which benefited from as well as contributing to the evolving discussion of contraceptive policy (ibid., 102).

Efforts to gain approval of the pill in the early 1960s by the MHW were derailed in large measure by the strong opposition of Shizue Kato, a socialist party member and family planning advocate who at that time was an Upper House member—although the pill was widely available widely over the counter from this time through the early 1970s (Gelb, 1996, 127). Emphasizing potential health risks and dangerous side effects, the two main family planning organizations, Nichibo, the Japan Medical Association, Japan Midwives Association, and LDP Women's Bureau all voiced opposition (Gelb, 1996, 111). Japanese women relied on abortions and condoms for birth control and the latter, the primary form of contraception, was actively promoted by family planning associations that sold them at a profit. Income derived from condom sales, particularly as Japan became the largest condom-producing nation in the 1980s, may have deterred family planners from advocating alternatives (Ogino, 1994, 77). In addition, family planners and midwives, as well as ob-gyns, may have feared a decline in revenue if alternative forms of birth control became available. The pharmaceutical industry, which advocated liberalization, could not compete with this formidable array of mobilized interests. Feminist women opposed the pill as well partially due to rifts with the more radical pro-pill group Chupiren. The Chupiren's militancy on this issue antagonized other feminists and retarded the development of a unified position on the issue (Norgren, 2001, 118).

In the 1970s, anti-pill forces contributed to an environment in which the pill could not be mentioned on radio or TV and was recalled from pharmacies.

However, by the 1980s, the ob-gyn and family planning groups had changed their minds and began to petition the government to test and approve the low-dose pill (Ogino, 1994, 77). And, at this time, other long-held interests that had been hostile to the legalization of the low-dose pill reversed their positions, including Nichibo, the Japanese Association of Obstetricians and Gynecologists and some women's groups. Former opponent Shizue Kato also now announced support for the pill. The new perspectives may have been influenced by generational changes within organizations, as well as increased knowledge that women elsewhere in the world had used the pill without dire health consequences.

Still, even during this period, few members of women's groups and individual women pressed for a change in the policy that permitted restricted use of the high-dose pill despite higher health risks. They feared turning women into sex objects, placing the burden of contraception on them and risking health due to side effects from taking synthetic hormones. Their antipathy may have been associated with concern about the "medicalization of reproduction," based in fear that drug companies were seeking to make quick profits without concern for women's health and that pill approval might jeopardize abortion access (Ogino, 1994, 84; Ashino, 1999, 89; Norgren, 2001, 115). The concept of individual choice played virtually no role in this perspective that stressed negative collective consequences. There was never a groundswell of opinion in favor of pill legalization among Japanese feminists or women in the public. Large majorities of women said they did not and would not wish to use the pill even if liberalized, citing possible side effects, as most claimed familiarity with the pill and its side effects (11 percent in the 1996 *Mainichi* survey, Gelb, 1996, 128; Ashino, 1999, 89). The use of contraception decreased dramatically from 63.6 percent in 1950 to 15.1 percent in 1992, an indication of lack of interest in this mode of contraception that weakened the case for policy change (Ogino, 1994, 74).

Ultimately, the Ministry of Health and Welfare froze the process during the 1980s and most of the 1990s, using AIDS as an excuse and citing concern for public morals, perhaps to prevent a further decline in the birth rate (Gelb, 1996b, 124,127). A key factor in the development of this policy was the ability of the HWM to control the Drug Council *shingikai* and to keep its proceedings secret, creating a lack of accountability and transparency that made policy change difficult for its proponents.

Contraceptive policy change. As noted, the voices of the women's movement were muted on the issue of pill liberalization for most of the late twentieth century (Ashino, 1999, 89). Not until the 1996 and after did groups like Repuro no

Genki no kai and the Professional Women's Coalition for Sexuality and Health galvanize into action, prompted in part by the 1994 Cairo Population Conference's Platform for Action (Norgren, 2001, 128). At the conference, Japan was the only country in attendance that did not support the low-dose oral contraceptive (Mainichi Shinbun 2000, 192). After attending international meetings, feminist groups, while still viewing the pill as a poor choice for contraception, began to advocate for its legalization based on the notion of rights and individual, alternative choices for women (Ogino, 1994, 87). However, during the next several years, the MHW equivocated and failed to approve the pill as promised, a position possibly now reinforced by the low-birth rate. By the end of 1998, Shizue Kato, now head of the Family Planning Federation of Japan, submitted a petition for speedy approval of the low-dose pill. The Professional Women's Coalition also began lobbying in earnest, through petitions and demonstrations. The final coup de grace came when—in just six months—the MHW approved the impotency cure Viagra for men in January 1999. Governmental embarrassment and an international outcry over the differential treatment for men and women led to the final approval of the low-dose pill in June 1999—with sales beginning September of that year (Norgren, 2001, 130). The role of *gaiatsu* is evident in this policy change as well; at an international population conference in The Hague in 1999 to assess five-year progress after the Cairo conference, Japanese feminists used the opportunity to attract attention in order to embarrass the government into changing its policy. At this conference, Diet member Komiyama Yoko cited the rapid approval of Viagra as evidence of bias against women (Ashino interview).

Once legalized, the costs and requirements for frequent checkups for women pill takers made the likelihood of widespread pill use limited. There are strict guidelines for pill usage, including health tests, and the relatively high cost (the equivalent of $550 to $950 per year) will act as a deterrent as well. One month before the policy change, only 12 percent of respondents planned to use it (Kihara et al., 2001). One year after passage only one half of one percent (or 100,000 of a possible 30 million) of Japanese women of childbearing age had gotten pill prescriptions (Kihara et al., 2001, 6). As of the 2000 *Mainichi* family planning survey, there had been no real increase in pill usage. Only 3.3 percent of married women and 3.8 percent of unmarried women say they want to use the pill; the majority fears unwanted side effects (Wagatsuma, 2000, 195; Piccininio and Moshter, 1998, 1). Only 1.5 percent of Japanese women take the pill, in comparison with 26.5 percent in the United States, although awareness of the pill increased to 82 percent in 1999, up from 62 percent in 1996 (Kihara et al., 6). One observer concludes that the long delay in approval of oral contraceptives "has given incorrect and inadequate information to Japanese people and created strong prejudice against the pill" (Wagatsuma, 2000, 199). In some ways, easy access to abortion may have complicated the contraceptive issue for women and government policy makers.

However, as the story of access to abortion and contraception makes clear, in the post-war period Japanese women's groups, animated by newly emerging internationally gender-related norms, have pressed their vision upon a reluctant Japanese government, bringing the reproductive policy full circle. The Criminal Abortion Law, which is rarely used but resulted in two arrests of doctors in 1993 and 1995 (Ashino interview), is the next issue slated for reform by pro-choice activists in Japan.

There are cross pressures at play with regard to Japanese reproductive policy, as there is concern with the continued low birth rate in Japan (see chapter five), and this has led to efforts to promote population expansion, with some initiatives being taken primarily at the local level to induce procreation (Ashino interview).

Conclusion

In both the United States and Japan, issues related to motherhood, abortion and birth control continue to be contentious in the public arena. Issues of reproductive rights and access, viewed as "core" concerns, have proven to be catalysts for feminist organizing and coalition building in both nations. The analysis suggests the importance of "feedback" effects through which policy creates new politics and political mobilization. In Japan, women's groups were not part of the policy process that produced easy access to abortion, but they have been mobilized to defend their rights on several occasions through the creation of multiple organizations and coalitions. This case study clearly suggests the ability of movement activists to overcome tendencies toward fragmentation and to exercise political agency, particularly over the 50-year time period. Women's groups successfully petitioned for the renaming of the Eugenic Protection Law although as yet they have not succeeded in decriminalizing abortion.

This chapter has sought, in part, to explain the disjunction between policy toward abortion and that related to contraception in Japan. In contrast to the abortion issue, the failure of the Japanese government to legalize the pill was in part due to the division and silence of movement activists on this issue. Their absence from the decision-making process meant that other interests—professional, medical and bureaucratic—dominated the policy discourse until very recently, ultimately permitting bureaucrats to frame the politics of contraception. In the final analysis, Japanese feminists were aided in the process of renaming the Maternal Protection Law and final approval of the low-dose pill by recourse to a rights-based perspective activated by *gaiatsu*.

For American feminists, the struggle to defend abortion rights and access has been an all encompassing task. The American case also demonstrates the importance of "feedback" effects, this time in a reverse manner related to the counter-mobilization of anti-choice forces, who have proven to be formidable adversaries. In this instance, the separation of powers and federal system have proven to a hindrance for women activists, as they have been forced to defend their rights on many political terrains including all branches of national and state government. Feminists have had to fend off persistent and effective attacks from the "New Right," made more powerful through their links to the Republican Party. The polarization of American parties and politics on this issue has limited American feminists to an alliance solely with the Democratic Party, making compromise on abortion difficult to attain. In the United States, the highly politicized nature of the abortion debate affects all aspects of decision making. Although feminists in and outside of government have been able to influence agendas related to abortion and reproductive rights, they have not always been able to achieve positive policy impact. Growing institutional power through the Congressional Caucus on Women's Issues (CCWI) and committee and party leadership positions have helped support their efforts. However, even women in Congress have been divided on the abortion issue (and are increasingly likely to be so, with the increase of right-wing Republican women elected). The first time the CCWI took a pro-choice stand was in 1992, with the influx of new members after that election year. The group has since retreated to a position of neutrality on abortion (Dodson, 1998, 135). In Congress, feminist advocates were unable to gain passage of the Freedom of Choice Act, 1989–1991, which would have placed the principles of *Roe v. Wade* into federal legislation, partially due to internal divisions among CCWI members. Pro-choice forces were more successful in placing the issue of restrictions on federal funding for Medicaid abortions on the congressional agenda in some years, although they have not always able to influence outcomes in terms of access (ibid., 140–41).

The CCWI has been influential in affecting policy related to clinic-related violence and harassment, via FACE. Women members of Congress put pressure on committee sponsors such as Schumer (D-NY) and Brooks (D-TX) to pursue the legislation. And, women occupying key committee and other positions for the first time in some instances (Schroeder, D-CO), Slaughter (D-NY) and Morella (R-MD) used their newfound institutional roles to insure that the bill did not die.

The occupant of the White House in the United States plays a significant role in aiding or retarding access to abortion, as well as influencing other policy, with partisan shifts in national politics greatly affecting policy outcomes. Former President Clinton, for example, ended the "gag" rule in international family planning funding and vetoed the Partial Birth Abortion Act. The Republican Reagan and both Bush administrations have reversed this course whenever possible. The impact of right-wing Republican presidents is felt in appointments to the federal courts as well; litigation, which proved to be such an effective tool for feminists with regard to equal employment policy, has been unable to stave off steady erosion of abortion rights since the very successful *Roe v. Wade* decision in 1973, given the increasing conservatization of the judicial process. Pro-choice forces have been able to prevent the passage of an anti-abortion constitutional amendment, but the cost in terms of movement energy and policy priorities has been high.

Chapter 5

Policies to Harmonize Work and Family Life in Japan and the United States

Introduction

Equal employment policies in Japan and the United States were analyzed in depth in chapter two. On the one hand, the United States seems to have made greater inroads toward gender integration of occupations than other advanced countries, including Japan (O'Connor, Orloff and Shaver, 1999, 4–5). Women have made major strides in the educational arena and executive and professional occupations in the United States, aided by affirmative action and a well-developed legal apparatus to protect women against sex discrimination, as well as feminist advocacy efforts. In contrast to their Japanese sisters, whose participation in the labor force has been far more problematic, American women have tended to work full time and for most of their lives. They have done so with limited childcare support and in the absence of other state policies that might help to resolve the tensions between work and family responsibilities. As noted earlier, equity policy in the United States tended, particularly in the initial era of second wave feminism, to stress gender sameness. In more recent years, although these views have shifted, the U.S. system has proven resistant to providing special support for care giving and other primarily female family-related roles. In this chapter, the forces that have shaped two policies related to changing family needs, the successful passage of the Family and Medical Leave Act (FMLA) of 1993 and the less successful effort to create a comprehensive national childcare policy, will be examined.

While Japan is clearly behind the United States with regard to policies related to equal employment and labor market access, it is arguable that it has gone further in the area of family-friendly policy, in order to attempt to create more favorable conditions for working mothers in an era of shrinking marriage and birth rates. These changes are particularly noteworthy given the conservative nature of the Japanese state. Both the United States and Japan are among the leanest OECD (Organization for Economic Cooperation and Development) states in terms of their overall welfare expenditures, making the policy changes to aid working women especially significant in the Japanese case (Peng, 2002, 4). While women's movements have influenced family policy in both nations, they have not always been dominant. In this policy arena, as well as in others, in Japan and the United States, ideological and other considerations (for example, pronatalism in the Japanese case) have constrained policy outcomes significantly.

At present, about 50 percent of all Japanese women work, in contrast to over 60 percent in the United States although for the first time as of 2000, the number of working women with children under three in the Unite States has dropped to 57.5 percent in 2001 from a record 60.9 percent in 1997 (Uchitelle, 2002, 5).

After considering the dimensions of family-friendly policy in Japan and the United States, a final topic to be considered in this chapter is the significance of the Basic Law for Gender Equal Society in Japan, enacted in 2000, which also promises to aid in balancing work and family life. This type of law, largely symbolic in content, has no functional equivalent in the United States or in most other Western nations; given these limitations, its importance will be evaluated.

Family Friendly Policy in the United States

In the United States, the prominent role of women in the labor force has not been accompanied by policies that might support employment, including publicly assisted day care, and maternity and parental benefits available on a collective basis (O'Connor, Orloff and Shaver, 1999, 79). Women in the U.S. have had considerable difficulty in gaining policy to support work and family life, given systemic antipathy to state intervention in what is cast as the "private" sphere. While European and other democratic nations (including Japan to some extent as will be discussed below) have increasingly provided working women with special benefits, such as paid parental leave and state-supported childcare, the United States has followed a different model. A reluctant welfare state, the United States utilizes a "pro-family, noninterventionist" model, limited primarily to families in need in a highly incremental fashion (Wisensale, 2001b, 216). In contrast to the effective policy-making role involving grassroots advocacy and "insider" politics that characterized pressure to pass the Violence against Women Act (VAWA), feminists influenced the passage of the FMLA as members of a more "elite" process only. They were forced to compromise and accept limited, unpaid leave. The complex process that comprises childcare policy in the United States has proven to be even more problematic: it is fragmented due to federal/state and public/private differences, as well as racial, class and other factors. "Feminists never made child care a national priority and would have found little receptivity in Washington had they done so" (Michel, 1999, 295). On the issue of childcare, no effective coalition between feminists, labor, childcare providers and advocates and other liberal forces ever developed.

The Family and Medical Leave Act of 1993. American feminists pressed for the adoption of the Family and Medical Leave Act (FMLA) signed into law in 1993 by former President Clinton after two vetoes by former President George Bush.

The law provides for unpaid leave for twelve weeks of childcare and other kinds of family leave, applicable to companies of over 50 employees, and if employees have worked relatively full time for past twelve months, via a gender neutral policy. The law covers about 11 percent of American employers and about 60 percent of the U.S. work force (Bernstein, 2001, 115; Wisensale, 2001b, 6). This law is framed as an individual rather than group right, in line with other U.S. policies (Gottfried and O'Reilly, 2002).

The FMLA, enacted in 1993, was a policy that became embroiled in partisan and interest group politics, delaying its passage after initial support from decision makers. While Democrats favored an extensive leave policy available to most workers, Republicans, more responsive to business interests, advocated a reduced leave period and the elimination of many workers from coverage (Marks, 1997). Unlike the VAWA, discussed in chapter three, which, after initial hostility in the 1980s, was virtually unopposed in the 1990s, during the eight-year period of the FMLA's consideration small business interests came to dominate the political debate and affected the outcome significantly. As the policy process unfolded, the discourse shifted from concern for families to concern for business. The ensuing debate focused on dealing with an effectively organized opposition, necessitating a continuing process of compromise. Some contend that during the legislative negotiations, feminists lost control of the issue and the act lost a clear identity (Stetson, 1991, 406). Although focused on balancing women's work and family roles and providing for a stable family, the law was ultimately presented as more of a family and labor, rather than a women's, issue (ibid., 416). After years of negotiation, the bill finally developed momentum because of the focus on family care, not just limited to "special treatment" for mothers, permitting a broad-based coalition to form (Wisensale, 2001a, 36). The result was a largely symbolic act, which nonetheless has impacted some women and male workers positively, although many workers had access to aspects of its provisions prior to passage (Bernstein, 2001, 115).

In its initial stages, the FMLA legislation was actively supported by feminist advocacy groups and many Democrats, as well as some moderate Republicans. It gained support from women's, labor, religious, disability and retiree groups, including the American Association for Retired Persons (AARP), and major labor unions. It was highly visible, receiving widespread media coverage and generally positive support. Initially packaged as no-cost legislation that would promote family and economic concerns, a broad constituency produced votes at the federal level (Wisensale, 2001a, 24). Feminist advocates for this policy represented nationally based, nonmembership organizations such as the Women's Legal Defense Fund (WLDF), National Women's Law Center (NWLC), Women's Equity Action League and National Federation of Business and Professional Women, as well as the National Association of Junior Leagues and the Institute for Women's Policy Research (Bernstein, 2001, 97–98). The latter group undertook a study to counter the adverse findings of the U.S. Chamber of Commerce, which concluded in a cost analysis that the FMLA would place an "undue burden" on business (ibid.). The Washington-centered coalition that organized around this policy after 1985 accepted the need for an incremental strategy that accepted unpaid leave in order to gain the passage of any family leave law at all.[1] The Congressional Caucus for Women's Issues (CCWI) adopted policy toward family leave as a major priority during the eight-year struggle for its enactment and helped to coordinate women's advocacy for it within and outside of Congress; its Chair, Pat Schroeder (D-CO), was the bill's first sponsor in 1985 (Costello, Miles and Stone, 1998, 30). The role of the White House incumbent proved to be crucial with regard to the FMLA as well, as for many of the other policies examined in this volume.

Maternity leave was available to American women after 1972 in accordance with an Equal Employment Opportunities Commission (EEOC) directive that ordered employers who allowed leaves for medical disabilities to offer them for childbirth as well (Kelly and Dobbin, 1999, 456). Some states, such as California, went further in providing job guaranteed and paid maternity leaves. After the passage of the Pregnancy Discrimination Act in 1978, which provided that women who were pregnant or affected by childbirth and maternity needs should be covered by the same disability benefits as extended to other medical conditions, the California state legislature amended the Fair Employment and Housing Act to provide women workers with an unpaid pregnancy disability leave of up to four months. In *California Federal Savings and Loan v. Guerra*, the statute was challenged as unfairly discriminating against male workers, a view with which some "equality" feminists and the U.S. District Court for Central California concurred (Radigan, 1988, 5). In consequence, a gender neutral bill to cover parental leave was first proposed in Congress in 1984 in meetings held by Howard Berman (D-CA) with the assistance of a group of feminist lawyers in Washington D.C.[2] Initially known as the Parental and Disability Leave Act, it would have provided for 18 weeks of unpaid leave (and twenty-six weeks of medical leave) with job reinstatement guaranteed. A civil right of action could be brought against employers who failed to grant such leave. The bill called for a commission to be convened to examine wage replacement within two years of the bill's enactment. By 1985, the bill's name was changed to the Parental and Medical Leave Act and exempted employers with fewer than five employees from coverage. Congressional Democrats Pat Schroeder and William Clay (D-MO) continued to sponsor the bill in the House. In addition, conservative Republicans such as Henry Hyde (R-IL) and Christopher Smith (R-NJ) were cosponsors, in an era stressing "family values" together with support from numerous women's and labor groups (Marks, 1997). The proposal received favorable press coverage. However, by the time subcommittees convened in 1986 to consider the legislation, bipartisan support had dissipated. Business organizations, including the National Association of Manufacturers (NAM) Economic Policy Council, representing large businesses, and those representing smaller ones, such as the Chamber of Commerce, National Federation of Independent Business and White House Conference on Small Businesses, actively opposed the bill. They feared increased financial costs and business disruption (ibid.). A "Concerned Alliance of Responsible Employer" (CARE) formed a coalition specifically to defeat the proposed legislation. Alleging costs of $13 billion per year, their effective opposition caused the bill to languish in House committees and subcommittees for the next four years. During this period, a succession of compromises was crafted, limiting coverage to large companies but broadening the range of "care" covered. As partisanship increased, most Democrats and a few Republicans favored the bill's passage while it was opposed by most Republicans and some conservative Democrats. On the House Education and Labor committee whose approval was necessary for the bill to pass, during this period no Republicans supported any type of leave policy (ibid.).

A bill was approved by the House Education and Labor Committee in June 1986, but most Republicans continued to resist its enactment. The bill's proponents awaited the 1986 elections before moving further, and when the Democrats regained control of the House and Senate, the time seemed ripe for action. Chris Dodd (D-CT) introduced the bill in the Senate for the first time.

Congresswoman Marge Roukema (R-NJ), a ranking member of the House Subcommittee on Labor Management to which the bill was referred, played a key role in supporting the bill after 1987, seeking a compromise which would exempt firms with fewer than fifty employees, and decreasing the period for disability leave. When Roukema and Clay added a provision to permit care for aging parents, the base of support was broadened and additional, although "grudging," Republican support was forthcoming (Marks). In order to gain the crucial support of moderate Republicans needed to secure the bill's passage, such as Marge Roukema (R-NJ) and Jeffords (R-VT), a bill was approved that resembled the law finally adopted in 1993. It specified that small firms would be exempted. Both family and medical leaves would be limited to short periods. To qualify, an employee had to have worked for at least twenty hours a week for at least a year. A firm could deny leave to its highest paid employees. Leave could be used to care for a child, spouse or seriously ill parent and the employee would be reinstated to the same position as before the leave.

On November 17, 1999 the Schroeder-Roukema compromise passed the full House Education and Labor Committee by a vote of 21 to 11, with only Jeffords and Roukema as Republican supporters (one Democrat opposed the legislation as well). This new compromise exempted 95 percent of the nation's employers, leaving over 60 percent of workers unprotected (ibid., 1997). In 1989, the proposed legislation, now known as House bill #770, included a provision to permit leaves to care for ailing spouses and was passed by the relevant committees. On the floor of the House, a compromise that exempted firms with fewer than fifty employees and limited the leave period to twelve weeks was passed by 237 to 187 in May 1990 (supported by 198 Democrats and 39 Republicans). The Senate passed the bill by a voice vote in June 1990, five years after the law was initially proposed. The proposed bill was enthusiastically supported throughout the entire period by the CCWI and its then director, Ann Radigan.

However, the Reagan and Bush White Houses vigorously opposed the concept of a government-mandated leave bill and former President Bush vetoed it on June 29, 1990. Leave proponents attempted an override but they fell short of the 285 votes needed, again splitting on partisan lines. The National Federation of Independent Business called the July 25 vote that defeated the override "a great day." Family leave advocates continued to press for the bill's adoption: in 1992 the Senate did override the presidential veto but the House could not (ibid.).

With the 1992 election of Bill Clinton, who enthusiastically supported the FMLA during his campaign as president, and the election as well of Democratic-controlled houses of Congress, the stage was finally set for the bill's passage. The final bill covered only employees who had worked for 1,250 hours during the past year. Full-time workers were granted leaves for childcare, adoption and family emergencies, as well as time off to care for ill relatives or to recover from personal injury or illness. While other nations—including Japan—offer total or partial compensation for leaves, the U.S. does not as it was felt that including provisions for paid leave would have resulted in the failure of the bill to pass (Marks, 1997). In addition, coverage is far from universal—firms must have fifty workers or more and employees in the top 10 percent of the firm's pay scale may be denied leave if their absence would result in "substantial and grievous injury" to the employer (Conway, Ahern and Steurnagel, 1999, 78, 169). The exemption of smaller businesses was in response to active lobbying on behalf of these interests.

The day after the bill's passage by both houses, Clinton signed it into law, on February 4, 1993, the first public bill signing of his new presidency. Clinton subsequently proposed consideration of paid leave and directed the Department of Labor to use surplus unemployment insurance funds to provide some sort of wage replacement, limited to care for children, although this has never come to pass. Highlighting the issue of leave, he addressed the need to expand the law's range in his 1999 State of the Union address, stressing the minimal impact on business costs of the law up to that date. During his administration, twenty efforts between 1993 and 1999 to strengthen the FMLA were introduced into Congress: proposals to include smaller companies and expand coverage to include additional family obligations. All failed—none ever even got out of committee (Wisensale, 2001a, 31).

Recognizing his inability to amend the policy further through legislation, the president shifted the policy venue to the executive branch, suggesting that the Department of Labor explore ways to use surplus unemployment funds to subsidize childcare and twelve weeks of accrued sick leave to care for an ill family member. The Department of Labor subsequently recommended that states experiment with use of unemployment compensation for this purpose. By 2001, twenty-six states sought to pass legislation providing for paid family leave utilizing this approach—all failed, demonstrating the continuing controversial nature of this policy.

Some (five) states do offer Temporary Disability Insurance (TDI) to new mothers, just as they do to other temporarily ill employees. To date, however, California is the only state in the nation which has succeeded in passing a law for paid coverage. Utilizing the state temporary disability program, the California Family Rights Act, was passed by the California legislature in November 2002. It provides for a six-week family care leave to care for a child, family member or same sex partner, to be taken by workers in companies with more than fifty employees. The policy permits benefits amounting to 55 percent of an employee's salary but not more than $728 per week, with employees bearing the cost of funding the program through payroll deductions ("Time for Families" *San Francisco Chronicle*, 24 September 2002, A20). Other states have enacted parental leave laws with fewer qualifications, but no monetary support.

While the FMLA bill marked a symbolic victory for many women and their families, many large businesses had implemented such policies before the law's passage. The small business community was the ultimate winner because it was not subject to the law's requirements. Many families could not afford to take unpaid leave and workers most likely to be covered are those in more "elite" (higher-paid and higher-status) positions (Marks). The twelve-week period for leave is shorter than most nations provide. Nonetheless, the law's passage may represent a federal recognition that both the workplace and American family have changed dramatically over the last decades (Wisensale, 2001a, 21). However, the United States remains one of only three industrialized nations (together with South Africa and Britain) that do not provide paid parental leave and it is the wealthiest of all (ibid., 35). Prospects for paid leave remain grim; the current Bush administration rescinded the 1999 Clinton order that permitted states to use unemployment insurance for employee leaves (although, as noted, none ever did).

The law as adopted provides for both childcare and long-term care, although not for a domestic, nonmarried partner, and, as of 2001, some 16 million people had used it for personal reasons or to care for a family member (ibid., 22; Waldfogel, 2001). A Commission on Leaves was established to monitor the law (Bernstein, 2001, 120). Their surveys have found that 88 percent of respondents who are familiar with the law have a favorable view of it; it has become widely accepted and has been legitimized in the public mind (ibid.).

As of June 1999, 16.5 percent of employees had taken parental leave, over half of very short duration, just 10 or fewer workdays (U.S. Department of Labor, 2002, 2). Of workers who took leave in 2000, 46 percent were men and 54 percent women; the largest percentage (47 percent) used the leave time for their own health-related purposes, 19.7 percent to care for ill parents and 30 percent to care for a new or ill child (U.S. Department of Labor, Table A 2-2, 13; Rosenberg, 2001, 46). In the 2000 labor survey, over 75 percent of those who could not take leave cited financial reasons (Waldfogel, 2001, 17; Wisensale, 2001a, 23). In some instances, however, employers are going beyond what is required by the FMLA and the use of leave taking under the FMLA is increasing and becoming more accepted (ibid.). Businesses also report positive effects on productivity and profitability as well as ease of compliance, suggesting widespread support for the policy as enacted, although not yet for paid leave in most instances (Waldfogel, 2001, 7).

A continuing source of contention related to the FMLA has been the failure of employers to provide advance written notice of prospective care leave to the employee; in such instances, the employer would be obligated to provide a full additional twelve weeks in addition to leave already taken. In April 2002, the U.S. Supreme Court in *Tracy Ragsdale v. Wolverine Worldwide* (US 00-6029) invalidated an advance notification regulation for FMLA promulgated by the Department of Labor. The court found that the requirement for individualized notice was improper, exceeding the Department of Labor's authority (Hatch and Hall, June, 1).

On May 27, 2003, the Supreme Court in *Nevada Department of Human Resources v. Hibbs* (US 01-1368) upheld the right of state employees to sue state agencies for denying them time off for family care, another stage in the struggle between state's rights and federal anti discrimination law. In a six-to-three decision, a victory for the pro-family friendly groups, the court supported the right of a state employee to recover money damages if the state failed to comply with the FMLA's family-care provision. Thirteen states argued for immunity from the legislation, while the Bush administration, civil and women's rights groups and numerous members of Congress, as well as five states opposed the concept of state immunity (Greenhouse, 2003, 12; Associated Press Online, 2003).

The incremental policy that the FMLA represents must be judged a qualified success, at least as a first step to recognizing that balancing work and family problems is a public responsibility. (See Bernstein, 2001, 132.)

Childcare policy. In contrast to the passage of the FMLA in 1993, the U.S. Congress has not addressed a national, comprehensive and universal approach to childcare policy. Since a near miss at the time of the historic veto of proposed legislation for universal childcare (the Family Assistance Plan) in 1971 by then-President Nixon, who opposed it as too intrusive regarding the private family, a more expansive construction of the childcare issue has been unable to penetrate the "institutional" policy agenda.[3] Instead, the government finances childcare through a myriad of programs related to welfare policy and the dependent care tax credit. Until 1990, the latter was the largest federal program for day care finance, although it provided no assistance to those who need it most: those with incomes below the tax threshold and those who utilize informal childcare (Kamerman and Kahn, 1995, 16). Other federal programs have supported aid for childcare targeted to the poor. Head Start, a subsidy program for compensatory pre-school education for the nation's poor three- and four-year-olds, begun in the 1960s, presently serves about 40 percent of that population (ibid.). Head Start appropriations tripled from 1989 to the late 1990s and enrollments doubled (Levy and Michel, 2001, 255). The 1976 Aid to Day Care Centers Act (ADCC) increased funding to raise standards for public day care centers while encouraging job creation for low income women (Michel, 1999, 251). Marking an important new federal commitment, the 1990 Child Care and Development Block Grant and At Risk Child Care program subsidized childcare for the working poor for the first time without strict income limitations and also sought to aid women who might otherwise have to return to welfare rolls. Under Title XX of the Social Security Act passed in 1974, the Social Services Block grant provides grants to the states for a number of social services including child care. It links childcare to "workfare" and other "at risk" populations (ibid., 251). The fragmentation of policy has both reflected and contributed to the absence of a concerted feminist mobilization for public day care.

In the United States, childcare policy is divided into two distinct sectors: public and private. In contrast to nations in which social citizenship includes generously supported childcare, leave and allowances for families and children, the United States operates on a different model. The concept of "maximum private responsibility" for childcare prevails, leave provision is meager and subject to widespread exclusions and wage replacement is nonexistent or relatively low

(O'Connor, Orloff and Shaver, 1999, 79). The private sector is subsidized by the federal government through a dependent care tax credit, permitting parents to choose their own system of childcare. Support for corporate childcare was also provided; in part a response to the women's liberation movement's demand for aid to working mothers. Since the 1980s the government has subsidized corporate sponsored day care, which now supports about 500,000 children; primarily benefiting middle- and upper-income parents (Michel, 1999, 266–276). In the public sector, state-funded childcare is viewed as part of a policy package mandating job training and employment (workfare) for parents seeking public assistance (Levy and Michel, 2001, 240).

Child care for the poor. In 1988, former President Reagan signed into law the Family Support Act, which sought to increase work, education and training for poor mothers, together with the expansion of childcare services to facilitate labor participation (ibid., 238). Increasing attention to childcare for the poor occurred primarily in the 1990s, linked to issues of welfare reform and school readiness (Cohen, 2001, 5, 304–5), although many poor women continue to lack access to affordable childcare. The U.S. Act for Better Child Care, introduced in 1987, authorized matching grants to the states to assist in providing affordable, available and quality childcare for low-income families (O'Connor, Orloff and Shaver, 1999, 79). The first federal programs to provide for quality improvement in childcare—the Child Care and Development Block Grant (CCDBG) and At Risk Child Care Program—provided for voucher-based choice for care by relatives, neighbors or employers, childcare homes or centers (Cohen, 2001, 126). The legislation increased funds for low-income families, allocating $2.5 billion by 1991 to 1993 to help poor families meet their childcare needs and for state initiatives to improve availability and quality. An Earned Income Tax Credit (EITC) was also adopted, to help defray childcare costs for the poor. Women's groups such as the National Women's Law Center (NWLC) and National Organization for Women Legal Defense and Education Fund (NOW LDEF) were active members of the coalition that pressed for this law (ibid., 133). However, male members of Congress, in the majority and in key decision-making roles, often took the lead on childcare policy, together with some female colleagues, including the CCWI (ibid.). The latter supported specific bills, despite the opposition of some caucus members (Hall, 003, 343). The establishment of a Child Care Bureau in 1995 helped to provide a more coordinated federal effort on policy and a center for lobbying activity.

The Personal Responsibility and Work Opportunity Reconciliation Act (PRWORA) passed in 1996 involves the devolution of workfare and childcare policy to the state level of the federal system, a process that was begun in the 1990s, removing federal standards of regulation (Levy and Michel, 2001, 240, 255). In an effort to cut federal expenditures, block grants to the states denied payments to unmarried teen mothers, and eliminated the notion of any entitlement or rights-based eligibility on the basis of need, instead substituting a system of time-limited benefits (Bashevkin, 2002, 78). Although feminist groups such as

NOW participated in a hunger strike against this sweeping policy change, they were unable to stop it from being adopted (ibid., 75).

Under the new program, Temporary Assistance to Needy Families (TANF), access to child care is at the discretion of local authorities, where bureaucratic decision makers determine access. While the new legislation did include a federal guarantee of childcare for those funded as part of the work fare program, the inadequacy of funding provisions led then-President Clinton, a supporter of welfare reform in general, to veto the bill passed by Congress twice (Cohen, 2001, 194). Aided by pressure from the nation's governors, the law finally approved increased funding ($4 billion over five years) for childcare in connection with welfare change (Levy and Michel, 2001, 246). Current law combines previous programs into a single block grant, the Child Care and Development Fund (CCDF) (Levy and Michel, 2001, 250).

In February 2000, at the urging from Clinton, who had been advocating for change since the enactment of welfare reform, the fiscal year labor appropriations bill passed by Congress contained dramatic increases in funding support for CCDF funding, infant and toddler care, after school and campus-based care, and a national childcare hotline (Cohen, 2001, 242). As noted earlier, for female legislators, now at an all-time high in Congress, through the CCWI and feminist advocates, childcare reform in terms of increased support for policy and tax credits remains a major priority. The National Council of Women's Organizations, representing more than one hundred women's groups, designated childcare as an official agenda priority as well in 1998 and established a task force under the leadership of the National Council of Jewish Women and NOW LDEF as co-chairs, to attempt revitalize policy initiatives around this issue (ibid., 246).

As is characteristic of the U.S. federal system, childcare policy has always involved a mix of state and national policy. States have invested their own resources to create new funding sources. As of 1999, 1.8 million children were served per month under the CCDF, an increase from 1.5 million the previous year (ibid., 264). But this program still reached only 12 percent of eligible children, and 28 percent of those served were in unregulated day care (ibid., 265). Women on TANF often lack access to affordable childcare and low-income working families also suffer from a huge deficit in available daycare, reinforcing the continuing struggle for child care provision (ibid., 272).

As suggested above, although more public funding is available for day care than ever before, the gap between demand and supply continues to grow (Levy and Michel, 2001, 256). The competing imperatives of cutting welfare rolls, increasing employment by poor women and providing public childcare services have proven contradictory. In consequence, states vary widely in their provision of day care, which is often provided by nongovernmental organizations (NGOs), exacerbated by the lack of federal standards and regulations (ibid., 257). "The maze of federal child care policies" means that standards and eligibility vary from state to state, placements are often unregulated, and many low-income families remain underserved (ibid., 169). As of 1998, only 10 percent of eligible families received federal childcare assistance (Department of Health and Human Services, 1999).

Private child care through tax policy. Tax policy is another instrument of childcare policy in the United States: providing tax credits for limited childcare expenses. These policies largely benefit middle- and upper-income women who finance childcare with this assistance on their own, or through employer subsidies (Kamerman and Kahn, 1995, 127). Childcare tax deductions, established in 1954, were converted to a tax credit in 1972; in 1962 and after employers were offered incentives to set up or sponsor services for their employees (Levy and Michel, 2001, 241). In 1997, a child tax credit was passed enabling most taxpayers with children to reduce their tax burden by $500. The credit was increased to $2,000 for children under 17 years of age in 2001, and was made refundable, so it could reach poorer families (Coalition on Human Needs, 2002). Through the system of dependent tax credits, the state supports parental decisions to place their children in paid childcare up to ages 13, while in the public sector the state subsidizes childcare as part of a mandatory system.

For the first time in a quarter century, the percentage of women with young children holding full-time jobs decreased in 2000; to 55 percent, with only one-third of those with infants under one year of age with full-time employment outside of the home (Tierney, 2002). Perhaps this trend is at least in part a reflection of the absence of comprehensive, universal and national "family friendly" policy in the United States.

Policy outcomes. In the feminist view, childcare and other supports for working women are integral parts of "social citizenship"; a concept almost entirely absent from the American political system. Feminists oppose the notion of compulsion to work as a trade-off for childcare, a view ignored by U.S. policy makers (Levy and Michel, 2001, 259). Feminist groups and their allies in Congress kept the issue of the FMLA alive for eight years and finally achieved an incremental policy outcome, although they were forced to compromise on the policy content. Concern for childcare legislation, however, has never occupied as a central role for American feminists as have sex discrimination or pro-choice policy, although advocacy groups such as the NOW LDEF and NWLC and others have been strong advocates of reform. Women members of Congress elected in 1992, as well, put childcare on the agenda as one of their major priorities and the CCWI has created a task force to deal with the issue, which it views as a high priority. Still, one scholar of American childcare policy making contends that "although the women's movement challenged the prevailing prescription for motherhood, it failed to mobilize a visible campaign for public child care" (Michel, 1999, 279). In this view, the "rights-based orientation" of the most visible branch of second wave feminism, NOW and the National Women's Political Caucus (NWPC) focused on formal aspects of gender equity such as employment and education but ignored the implications for women's social citizenship of the absence of day care (ibid.). While, as noted above, some feminist activists have actively supported efforts to reform childcare, the failure of other advocates to put this issue on the front burner may be due to several factors. Some point to the divided constituency for childcare, with cleavages based on class and race, as well as type of service provision (public and private) (ibid.). Issues related to class play a role, since for many middle income women state-funded childcare is not a key issue. Growing ideological differences among women inside and outside of Congress have prevented a monolithic agenda from developing on this issue, and the plethora of different approaches and policies have complicated policy making as well (Cohen, 2001, 299–300). Other policy concerns may have seemed more pressing: feminists may initially have resisted the notion that women were responsible for childcare and rearing, which may have been seen as reinforcing traditional stereotypes (ibid., 299). Finally, the near impossibility of obtaining universal childcare coverage may have led U.S. feminists to prioritize other issues as more attainable.

Family Friendly Policy in Japan

While equal employment policy per se has been far more advanced in the United States than Japan, with regard to policies to help support working women or "women friendly" policies, it is arguable that Japan has gone further than in the United States. These changes are particularly noteworthy because of the conservative underpinning of the Japanese state that has undertaken the partial restructuring of the welfare state and women-related politics, partially through pressure from mobilized women's groups and the politicization of social policy issues (Peng, 2001). The bureaucracy may have demonstrated increased flexibility and the political system more responsiveness on such issues, due to concerns related to the political economy and fragmenting of the dominant Liberal Democratic Party (LDP).[4] Policy change has continued to develop in an expansionary direction in order to attempt to reconcile aspects of family and work life.

Policy changes have occurred because the Japanese state has become increasingly concerned with gender specific issues, as the birth rate dropped to among the lowest in the world, 1.3 percent in 1999 (*Nikkei Weekly*, 8 January 2001, 3; 24 June 2002, 18). A 1997 survey found most respondents indicating that the birth rate is in decline because of the large expense of providing education to children (58.2 percent of respondents), as well as the lack of financial security (50.1 percent) and the difficulty of raising children while continuing to work (44.7 percent) (Foreign Press Center 1997, 4).

Women have delayed their marriage age (nonmarriage for women ages twenty-five to twenty-nine increased from 20 percent to 50 percent from 1975 to 1995), while the years of employment increased (Peng, 2002, 15) and there appears to be widespread discontent among Japanese women who find it difficult, if not impossible, to combine work and family life. The percentage of women who never married in their twenties increased from 18 percent in 1970 to 48 percent in 1995; 20 percent of women in their thirties were not married in 1995 (Schoppa, 2001, 79). Of course these trends contribute to the decline in the birth rate. Nonetheless, some caution should be exercised in interpreting this data. While the birthrate continues to drop, with the fertility rate at its lowest point ever, the marriage rate has increased for the first time in twenty-five years, now reaching 6.4 percent (in contrast to the United States, at 8.5 percent; *Nikkei Weekly*, 1 April 2002 and 24 June 2002, 18). The age of marriage is continuing to rise, however.

As the Japanese state has sought to balance decreased fertility and increase female labor force participation (Gottfried and Reilly, 2002), numerous efforts have been made by the state to help women combine motherhood and work, in order to further pro-natal objectives, utilizing a "pro-family/pro-natalist" model (Wisensale, 2001b, 215). This may be viewed as an example of "cognitive" policy development as discussed in chapter one; in which targeted policies are developed to connect problems and solutions. The result has been the vast expansion of social programs for working mothers and parents, and expanded day care places for children. Ito Peng points to the role of women activists in groups such as Committee for the Betterment of Aging Society (CBAS), begun in 1983, in mobilizing attention to the need for policy reform in the area of care policies. The fragility of the LDP political dominance after 1989 may have been a factor in opening the "policy window" related to social care (2002, 10–11) Higuchi Keiko, the head of CBAS, was invited to join the Ministry of Health and Welfare's Council on Health and Welfare for the Elderly in the mid-1990s, the *shingikai* (advisory council) on this issue—conferring legitimacy on and coopting members of women's movements in a manner similar to that described in the late 1990s with regard to domestic violence (DV), equal opportunity (EO) and Gender Equality legislation (ibid., 13). The inclusion of women's groups in a dialogue with these bureaucrats marked a new dimension in women's policy participation.

Care and leave policies.   One approach that has been employed by the Japanese government is a child allowance system which went into effect in 1992 and pays a monthly sum of 5,000 yen per month for the first two children and 10,000 per month for the third (about $50 and $100, respectively) (Foreign Press Center, 2000, 1). There are special benefits for single mother households as well. Maternity Leave (*shussan kyuka*), established in Japan in 1947, provides for six weeks of prenatal and eight weeks of postnatal leave for single births. However, while this leave policy is far ahead of the United States, remuneration is low and many women do not qualify for maternity leave. The Child Care Leave Law (*ikuji kyuka*) of 1992 established a national standard of paid leave at 60 percent of wages for a fourteen-week period; 22 weeks for multiple births (Curtin, Japan–U.S. Forum, email, 10 December 2001). In 1995, the Child/Family Care Leave was enacted and introduced to all business establishments (in addition to those with over thirty employees in the earlier act). This provided for a childcare and nursing leave until the child is one year of age (increased to three years of age in April 2002). Amendments to the Employment Insurance Law provided that unpaid family care leave of up to three months for any family member could be requested. An amended childcare law entitled fathers to take leave to care for a sick child and mandated employer contributions to offset the cost of childcare. Implemented in 1999, this seemingly gender neutral approach granted family care leave to either partner, who could receive 25 percent of wages, which rose to 40 percent in 2001 (Gottfried and O'Reilly, 2002; Peng, 2002, 22; Schoppa, Japan–U.S. Forum, email, 11 December 2001). As of November 2001, a Revised Law on Child Care and Nursing Care Leave banned employers from firing or mistreating employees who have taken leave. At this time employers were told that they should not treat employees who take leave "disadvantageously," meaning that employees not lose their jobs or be moved to lesser ones upon their return (Curtin, 2002, 1). Employees who care for children or elderly relatives are entitled to exemptions from overtime work and consideration regarding transfers. In addition, shortened work days are permissible for employees with children up to the age of three (as opposed to one year of age, as before). However, as in the case of the EEOL, these provisions lack any enforcement procedures.

As of March 1999, 97.6 percent of childcare leave was taken by women, with 54.4 percent of leave takers being women who had given birth. One study of firms with more than 4 employees found that 53 percent of women took childcare leave; 77 percent in firms with more than thirty or more employees (Curtin, ibid.; Ichikawa Fusae, March 2001, 3). This represents an increase from 1996, when 44 percent of women took such leave (Shirahase, 2002, 5). However, although women took 90.7 percent of family care leaves, only 0.06 percent of all workers actually took such leave through September 1999 (ibid.). They are discouraged from doing so because of a negative atmosphere in companies surrounding leaves and the financial difficulties that may result, particularly given the current frigid economic situation (Ichikawa Fusae, March 2001, 3).

Childcare services. The Japanese government promised an improvement in childcare services, including extended hours, infant care, and private child facilities at corporate quarters, as well as after-school care programs, as a result of the initiatives emanating from the 1994 Angel Plan to address problems of declining fertility through a widened welfare state based social care network (Gottfried and O'Reilly, 2001; Peng, 2001, 46). The New Angel Plan, adopted in 1999, mandated an increase in the number of babies admitted to public day care by over one-third by 2004. As of 2002, 22 percent of preschool-age children are cared for in public day care facilities, compared to 1 percent of those in the United States from birth to two years old and 14 percent of three-year-olds (Peng, 2002, 7), although far more women with young children are employed in the United States. Women's work opportunities are constrained by long commuting times, particularly in the Tokyo area, limiting job and day care options. In Tokyo, 30 percent of approved day care centers do not accept children younger than one year and 60 percent close for the day at 6:30 P.M., not late enough for many working mothers (Ikeya, 2002, 1, 19). Japanese women complain about high expenses for childcare, long waiting lists (particularly in urban areas; over 40,000 in 1997, doubled from 1994; Peng, 2002, 7; Wada, 1) and continued inadequacy of service for younger and sick children (ibid., 5). Only 21 percent of day care centers offer extended hours to accommodate the demand of working parents who often work more than forty hours per week (*Mainichi Interactive*, 2001, 2). Older children (between the ages of three and six years, are those primarily served by this childcare system, as many Japanese parents continue to believe the so-called three-year-old myth— that mothers should stay home to care for their children who are under three (Peng, 2002, 7).

In 1996, a mandatory system that gave the state control over child placement in public day care was replaced by an individual contract system; this has allowed more parental choice as well as competition among centers for enrollees (ibid., 23). One consequence has been the entrance of private childcare centers into the market and subsequent closure and decreasing availability of public sector centers (ibid.), a trend reinforced after the national government's decision in 2000 to deregulate requirements for nursery care (Wada, 2001, 6).

Publicly supported childcare is of high quality and is subsidized by the national and local governments (the government utilizes spatial and care giver/child ratios) (Ikeya, 2002) but it is difficult to gain a place unless infants are in a high priority category (if they meet the cut off date and other criteria; Schoppa, Japan–U.S. Forum, email, 13 December 2001). The cost of unregulated private care, subject to occasional scandals involving abuse, can average up to the equivalent of $1,500 a month, in contrast to public care which charges fees according to a sliding scale (Yamamoto and Struck, 2002). In a kind of "catch-22" situation, it is difficult for women who wish to return to work after child bearing to get a childcare place and they cannot get a position unless they do so.

In 1998, 24.5 percent of women who continued to work after child birth used day care centers but most of those also received help from family members for child rearing (one-half of those who use day care and two-thirds of those utilizing parental leave; Shirahase, 14; Mesler, Japan–U.S. Forum, email, 12 December 2001; data from Ministry of Labor Women's Office, Welfare Services Section, fiscal year 2000). More than 70 percent of women stop working after giving birth; according to Schoppa and others just 22 percent of women with children under three work and half of these work part time; just 10 percent of women in this group work full time (Shirahase, 2000, 14; Schoppa, Japan–U.S. Forum, email, 13 December 2001). Tax credits for three generation households that provide care for the elderly and care allowances for family members reinforce the system of limited work for women with children and elderly parents or in-laws, as do married women's tax credits that permit housewives to earn up to 1.3 million yen tax free for part-time work (Peng, 2001, 8).

As of 2002, the Japanese government announced increased day care places for 150,000 children to be implemented in 2004 (Ikeya, 2002, 1). Despite this and other new initiatives, the number of working women with children declined from 1997 to 2000, the period in which many of these new "family friendly" policies were instituted (Schoppa, email, 12–13 December 2001). It seems clear that incentives for women to work in the male-dominated Japanese economy remain limited even with better family support systems, as long as the fundamental economic structure remains unreconstructed (Shirahase, 2000, 15; Peng, 2001).

Other policy proposals. In keeping with renewed attention to gender related policies, discussion of pension and tax reform by the Ministry of Health Labor and Welfare has been undertaken to allocate pensions more fairly after divorce, a problem particularly affecting elderly women. Under consideration is a plan that would divide pensions more equitably, individualizing the system and ending the current practice through which men get the dominant share of pension funds. The system is currently household based, with those having a single employed worker receiving favorable treatment. In addition, this policy has been particularly difficult for full-time housewives married to male salary workers. The new plan, if approved, would be implemented in 2004 (*Yomiuri Shinbun*, 22 October 2003). Tax reform is also under review, so that women who work for less than 1.3 million yen and are currently tax exempt would be taxed. Full-time housewives who receive tax reductions under this system would now be taxed in some way. Revising this system would also impact on part time workers, who are largely women as well. While this proposed change is couched in the language of gender equality, it would provide the government with an additional source of revenue and lessened benefit payments, adversely affecting some women (Ando, 2002, 3). It is also unclear in the present economic climate how the tax policy change would affect women's currently limited employment options.

Japanese Basic Law for Gender Equal Society

The final policy to be considered as a tool to balance work and family life in Japan is the Basic Law on Gender Equal Society (also known as the Law for Cooperative Participation of Men and Women in Society), passed in June 1999. Japan has sixteen basic laws, but no precise legal definition of what they are according to one scholar (Osawa in Ueno, 2001). Basic laws are intended to address fundamental issues of the state system creating connections between the Constitution and the lawmaking process and policies in significant fields. They are presumed to take priority in relation to other laws in the same policy area. The basic law system creates a framework that leads to enactment of other legal measures and laws by the national and local governments, providing a basic guideline within which bureaucrats and Diet members may formulate new policies and laws and judges will be asked to hand down decisions. While some traditional legal scholars argue that basic laws cannot not be categorized as actual laws because of their lack of provisions concerning people's rights and obligations and their abstract, non-programmatic nature, making a basic outline of a significant policy and systematizing related laws and policies has become more common in the complex modern Japanese state (Kobayashi, email, 13 February 2002). Other basic laws (e.g., for the environment) have represented formal governmental responses to discontent, largely symbolic in content, as part of a gradual political process, with the idea that more concrete policies may or will follow later (Broadbent, 1998, 128; McKean, email, 10 February 2003).[5] In the analysis to follow, the significance of such a largely symbolic law on gender equality policies will be considered.

The term "gender equality" was first used in Japan when the former Prime Minister's Office for Women was redefined as the Office for Gender Equality as part of a reorganization in 1994 (fiscal year 2000, 1).[6] The office was created under the fleeting leadership of Hata Tsutomo, a non-LDP prime minister, who may have been seeking to appeal to women voters. The Japanese government in the mid-1990s began to realize that greater gender equality could have a positive impact on the moribund economy and the declined birth rate, although such recognition was always balanced by competing discourses of traditional values and business as usual (Osawa interview). In 1997, then Prime Minister Hashimoto Ryutaro included gender equality in a speech outlining six areas for reform, including fiscal educational and administrative reform (ibid.). This led to the submission of a report on A Vision of Gender Equality (vision statement) submitted to the prime minister by the already created Advisory Council for Gender Equality of the Prime Minister's Office.

The passage of the basic law, similar to much of the other legislation analyzed here, appears to have been motivated by the "endogenous external pressure" from the international arena and prompted by internal feminist interest group efforts used to prod the Japanese government (Osawa interview). In this instance, the 1995 Fourth World Conference on Women in Beijing was a major catalyst for the adoption of new legislation. (See Dorsey, 2001, 436–64; Keck and Sikkink et al., 1998.) Groups such as the Beijing Joint Accountability Committee (Peking JAC) and other feminist groups, including members of the Diet, had petitioned then Prime Minister Moriyama in 1995 to create national machinery for women: a Ministry for Women's Affairs and Women's Headquarters. The impetus provided by the Beijing + Five meeting in 2000 in New York City also helped to galvanize support from bureaucrats for new legislation (Osawa, 2001). The Basic Law on Gender Equal Society "incorporated the results of the Special Session of the UN General Assembly, Women 2000" (Gender Equality Bureau, 2001, 2; Osawa interview).

Nakajima Michiko, a lawyer and advocate, has questioned the commitment and understanding of the Japanese government to international pressures, claiming that the Japanese government has tried to steer clear of references to the international conventions or declarations that it has ratified (Nakajima, 2000). In the case of Japan's 1999 Basic Law on the Cooperative Participation of Men and Women in Society, Nakajima believes that fundamental aspects of the UN CEDAW have been left out (ibid.). A high-level bureaucrat from the Prime Minister's Office for Gender Equality is quoted to show the lack of government understanding regarding the significance of international conventions which it ratifies: "what has been pushed by international currents and trends until now will be autonomously planned by ourselves in the future . . . Japan will not make plans due to external pressure, such as making an action plan because the UN has made a world action plan, or make a year 2000 plan because the Beijing Platform of Action required it. With this basic law, Japan will create a basic plan for a gender-equal society as our own independent obligation" (ibid.).

Nonetheless, the preamble to the basic law (Law no. 78, 1999) utilizes the language of international feminism, stressing "human rights" and calling for genuine equality between men and women, emphasizing the ability of each citizen to exercise individuality and ability regardless of gender, in language reminiscent of international documents. Among the law's provisions are efforts to secure "nondiscriminatory treatment" of women including positive action, to harmonize work and family life, secure equal employment and eliminate violence against women (the latter two were added in a Basic Plan for Gender Equality, subsequent to passage of the law) (Gender Equality Bureau, 2001, 3–4; Basic Law for Gender Equal Society approved by the Cabinet, 12 December 2000). The basic law does not contain any responsibilities for companies and lacks provisions for a monitoring system, such as an ombudsperson, as initially recommended (WWIN, 2003). It is generally agreed that this legislation is vague and will require enforcement to become meaningful. How and why did this law come about and what is its significance in the Japanese context? While some view it as useless and inadequate, others see it as a resource for changing future policy. It is also praised as creating the basis for "national machinery" intended to further the role and status of women in Japan through the institutionalization of a government agency (Asakura and Osawa interviews; Stetson and Mazur, 1995, 2–3).

The significance of the basic law. The basic law was a government initiative, driven by bureaucrats primarily from the Prime Minister's office, although NGOs such as Peking JAC and other groups including the International Women's Year (IWY) Liaison Group, presently comprised of forty-nine groups, played a role in the deliberations, as has now become more common practice regarding gender based legislation. The coalition government under the leadership of the (somewhat) reformist Prime Minister Hashimoto Ryutaro (1996–1998) included the female headed Socialist and New Sakigake parties. The latter stipulated the creation of gender equality national machinery and the passage of a basic law on gender equality as the price for their coalition cabinet support (Osawa, 2000, 5). The Democratic Party also prepared an alternative version of the legislation. A series of six town meetings to include public comments were held after the preparation of an interim report; it is estimated that about 2,000 people participated in these (Osawa interview). Women's voices influenced the preamble and gained recognition of women's rights as human rights, but they were not able to influence the bill's content to the same extent. Observers note disjunction between the more progressive language embodied in the initial vision statement and the far weaker language of the actual legislation, with regard to issues of indirect discrimination, surname change and the like (Yamashita interview). There was much controversy over the naming of the law; whether it should be called the Danjo Kyodo Sankaku Shakai Kihon-Ho (joint participation by men and women or "gender-equal society") or Danjo Byodo (gender-equality) law. The first title was adopted (modifying the original) and calls for "gender-equal society" (meaning joint participation by men and women) rather than the second, more controversial term, "gender equality" favored by most feminists. The revised name as a frame for the policy may have been more appealing to conservative politicians, who feared the idea of equality of outcomes rather than equality of opportunity, as the law presently suggests, given their opposition to affirmative action, feminism and positive discrimination (Osawa, 2000, 6).

The bill has had at least two significant results. The administrative structure to implement the new basic law was given impetus by the reorganization of government ministries and agencies, operationalized in 2001. One result was the strengthening of the Bureau of Gender Equality, which replaced the former Office for Gender Equality, and the Council for Gender Equality, established in the newly created cabinet office in January 2001 in the aftermath of national administrative reorganization, aimed at enhancing the functions of the Cabinet and Prime Minister's Office. Among its four consultative organs is the Council for Gender Equality. Headed by the Chief Cabinet Secretary, the council is intended to serve as a force for "mainstreaming" gender policy. It is supposed to have more power than individual ministries, to act as policy coordinator by providing opinions to other ministries and agencies through review and advisement, monitoring and investigation, in addition to disseminating surveys to assess effectiveness of specific policies (Osawa, 2000, 13). The council has expanded its membership, and now includes twelve cabinet ministers and twelve "experts" (the latter include intellectuals, representatives of women's organizations, the media and unions).

This set of presumably enhanced powers for the equality council and bureau, are referred to in official documents (e.g., the basic law) and by some feminists as having created "national machinery" in Japan of the "state feminist" variety to advance women's rights, pursuant to the directives of the Fourth World Conference on Women in Beijing, 1995. According to Osawa Mari, the budgetary growth rate of this agency was the highest of any in the government, although it is still small and largely directed toward research and international exchanges rather than advocacy (Osawa interview). The Gender Equality Bureau, the administrative arm and secretariat of the council, may act to formulate plans "not falling within the jurisdiction of any particular ministry" (Gender Equality Bureau, 2001, 2). A Liaison Conference for the Promotion of Gender Equality links the work of these bodies with NGOs and local governments (Osawa, 2001, 7). Nonetheless, since its creation, the role of the bureau as policy advocate has been relatively weak (Yamashita interview).

Some female intellectuals or "Feminists in the Establishment" (*taiseinai* feminists) associated with the women's movement have been incorporated into the new bureaucratic structure, similar to practice described with regard to care, EO and DV policy. Professor Osawa Mari of Tokyo University is head of a Gender Equality Program Review and Evaluation Committee. Professor Higuchi Keiko is head of a Commission on Policy for Equal Employment Opportunities. Cooptation of movement activists may bring women closer to policy-making roles and provide them with new access to power or it may bring them into the policy process without acceding to their demands.

A second outcome of the basic law is that it be operationalized by prefectural and local governments, in order to become more than a symbolic document. This is an expectation, not an obligation (*doryoku gimu*), which involves prefectural and local governments developing basic plans for gender equality and then passing appropriate ordinances to follow them up (Ueno, 2001). Ultimately, the basic law requires prefectural and local, rather than national, implementation.

Some contend that a third outcome has already been manifest: that the new law has created a foundation that makes other legislation more possible, for example, the DV law, about which it initiated reports in 1996 and hearings in 1997, as discussed in chapter three; EEOL amendments; and other gender-related reform efforts (Kawahashi, Nagai, Owaki interviews). Recent proposals that emanate in part from the Council for Gender Equality include tax and pension reform, currently under review. Others feel that the provisions of the basic law related to indirect discrimination, part-time work and positive action may bear fruit as resources for women plaintiffs fighting sex discrimination (Ueno, 2001). Critics contend that the new law failed to adequately address the issue of indirect discrimination, on which the government argues there is no consensus (WWIN, 2003).

The adoption of the basic law. The law was formulated by a *shingikai*—an advisory council in which women's voices were reflected in the hearings held for women (Owaki interview), following the 1995 Beijing world women's conference directives that urged an increase in the power of national machinery for women (i.e., the establishment of government policy structures to further women's status and rights; Stetson and Mazur, 1995, 1, 3).

As early as 1985, after the Third World Women's UN Conference in Nairobi, Japanese women's groups demanded the establishment of "national machinery" for women's policy. The law's specific origins date back to a research group in 1992 that sent members to seven developed nations to investigate their approaches to national machinery (Furuhashi interview).[7] The process of policy adoption was in part a reflection of a political tug-of-war, between the Ministry of Labor Women's Bureau (MOL WB) and the Prime Minister's Office, over responsibility for women's issues. Conflict, which involved women's groups, related to the marginalization and structural weakness of the MOL WB and the ability of the Section of Gender Equality, as it was then known, to coordinate comprehensive policies and invoke the power of a strong ministry, the Prime Minister's Office (Kobayashi, 2002, 214). Arguing that the MOL was too narrow in its focus solely on labor-related issues, and with its ability to co-opt a wide range of women's groups into its advisory council, the Prime Minister's Office ultimately won and the first Council for Gender Equality was established (Furuhashi interview; *Asahi Shinbun*, 1 December 1994).

The initial report of the research group had few concrete outcomes, other than the appointment of gender equality officers in each ministry. In 1994, a *shingikai* on gender equality was established. Members included Furuhashi Genrokuro, a veteran bureaucrat, and Nuita Yoko, its head and a long time advocate of reforms for women. The advisory group met over sixty times between 1991 and 1997—its members included such women as Osawa Mari (Tokyo University), Muraki Atsuko (of the Ministry of Labor) and Mikami Akiteru (of the Prime Minister's Office), who all played important roles. The group's vision statement, which formed the basis for the later legislation, was adopted in 1996; although at that time legislation was not contemplated, ultimately public opinion supported it and the bureaucracy acquiesced (Furohashi interview). The vision statement was initially intended as a protest by feminists on the then Council for Gender Equality against a proposed draft of a report written by a low-ranking bureaucrat at the Prime Minister's

Office, which was deemed unacceptable. Instead, the Statement stressed a far-reaching conception of a gender equal society embodying drastic social and economic reforms (Osawa, 2000, 7–11). It included specific proposals including reform of the Civil Code to permit retention of maiden names after marriage and correction of gender bias in pensions and other benefit programs, all aimed at challenging the dominant "male breadwinner" model prevalent in Japan.

In June 1997, a new advisory council on Gender Equal Society was established, with Furuhashi, a former vice minister of the Management and Coordination Agency, as head (ibid.). The moderate reformism of Hashimoto Ryutaro, the LDP prime minister from 1996 to 1998, helped to promote the new law's passage during this period when much of the groundwork was laid. Hashimoto's receptivity may have been attributable to his three daughters' insistence on the need for new legislation (Osawa, 2000, 4). During this administration, gender equality-related machinery was strengthened in a restructured central bureaucracy (ibid., 5). The political environment at that time which involved a coalition between the LDP, New Party Sakigake and the Social Democratic Party of Japan, also facilitated consideration of the policy; the bill was one of the fruits of coalition government, similar to other legislation discussed here (anti-pornography, anti-stalking, DV). The leaders of the two coalition parties were female at the time, Domoto Akiko of the Sakigake and Doi Takako of the Socialist Party of Japan. Domoto, though the head of a minor party with just five Diet seats, was particularly forceful in pressing Prime Minister Hashimoto for gender reform (Osawa, 2001, 2). The opposition parties and women's groups pressed for a strong preamble—their language was not incorporated during the bureaucratic negotiations but was added in the Diet deliberations (Furuhashi interview). Other active participants were the head of *shufuren* (housewives association) and Nuita Yoko, the prior advisory council head and a well-respected women's advocate. It is possible that agreement to pass this basic law was a trade-off for the government's failure to create an independent Ministry for Women's Problems, which would have represented a more direct approach to the creation of "national machinery" (Ueno and Osawa, 2001, 10–92).

In February 1999, the cabinet passed a bill proposing the basic law and it was introduced to the Diet. Its sponsors feared that opposition amendments unacceptable to the LDP might kill it but women's groups negotiated with them to accept this version (Furuhashi interview). The UN women's conference (Beijing + Five) in 2000 in New York City helped to galvanize bureaucrats in support of the basic law (Osawa interview). This bill, like the DV legislation discussed in chapter four, also passed unanimously in both houses, perhaps less surprising in this case as it was government sponsored, as are most Japanese bills, and because it lacked concrete provisions. As was the case during consideration of the EEOL, there was a provision for public comment. The Council for Gender Equality received over 3,600 comments, the first time that more than 1,000 had been received in a similar process. However, this number was far fewer than the 20,000 comments in response to the EEOL revision discussed in chapter two, a policy that elicited far greater interest (Osawa in Ueno, 2001). Poll data reveals that only 10 percent to 15 percent of Japanese people have any familiarity with the new law (Osawa interview).

The basic law that was passed was heavily influenced by recommendations of the Council for Gender Equality. Article 8 states that the state is responsible for the comprehensive formulation and implementation of policies, including positive action (Gender Equality Bureau, 2002). Article 17 specifies grievance procedures, although no independent mechanism for complaint resolution has been designated. Articles 8 and 9 state that prefectural and local governments are responsible for taking positive steps to implement the law[8] (Hashimoto, 2002, 1). As a way of following up on this policy, the National Personnel Authority in May 2001 published guidelines for hiring and appointing women to the national civil service; at that time, there were only 1.2 percent in the highest positions. They suggested that each ministry should set goals and consider the ratio of women to total employees and quotas at the time of examination for the service. A major effort that has been promoted by the Gender Equality machinery has been to increase women's participation in advisory councils and committees, which rose from 2.4 percent in 1977 to 24.7 percent in 2001 (ibid.).

Local enforcement. Perhaps the most significant impact of the basic law to date has been at the local level. Articles 8 and 9 of the basic law specify that prefectural and local governments are responsible for making efforts to take positive measures to promote a gender equal society (*doryoku gimu*). As of January 2003, 40 of the 47 prefectures and 98 municipal governments had enacted plans of action and ordinances to follow them up (Saito Fumie, email, 12 February 2003). Other governments are still preparing to do so (Hashimoto interview). Proposals for policies related to gender equal society have emanated from administrative leadership, citizen groups or assemblies and assembly members, and, as in the DV and other legislative initiatives, the presence of women in government can make a difference.

In Saitama and Yamaguchi prefectures, female deputy governors played a key role in enacting ordinances that emanated initially from women's groups. Bando Mariko in Saitama (the former head of the Women's Bureau of the Labor Ministry) initiated a committee to research gender equality in advance of the law's adoption (Hashimoto interview). Women governors in Kumamoto and Chiba prefectures, including Domoto Akiko in the latter, a key player in the enactment of the national basic law, have sought to promote gender equality policy (Hashimoto, 2002). Some contend that a clear legacy emanating from local government support of delegates to UN meetings (such as the Fourth World Conference on Women) exists with regard to those local governments that have succeeded in passing progressive gender-related ordinances, another example of the significance of transnational feminism. In this view, feminists have brought back the lessons learned at international conferences to create local networks and continued pressure for policy change (Yamashita interview). They have built upon an infrastructure of local women's centers and female assembly members to create structures of support.

Many governments have utilized public hearings, although they were not mandated, in order to develop equality plans and then ordinances to implement them.

While the policies adopted are not binding, but rather require a good faith effort, numerous towns and prefectures have taken these initiatives seriously. Some local governments have developed local ordinances that involve ombuds systems in order to resolve human rights complaints. In Okayama and Hiroshima, private companies have been asked to submit records (*joetsu*) related to gender equality measures (Hashimoto, 2002). Others have established an independent compliance system to monitor compliance efforts and mediate complaints. Although quotas per se are prohibited by the Japanese Constitution, ratios have been employed in some localities and prefectures—either a 50:50 or 60:40 ratio of female to male representation on local advisory committees. In some cases (Fukuoka) a 30 percent target for women in office has already been achieved (Hashimoto, 2002). Ordinances have also addressed other gender-related issues including sex segregated public high schools and the Japanese custom of calling boys' names first when the daily school register is read. Policies adopted vary with each locality: some prohibit indirect discrimination. Councils for Gender Equality handle complaints, while the governor may have a dispute resolution role as well. In Tokyo, the governor may ask companies to report to the metropolitan assembly regarding their revised practices, with the possibility of publicizing the names of companies who do not comply (the latter sanction has not been invoked to date). No ordinances stipulate punishment for violation of these new initiatives at any level.

Despite these apparently positive efforts, in other instances, local and prefectural governments have opposed the adoption of gender policies. In Tokyo, for example, under the conservative leadership of Governor Ishihara, the Tokyo Josei Women's Foundation was abolished; it ceased to exist at the end of 2002 and prefectural leadership was put in control of the remaining services. Budgets for many women's centers have been cut. In Osaka, Japan's other major urban center, right-wing assembly members who alleged that gender equality efforts would destroy the family, as well as Japanese culture and society, prevailed in the policy process. Osaka has passed a weak ordinance recognizing differences between men and women, due to conservative pressure. In both of Japan's leading urban areas, Tokyo and Osaka, the policy outcomes have been disappointing to feminists. In Okayama City, the final version of the ordinance enacted excluded a specific quota for women in managerial positions.

Many in Japan speak of a "backlash" against even those modest policies adopted to date; in Chiba prefecture Governor Domoto Akiko's efforts to adopt a more proactive policy, involving affirmative action in order for companies to bid for contracts, have thus far been ineffective. Right wingers, including housewives—led by a male former Diet member (Murakami) who maintains that gender equality is as radical as "communism"—appear to be winning the struggle to develop prefectural policy (Hashimoto interview; email, 30 December 2002). A group called the Nihon Kaigi (Japan conference) and its women's branch, Nihon Josei Kaigi, attack the concept of "gender equal society" as denying the differences between men and women, and demands that such differences (e.g., respect for women's role as traditional homemakers) be acknowledged in provisions of the regulations being drafted (WWIN, 2003; Yamashita interview).

In Yamagata prefecture a vice-governor with good connections to women's groups who sought progressive policies was ousted by the more conservative governor (Hashimoto, 2002). Women intellectuals who serve on the Council of Gender Equality, such as Osawa Mari, have been vilified in the conservative press as radical feminists who are challenging "family values" and introducing Communist ideas in the guise of "gender equality" (*Nihon Jiji Hyoron*—Japan Current Events Critique; 15 March 2002, 8). The notion of gender-free education proposed by Ministry of Education bureaucrats has also been attacked. Other national newspapers, including the *Yomiuri Shinbun* and *Sankei Shinbun*, have engaged in unremitting, front-page publicity for these anti-gender equality interests. The hostility has spilled over to other policy issues, including education reform, adoption of local ordinances on gender equality and the proposal for civil code reform relating to women's surnames.

Specific policy outcomes. While it is difficult to document a precise relationship between the basic law for Gender Equal Society and specific policy outcomes, several new policy initiatives which may be linked in party to the passage of the basic law include the DV law discussed in chapter three, efforts to amend the Civil Code to permit retention of the wife's surname (selective surnames) analysis and revision of gender-related inequities in taxation, retirement and pensions, and insurance and corporate allowances (Osawa, 2001, 9). A special committee for balance between work and life, chaired by a well-known academic feminist, Higuchi Keiko, proposed elimination of waiting lists for day care centers, and amended childcare and long-term care leave policies, to which the national policy-making process has paid some heed. The latter two policies have been enacted into law via the Revised Childcare and Nursing Care Leave, November 9, 2001.

Selective surnames—an emerging policy area? The issue of amending the Civil Code to permit dual surnames, to be retained if married women choose, has gained momentum on the systemic agenda in Japan even though it has failed to achieve policy acceptance in the decision-making process. While this reform has been a long standing demand of Japanese feminists, the revision of code number 750 has been actively resisted by the Japanese government for years, despite the promise of "revision in the future" in a report to CEDAW by the Japanese government in 1988 (Yamashita, 1993, 82). Based on the century-old *ie*, or patriarchal, household system, the bride lost her identity when she became part of her husband's family. Today, wives are required to use their married names on drivers' licenses, health insurance cards and other official documents. Official change in this policy was first proposed in 1991; in 1996, the Judicial Advisory Council (or *hosei shingikai*), a conservative advisory body to the Justice Ministry, proposed a draft bill to revise the code. It is most unusual for a favorable proposal by a strong council such as this to fail to pass (Kobayashi, email, 9 August 2002).

However, this effort, as well as many others, failed to achieve consensus due to reluctance to establish traditional practices. As in the case of DV, a survey of public attitudes toward this reform was undertaken by the Cabinet office, under the aegis of Justice Minister Moriyama Mayumi, in an effort to garner widespread support (*Japan Times*, 2001, 15). The Cabinet Office survey showed that 68.1 percent of women and 61.8 percent of men supported the use of two surnames, an increase of 10 percent from the previous survey a decade before (ibid.). The Council for Gender Equality recommended a Civil Code revision, through a twelve-person panel, in October 2001. In 2001, after years of opposition, the LDP agreed to consider the issue. The combined efforts of the Justice Minister, the positive poll numbers, the record number of female lawmakers (then seventy-four) and the exit of a primary opponent of change due to a scandal, seemed to augur well for change (Magnier, 2002b). However, due to opposition within the LDP and other parties, from women as well as men, none of these efforts proved successful.

Women advocates of change hoped for a positive outcome to this policy initiative while Moriyama Mayumi retained her position as Justice Minister in the Koizumi cabinet (Yamaguchi interview). However, Moriyama judged that opposition, both within her own LDP party and from opposition party members, particularly from two right-wing Democratic party women, was too great and abandoned plans to introduce a government-sponsored bill (ibid.). She asked Noda Seiko, who had been involved in legislating against child pornography and prostitution, to help sponsor the change from within the Diet (Moriyama, Noda interviews). Chairing a project team similar to the one utilized in the DV Law reform process, Noda, a Diet member who is in a common law marriage, made efforts to gain support from LDP members and opposition party women (Yamamoto, 2001, 6; *Japan Times*, 2001, 3; Noda interview). Her efforts have been opposed by the Nippon Josei no Kai (Japan women's group), which argues that this policy change will trigger the collapse of the family. Conservative LDP members also fear that passage would foster too much "individualism" in society (*Asahi*, 2001, 22; *Japan Times*, 2002). Noda has indicated that although the LDP is hostile to member-sponsored legislation, she would attempt to put together a coalition of Diet women to press for this policy reform (Noda interview). However, this policy has proven more resistant to *giin rippo* than DV and other policies discussed to aid "miserable women and children." This proposed reform may more directly challenge the *ie* system that lies at the core of Japanese society and patriarchy and it is viewed with hostility by numerous Diet members (including perhaps up to half of LDP Diet-women) while others avidly support the change (Moriyama interview). If the bill were passed, it would require individual permission from a specially designated court, creating selective surnames as an "exception," rather than providing for a general policy that would permit married women to opt out of the single surname system. However, even this limited approach has not succeeded in gaining support (Moriyama, Noda interviews). Nonetheless, central government offices, many local governments, sixteen prefectures and some private companies have already institutionalized such policies (Yamamoto, 2001).

Conclusion

In the final chapter, the reasons for failure of some policies to become law, both in Japan and the United States, to move from the problem or "systemic" to the "institutional" or decision-making agenda (Cobb and Elder, 1983) will be explored further. Such issues include the selective surname issue in Japan, as well as a strengthened EEOL. In the United States, policy related to universal childcare is in this category.

This chapter has demonstrated major progress in both nations related to "family friendly" policy, as well as continued obstacles to its full realization. In the United States, the enactment of the FMLA, providing for unpaid leave, and some childcare policies largely tied to welfare for public care, as well as tax credits to purchase private care, have been adopted in recent years. However, the United States still lacks a universal and comprehensive policy for childcare and although it represents a significant symbolic gain endorsing public recognition of the need to balance work and family, the FMLA is one of the few parental leave programs among industrial states that provides no financial support, limiting its applicability. Utilizing an incremental noninterventionist model, the United States remains behind most other nations with regarding support for working mothers, a hurdle that American feminists have been unable to overcome.

Childcare, parental leave and allowance policies in Japan, although closer to European models and more generous and accessible at least on paper than those in the United States, have been motivated by pro-natalist efforts to increase the birth rate among reluctant working women. At present, they have not succeeded in reversing the low birth rate, as Japanese women's work options continue to be limited by the inhospitable structure of the labor market, with few ports of entry and long working hours for those who are employed full time. In addition, company pressures to forego leaves and other benefits may reduce their applicability for many workers, making them difficult to operationalize in practice. In both nations, financial pressures may also prevent workers from taking needed care-related leaves. In both nations as well, countermobilization by groups opposed to change have been prominent in the policy process, as this chapter makes clear. In the United States, small business groups were able to dominate the discourse related to the FMLA, significantly reducing the law's scope. A bimodal approach to day care prevails, with women's groups unable to stem the tide of punitive approaches to welfare-related care policy, while tax credits for private care have expanded. In Japan, opposition to the selective surname issue and extensive backlash against even the largely symbolic Basic Law for Gender Equal Society have suggested the limits of policy change, as well as perceived threats to traditional norms from even a marginally more successful feminist movement. It may be too early to gauge the full impact of gender equality policy in Japan, although at the very least it represents a new potential resource for Japanese women, with the establishment of the Council for Gender Equality.

In each of the policy arenas examined in this chapter, women's groups participating in a policy community with bureaucrats or legislators or both, have played an important role in bringing issues related to balancing work and family to the fore. As noted, Japanese feminists have also relied on international equity norms to produce policy change, while U.S. women have not been able to benefit from similar recourse to a transnational dynamic, characterized here as the politics of "externality" versus "insularity."

Conclusion: Assessing Policy Change

Introduction

At the beginning of this book, a central theme was established, asking how the role of women's movements in gender-related policy making might be evaluated in two seemingly very different cultures. Through developing case studies on related policies in each nation, the analysis sought to investigate the conditions in which women's "agency" may be likely to have a more significant political impact in creating policy, examining the political meaning of gender in two distinct cultures and political systems. This study fits best within the framework of qualitative analysis, as a set of "first step" studies of relatively uncharted areas identifying the complex forces at work in a small number of cases through "thick description" and "process tracing" (Mazur, 2002, 173).

While feminist policy making does not have a single profile or common pattern either within or across national borders, some factors are significant at least in several of the cases examined. (See ibid., 177, for a similar argument.) The findings suggest some insights into the strategies employed by women's movements, the significance of increased women's representation in political office, the kinds of policies that have been most successful in each context and, particularly in the case of Japan, the important role played of transnational feminism and new international venues for the articulation of gender equity norms. In emphasizing the centrality of women's movements and women's centered policy coalitions, as often decisive factors in creating feminist policy, this study takes issue with other recent scholarship that questions their impact in both formulating and implementing policy. In addition to suggesting that increased descriptive representation by women does not necessarily lead to substantive policy change, Mazur contends that: "[while] Women's movements, women centered feminist policy coalitions and strategic partnerships are clearly a part of feminist policy formation; they do not appear to be the decisive ingredient" (ibid., 197).

At the outset, this research comparing gender policy in the United States and Japan sought to test four hypotheses: (1) that increased numbers of women in office impact substantive policy; (2) that cross partisan agenda setting by elected female representatives may have an important policy sponsorship role; (3) that "advocacy coalitions" or policy communities comprised of political insiders and outsiders develop a basis for collective action and policy influence, and finally; (4) that, in the case of Japan, emerging international standards of gender equity through *kansetsu gaiatsu*, have proven to be a crucial resource with which to advocate for a rights discourse and pressure the Japanese government. It appears that each of these has been confirmed at least in part.

Major differences between the two countries relate to the view of and integration with the world, with the United States maintaining a stance of "insularity" and rejecting international inputs on gender policy and Japan increasingly receptive, at least on with regard to passage of legislation, to a model incorporating "externality." The second conclusion emphasizes greater similarities in policy making, based on changing power balances within existing institutions such as elective bodies (the Congress in the United States and the Diet and some local governments in Japan). Theories of "institutional dynamism" demonstrate that increased representation for women, as new participants in older structures may help to redefine the ends of policy from a gendered perspective. (See Bishop, 2002, 5 for a similar point.)

The Significance of Women in Office and Cross Party Alliances

This study has suggested the political importance of increasing numbers of women in office. They play a role in agenda setting, bringing new attention to bear on women's issues, and also in linking the demands of movement activists with the structures of policy making through the establishment of policy communities. While nowhere near a majority in either nation (in particular, female representation in the more powerful Japanese House of Representatives remains low), an enhanced women's presence in the legislative process has often helped to produce greater policy success. In the cases studied here, the fact that women in the legislatures of both nations gained experience, seniority, more influential positions and voice over time meant that they were able to shape policy alternatives to a greater extent as a result.

In the United States, there continues to be incremental improvement in women's access to congressional office, most notable in 1992 and 2000 when more women ran and were elected to seats, as well as a record of policy impact produced by independent-minded women members of Congress relatively unencumbered by party control. As of the 107th Congress, in the House and Senate, women held the most important positions ever on powerful committees (though they chaired no full committees) and within the leadership of both parties. They chaired five subcommittees in the House and held ranking positions on others. In the Senate, they chaired seven subcommittees and held ranking positions on five others (Hall, 2003, 345). Many of these are particularly important for women's policy making including assignments on Appropriations and Labor Health and Human Services committees (ibid.). The election of Nancy Pelosi (D-CA) as House Whip, in October 2001, and others to key positions in both parties—for example, Kay Bailey Hutchinson (R-TX) as Secretary of the Senate Republican Conference and Barbara Mikulski (D-MD) as Secretary of the Democratic Conference—indicate new prominence for women in party leadership roles (ibid.). Clearly, access for women as representatives and leaders on influential committees and in key positions has increased attention to some issues related to women and families, such as reauthorization and funding of the Violence against Women Act (VAWA) in 2000, now viewed as a mainstream policy. Women legislators appear to feel a special obligation to represent the views of their women constituents (Carroll, 2002) and are increasingly able to advocate on behalf of these interests. The validating presence of other women legislators has helped women in Congress to place women's issues higher on the policy agenda. Successful legislative efforts have represented collaborations between movement outsiders and women inside government creating policy communities, which have been effective; alliances with other interest groups such as unions and male members of Congress facilitate policy change as well. In most of the policy areas analyzed, including the VAWA and its continued funding, legislation related to the Federal Access to Clinic Entrances Act (FACE), limiting access by anti-abortion groups to clinics, the Family and Medical Leave Act (FMLA), and childcare, the policy agenda has been shaped to some degree by elected women representatives.

The formally organized Congressional Caucus for Women's Issues (CCWI), established in 1977 as a non-partisan coalition, has played a significant agenda-setting role, creating pressure to pass legislation even when encountering significant internal opposition. There have been strains in the CCWI as both numbers (now at a record sixty-one) and more diverse partisan perspectives have gained strength; it is increasingly a challenge to craft an agenda with a membership representing the entire ideological spectrum (Hall, 2003, 345). Republican members of CCWI (including Connie Morella, who served as its co-chair in the 104th Congress, as well as Susan Molinari and Marge Roukema) have appealed to their leadership for support with considerable success. Their role has been of particular significance, given enhanced congressional power for the Republican Party in the last decade. The caucus agenda-setting process changed during the early 1990s so that complete consensus from all members was no longer required: on abortion and welfare reform this proved to be helpful as a means of rallying member support.[1] But, it also meant that a number of Republican women refused to participate (ibid., 342). As a consequence of divisiveness of the abortion issue in particular among CCWI women since the 104th Congress, after mid-1997 a policy of abortion neutrality has been maintained. Emphasis is placed on creating agreement on less controversial issues, such as funding for the Violence Against Women office in the Department of Justice and support for women's health research (ibid., 343–45). Problems occur when numbers and diverse opinions increase, foregoing efforts to achieve unanimity on controversial issues as suggested above. Conflicts may limit future CCWI effectiveness, and confine agenda setting to more neutral policies such as health care for women. In addition, the caucus is based in the House: Senate women have shown little interest in joining or forming their own, and their numbers rival those for congressional women at present (ibid., 347). The next quarter century will bring new challenges to the fore for the CCWI in establishing priorities and acting as a collective legislative presence. In both nations, the future of non incremental increase in women's descriptive representation and cross-party efforts remains unclear, given significant institutional obstacles in each.

In Japan, a crucial byproduct of increased representation for women in legislative politics discussed in this volume has been greater reliance on *giin rippo*,

Diet member's sponsored legislation. While *giin rippo* as a more general trend is not limited to women's issues, as Robert Pekkanen and others note, often such bills have been the product of opposition parties and as such they have been doomed to failure (2000, 112). However, in several cases, Diet women across party lines have successfully collaborated on legislation.

What characterizes successful efforts? It appears that legislation dealing with protection of victims has been most accepted to date. Second, successful policies may involve a limited government budgetary commitment which makes them more palatable. Finally, the adoption of these laws has involved compromise and collaboration not just among women, but also among the Liberal Democratic Party (LDP) and opposition parties. In the absence of key LDP support, they cannot succeed. Bills proposed by opposition parties alone and collaboratively, fail and are discarded (Kobayashi, e-mail, 9 August 2002). Successful gender-related policy adoption has also involved active lobbying by women's groups who have gained the ear of female Diet members, often through their association with opposition parties but occasionally with sympathetic members of the LDP as well. Such citizen groups help publicize issues and keep them in the public arena with continuing scrutiny from the media (Pekkanen, 2000, 133).

Cross-party sponsorship cannot prevail in those instances where the LDP is divided, and/or opposition party members are also opposed to policy. The key to effective cross-party collaboration by Diet women necessarily involves participation by LDP Diet women, and their leadership on policy initiatives is needed as well (Kobayashi, e-mail, 13 August 2002). This was true in the DV law in the House of Councilors, through the Study Group (*chosokai*) and Project Team effort and also in the House of Representatives for the anti–child pornography/anti–child prostitution bill. The selective or dual surname legislation has encountered much opposition from male and female LDP members (among others) and cannot garner the same support, despite efforts to use the *giin rippo* process again by an LDP Diet woman (Noda interview). Another factor upon which members' legislation is premised is the existence of coalition government, which necessitates compromise and bargaining between the LDP and the opposition parties. The exigencies of electoral instability and the potential of female swing voting in unstable electoral conditions may play a role as well (Pekkanen, 2000). Finally, successful efforts to date have involved international gender equity norms as applied by Japanese women, although this may not always be the case in the future. While LDP women, although active on other issues, expressed their dismay with the revision of the Eugenic Protection Law, particularly the name change to Mother's Body Protection Law (*botai hogo ho*), on this issue they did not make common cause with opposition party women who also opposed the name and content of the new proposal. Each party supported its own bill and the result was one disappointing to feminist interests. On some issues, LDP Diet women may be constrained by the opposition of their male counterparts, or they may wish to claim sole credit for legislation for their own reelection benefit or that of their party, making cooperation difficult (Kobayashi, e-mail, 13 August 2002). It is therefore premature to speak of gender-based Diet members' legislation as a definite and enduring trend. Nonetheless, informal groups of Diet women will continue to be active in proposing some legislation; they are presently redoubling efforts to revise the DV law through a cross-party project team similar to the one employed earlier in 1999–2001.

Diet member bills, particularly those sponsored by suprapartisan groups of women in conjunction with policy advocates, may be transforming aspects of Japanese law making, with important consequences for civil society and parliamentary decision making. While in earlier periods such collaboration was attempted, the conditions for success, including women in sufficient numbers able to take on leadership roles, the exigencies of coalition politics and other factors were lacking. Diet member bills as alternatives to bureaucratically drafted bills submitted by the cabinet which account for the vast majority of Japanese legislation, bear watching.[2] These efforts challenge the notion of bureaucratic decision-making dominance, pointing to new possibilities inherent in Diet policy making, with members acting individually and collectively as decision makers. A broader trend may be at work in Japanese politics, marked by greater influence for NGOs, which have gained more of a foothold in the legislative process than was true earlier, as some Diet members initiate policy in conjunction with social movements and citizen groups (Sasaki, 109). This phenomenon may be attributable in part to the passage of the Freedom of Information Act, passed in 1999, perhaps contributing to greater openness in legislative policy making Sasaki claims that it has (ibid.).

Another aspect of women's increased representation in policy making in Japan and the United States relates to the role of "femocrats," or female bureaucrats who may help to advance a feminist agenda. This phenomenon may be less visible in the United States, given the absence of comparable administrative agencies devoted to women and, arguably, a less significant policy-making role for bureaucrats in initiating policy.[3] As noted earlier, the United States has not followed UN directives regarding the establishment of "national machinery" for women in keeping with its politics of "insularity." Nonetheless, Equal Employment Opportunity Commission (EEOC) staff members have sometimes functioned as "femocrats," particularly as they expanded the meaning and significance of Title VII in the decades after the enactment of the Civil Rights Act of 1964. The Ministry of Labor (MOL) Women's Bureau and the Bureau and Council for Gender Equality have created a base for advocacy of women's issues in the Japanese government as "state feminists," although they may be relatively weak entities in terms of their decision-making clout. (See Kobayashi, 2002b, who argues this position forcefully.) For the first time, some feminists have gained a policy-making role among Japanese bureaucrats, although the dangers of cooptation may be significant. Much of the evidence in the Japanese cases related to the EEOL, and its amendments as well as the Basic Law for Gender Equal Society, suggests the importance of femocrats bringing feminist issues to the fore in policy making at multiple levels of politics.

Creation of policy communities. In both nations, advocacy coalitions, or policy subsystems/communities,[4] bring new feminist values and initiatives to the policy arena, although they appear to more effectively mobilized, and have had greater access and legitimacy, in the United States than in Japan. "Policy communities" link women inside and outside of government in common efforts. Such coalitions have been more highly developed in American politics, where women's movements have been effectively mobilized at the national level for a longer period and where numerous female legislators have internalized the values of feminist/women's groups to which they belong than in Japan. In addition, the existence of membership organizations with state and local branches, such as the National Organization for Women (NOW) and the National Coalition Against Domestic Violence (NCADV), have permitted mobilization of impressive grassroots lobbying support on behalf of feminist issues, such as the VAWA. Of course, not all policy enactment involves an expansive grassroots pressure group effort. In the United States, the successful effort to pass the FMLA came about at the national level, through interest group representatives and political insiders, without recourse to grassroots mobilization.

In contrast to the U.S. experience regarding many of the policies analyzed here, the more localized and fragmented nature of the Japanese feminist movement, until recently, made it more difficult to impact national policy. However, the Japanese women's movement appears to have overcome some of the tendencies noted by earlier scholars toward fragmentation and has demonstrated ability to prod an often reluctant government into making policy related to women, on such issues as the EEOL, abortion and contraception.

Other cases demonstrate an insider/outsider approach linking policy makers (including legislators, bureaucrats, academics and movement activists) in an "issue network" framework. (See Sasaki, 2002, 108 for a similar point regarding Japanese politics.) In both the United States and Japan, the domestic violence (DV) case has provided the best representation of this approach. In Japan, in recent years, links have developed especially been especially between female legislators, academics and experts and activists on a range of policies, often utilizing international women's rights as a resource.

Group connections to bureaucrats are rarer in Japan than in the United States, given the lack of transparency of the administrative process, although they do occasionally exist. In the case of DV legislation among those considered here, after initial opposition, some bureaucrats were converted after they received information from Diet women and movement activists of which they had been ignorant (Komiyama interview). The childcare policy-making process demonstrated new linkages between bureaucrats and feminist activists. The MOL Women's Bureau was able to play a limited advocacy related role on labor policy for women related to the EEOL, and was subject to pressure from advocates of change both in 1985 and 1997. However, it never developed the kind of policy alliances that might have aided in the creation of a more effective anti–sex discrimination law (Kobayashi, 2002b, 178). On many issues, advocacy coalitions have been effective in calling for policy change, such as the broad-based aggregate comprised of diverse women's groups, professionals and Diet members to defend access to abortion in the 1970s and 1980s. In contrast to their pro-abortion activism, in other instances, for example, the legalization of the low-dose birth control pill, Japanese feminists and Diet members were divided and relatively silent throughout most of the process.

Their absence from the parliamentary and bureaucratic decision-making process related to policy change until fairly late in the game meant that that other interests dominated the political discourse and delayed the adoption of the birth control pill. Once women's groups mounted a collective effort and mobilized an advocacy coalition, they had a significant impact on the policy outcome.

Policy communities may also include alliances with members of the executive branch and bureaucracy, other interest groups and movements (including women's groups) and male members of the legislature who are outside of the feminist constituency. Such coalitions vary with the nature of the issue and the policy sub-sector involved. In Japan, abortion politics proved to be a particularly effective policy with which to rally health professionals, family planners, male Diet members and members of opposition parties and labor. Opposition parties (Socialists, Communists) in Japan have sometimes played an important role in highlighting gender-related concerns on employment and other issues as well, although as noted, they cannot prevail in the absence of LDP support. Labor has sometimes functioned as an ally as well, as in seen in the central coordinating and policy role played by Rengo during the negotiations for the 1997 amendments to the EEOL. However, the weakness of trade unions in the Japanese neo-corporatist state (in which labor is not a participant) has diluted initiatives to expand social- and gender-related citizenship.[5] Male-dominated company-based labor unions have often failed to support the legal and other demands of their female workers. They have limited their role in the litigation process and forced women to turn elsewhere, to Josei (women's) and more radical unions that represent less traditional approaches.

In the United States, like Japan a nation in which a labor/Left presence is extremely limited, organized labor has been a frequent supporter of the feminist movement on issues particularly related to equal employment and domestic violence. The feminist network is a part of the larger civil rights community, which has given it a strong vehicle for gaining coalition support from religious, labor and other civil rights organizations, although on controversial issues such as abortion, customary partners have been less willing to join forces. Efforts to develop new alliances (with such groups as the American Association of Retired People [AARP]) may show promise, as the focus and scope of acceptable legislation and policy is broadened beyond women's interests only, as the FMLA, family care policy and abortion-related hospital merger struggles suggest.

***Kansetsu gaiatsu*—utilizing international gender equity norms as a resource in Japan**. One of the most important findings presented has been to highlight the vigorous activism of Japanese women, who have added an important dimension to their claims for change by buttressing them with appeals to international feminism and new transnational gender equity norms. This has been characterized as the "politics of externality."

Utilizing models learned from international conferences and other venues, as well as new global directives in a period of greater internationalization, advocates have pressed for a number of initiatives in Japan, ranging from the DV and anti–child pornography, anti-prostitution law, to the process of amending the

EEOL, to altering the discourse around abortion and the legalization of the low-dose birth control pill. A "rights" discourse, stressing appeals for recognition of women's rights as human rights, has informed most of the activism examined in the case studies. This discourse, in turn, has utilized *kansetsu gaiatsu,* which has led to articulation of new norms of gender equity and rights. As the case studies suggest, the Japanese government has been shamed into adopting policies in order to keep up and save face with western democratic states and some Asian nations as well. *Kansetsu gaiatsu* as a resource and rallying point for Japanese feminists has led to a new policy dynamic. Activists have employed the notion of individual rights not only to gain the adoption of legislation, but also to monitor policy through the agency of international organizations once adopted, seeking to embarrass the recalcitrant Japanese government into greater compliance with its commitments. Feminist groups have both been informed by the international meetings they have attended and in turn have continued to inform them about Japanese governmental shortcomings. Admittedly this process has limitations, given its restricted scope and often indirect and symbolic quality (Mazur, 2002, 193). The Japanese government has often responded to rights-based appeals with legislation that has done little to change actual conditions related to gender inequity.

The United States has maintained a "politics of insularity," an entirely different approach to extranational influences. A former leader in the twentieth century's global struggle for gender equity and other policies, and admittedly successful in creating career opportunities for working women, the United States has remained aloof from the strictures of international treaties, in the interests of national sovereignty. It does not view itself as subject to the demands of global feminism and international rule making. Symptomatic has been the failure to ratify the UN Convention on the Elimination of Discrimination against Women (CEDAW) as most of the world's nations have done (169 to date) and the insistence on maintaining the model of "maximum private responsibility" and nonintervention in the family. By failing to engage in the emerging dialogue created by the UN and other transnational policies that serve as important "touchstones" for feminist policy making, the U.S. government has ignored important social supports for working women who must balance home and work responsibilities. Despite the considerable policy accomplishments related here with regard to equality in the labor force and domestic violence, among others, U.S. policy making has neglected important aspects of gender equity policy.

The weak U.S. welfare state and renewed interest in "new federalism" and state autonomy make it difficult to develop policies that support working women as mothers. As noted, there is a huge contrast between the rights-oriented approach that has proven so significant in advancing women's interests in the labor market and the recognition of the importance of "social citizenship," which would bring American policies into greater harmony with policies for working mothers elsewhere. Apparently, in the minds of decision makers, social expenditures and commitment to policies that may treat women "differently" from men do not easily fit prevailing models of rights for women. Feminist activists may not have done enough to prioritize CEDAW ratification as a key policy concern, although, similar to childcare, their ability to achieve policy change on this issue is probably virtually nil. The U.S. failure to engage with international institutions that articulate a more supportive vision of gender equity related to harmonizing family and work roles, due to a strong commitment to national sovereignty and superpower status, may limit options for American working women even further in the future.

Implications for Theories of Policy Change: Streams, Cycles and Others

At the outset, it was posited that no one theory of policy making and change would explain all of the cases, either within or across national borders. That prediction has proven accurate. However, several theories do have applicability to some of the cases analyzed.

Policy windows and streams. The case studies suggest that in both nations "policy streams," which bring together problem recognition, policies and politics through periodic "couplings" that create "policy windows," help to explain some of the outcomes. These openings are said to occur only for a short time, until they are replaced by wavering attention and new issues (Kingdon, 1995, 88, 181). Policy specialists and members of policy communities float ideas and alternatives as a way of addressing problems in the "policy stream." In the "political" stream described by policy theorist John Kingdon, changes in national mood, electoral turnover and interest group pressure may combine to produce policy change. Such critical openings are often driven by perceived electoral instability and the potential role of women as voters in decision making. In the United States the threat of a "gender gap" after the 1992 "Year of the Woman" may have aided in the adoption of the FMLA and VAWA in 1993 and 1994 respectively. In Japan, continuing electoral instability may similarly contribute to policy-making access for women's groups. The role played by policy entrepreneurs, discussed below, who invest resources to push alternative programs helps in creating attention to the problems and in bringing disparate "streams" together to create policy change (ibid.).

Nonetheless, there are several problems with the concepts of "policy streams" and "policy windows" as explanations for gender-related policy making as described here. First, the power of ideas and ideology—changed values and beliefs—appears to be neglected. For example, the key role played by a women's rights discourse, first in the United States and more recently in Japan, would not be given a central place in the "policy windows" framework. Gendered definitions or frames have created new approaches to problems requiring policy attention; the key contribution of feminist theory in redefining wife battering as a public, rather than private, issue, might be ignored by concepts that fail to take appropriate note of ideas. Second, the significance that external or transnational macro-political factors may play, particularly in the Japanese case, is ignored in the "policy streams" analysis. Perhaps its focus is largely on U.S. domestic policy making, in which, as we have seen, international factors play a limited role. In contrast, in Japan, *kansetsu gaiatsu* has played a key role in prying open a reluctant system, as international conferences have "triggered" governmental response. The lengthy period of time required in the United States and Japan for adoption of some gender policies (FMLA, DV and selective surname change) leads analysts to wonder exactly what forces do produce that opening when it occurs: "Processes like agenda setting do seem a bit unpredictable. Even savvy policy insiders are sometimes surprised by major developments" (Kingdon, 1995, 224). Such statements emphasize the randomness and unpredictability of policy making a la the "garbage can" model, in which change depends on uncertain factors, suggesting that patterns are not easy to find until after the policy has changed (ibid., 86–88). Finally, the "streams/windows" approach ignores the recurrence and continuation of attention to specific policy concerns. Most of the policy issues addressed here appear to take on a life of their own, perhaps propelled by "policy communities" that have gathered around them. Virtually all are the subject of ongoing policy, albeit incremental, as opposed to discrete approaches which are negotiated anew. Sometimes, as in the case of DV policy in Japan and the VAWA in the United States, enacted policies specifically call for renewal and evaluation, so that they are insured a continuing place on the political agenda.

Policy cycles. The foregoing analysis suggests the need for attention to another policy concept that sheds light on several of the case studies presented in this volume: that of policy cycles or "secular" trends in policy—continuously high activity during a particular era on specific issues (Baumgartner and Jones, 244–5). Some issues "remain on the policy agenda for quite some time" and spread rapidly (ibid., 87). A related construct also stresses the importance of "spillover" effects, which help to foster change in another, similar or adjacent area, largely due to the existence of new coalitions and political entrepreneurs (Kingdon, 1995, 190–98). Periods of policy change link issues in a "policy cycle," which may be characterized by new ideas such as gender equity.[6] The cycles also appear to be responses to changing social and electoral conditions, for example, the relative fragility of the LDP as its power base eroded and the increased lobbying efforts of Japanese women's groups on a variety of issues, relying on new supranational support. (See Cobb and Ross, 1997, 10.) The "policy cycle" approach may best describe intensified attention to gender-related issues in Japan in the current period. During the last few years in Japan, there has been legislation on: pill legalization; the amendment and renaming of the Eugenic Protection Law (now the Law for Protection of Mothers' Bodies [*botai hogo ho*]); the laws to prevent stalking and child pornography and prostitution; the amended EEOL; and the Basic Law for Gender Equal Society. All of these policies have been enacted since 1995, when Japanese feminists utilized the Fourth UN World Conference on Women to prod the government. As suggested above, there is a need for more attention to "macro" forces in setting policy agendas and sustaining policy momentum. A similar era existed in the United States at an earlier time—in the 1970s—after the emergence of second wave feminism as a significant political force when such policies as equal credit, equal access to education and pregnancy discrimination initially gained congressional attention. (See Gelb and Palley, 1996; Costain,

1992.) Again in the 1990s, the election of Bill Clinton to the presidency, and the increase in women's congressional representation and appearance of a "gender gap" in which women voters favored Democratic Party candidates, created favorable conditions for a brief increase in attention to women's issues; the phenomenon known as "punctuated equilibrium" in which occasional change occurs as a result of disruption (Baumgartner and Jones, 23).

Policy entrepreneurs. The case studies reveal as well that male and female "policy entrepreneurs" have been active in sponsoring legislation in both countries. Joseph Biden, chair of the Judiciary Committee in the U.S. Senate, and other committed male and female legislators from both parties were key promoters and sponsors of the VAWA and the FMLA, while the CCWI has often played a key role in agenda setting as well. In Japan, women acting singly and collectively have been the primary advocates of new gender related laws. A number of legislators linked to feminist causes have been active in advocating on issues of interest to women, through the project team approach utilized to endorse the DV and other policies.

Policy entrepreneurship need not be limited to legislators or even government officials. Entrepreneurs or sponsors may include those holding bureaucratic positions, such as directors of the former Ministry of Labor Women's Bureau, the Gender Equality Bureau and other agencies in Japan. During the present era, Justice Minister Moriyama Mayumi has occasionally been a moderate advocate for women's interests.

Support from executive leadership may prove crucial although it is more likely to occur in the U.S. presidential system, which provides a potentially stronger base for powerful executive based policy advocacy than does Japan's weak prime minister: "presidential involvement can be decisive" (ibid., 241), both in a positive and negative manner. In Japan, Prime Minister Hashimoto supported the consideration and adoption of the Basic Law on Gender Equal Society. Former American president Bill Clinton was instrumental in the passage of the FMLA, the licensing of RU 486 and in supporting the VAWA as well. Republican presidents have retarded the adoption and implementation of these policies.

Policy entrepreneurs also include movement activists and leaders—for example, labor lawyers in the United States and Japan, who advocate tirelessly for policy change on equal employment issues. In Japan, activist groups such as the Working Women's International Network (WWIN) have sought to strengthen weak Japanese law through litigation and pressure exerted though national and international venues for more than a decade. The NOW Legal Defense and Education Fund (NOW LDEF)and the National Women's Law Center (NWLC) in the United States have been central to the continual effort to redefine and broaden Title VII, among other initiatives.

Other theories. In some instances (abortion in Japan and Title VII in the United States), women's groups played no role in the decision-making process that led to policy change or adoption, but in both countries, policy enactments have created the new institutional venues suggested by Baumgartner and Jones (238–9). These examples demonstrate that even in the absence of women's participation in the initial policy-making process, the creation of policy can lead to new opportunities for issue advocacy and redefinition. This suggests the importance of a "feedback" phenomenon in which policies develop a life of their own, creating new "subsystems" as new participants, communities, interests and demands form around them to articulate new policy goals.

Consideration of the types of policies likely to achieve the most success incorporates the notion of "cost/benefit" analysis as well. Costs include those imposed on business or government sectors who may be willing to accept change if the costs of noncompliance are greater than they feel can bear. Such costs may be monetary or psychological/social, including public embarrassment and saving face. (See Gelb, 2003.) In Japan, the perceived costs include international disapproval; in the United States, costs relate to government imposed sanctions on non-compliant employers.

"Cognitive" policy development, or policy designed to foster certain national goals to address national problems through policy adoption, may be operative in as well in some instances (Campbell, 1992, 356). American policies related to women have in general not been directed to the realization of national priorities in any discernible manner given the fragmentation of the policy process, with the exception of the welfare reform policies, which address work-related demands for poor women. In contrast, in Japan abortion and contraceptive policy have been linked to national goals, first to decrease and then to increase the population. In the present era as well, social policy aimed at balancing the demands of women with families who wish to work has produced a host of "family friendly" efforts. However, these efforts have not reversed trends toward low birth rates, perhaps, as suggested above, because they fail to address the inequitable working conditions that foster discontent (Peng, 2001; Schoppa, 2001). Major changes in the economy and society, including the expectations of mothers and wives, and of women workers by companies, will necessarily precede greater opportunities for Japanese women.

In still other instances, what has been described as "policy containment" or "agenda denial" (also known as "non-decision making") prevails; often involving redefinition of an issue away from the concerns of its proponents. In such instances, policies fail to move from the public agenda to the formal or institutional agenda, although the problems they embody are discussed and acknowledged in a public way (Cobb and Ross, 1997, 7, 20). Thus far, the "dual/selective" surname issue in Japan appears to be of this variety, as is the issue of governmental support for working women with families in the United States. In Japan, although the EEOL has entered the formal policy agenda, it has been defined narrowly, and does not address the range of difficulties experienced by working women in the labor force.

While several theories of policy change derived from the U.S. experience do seem applicable to some gender-related cases in Japan, this analysis suggests that they are limited in others. Certainly, no one theory has demonstrated complete explanatory power.

Additional factors explaining policy success and failure. One of the key conclusions of this book has been that women have "agency" in affecting policy change in both countries; that women's increased political participation and representation, as well as group mobilization, has significant policy outcomes. Although policy change is contingent on historical, cultural and other factors, many aspects of policy making demonstrate considerable similarity across both nations. Similarities involve strategies employed by women's groups as well as deep-seated resistance to feminist claims, albeit on different issues in each nation. Differences relate to the role of symbolic policy, more common in Japan, and efforts at implementation and resource commitment, more likely in the United States.

Similarities

Feminist strategies and approaches. Systemic and cultural differences affect the strategic choices available to feminist advocates in each nation, although the repertory of tactics appears remarkably similar. The range of strategic options open to advocacy groups is greater in the United States than in Japan, partially due to federalism, the separation of powers with multiple entry points which permits policy intervention, as well as due to the greater openness and transparency of the bureaucratic and policy-making processes. While their claims are often viewed as controversial and, as noted, besieged by countermobilization, American feminists have achieved a degree of legitimacy in political decision making perhaps still far off for Japanese feminists, in a system which has not been receptive to change-oriented groups.

As noted above, government-sponsored, bureaucratic initiatives in sponsoring most legislation have been far more significant in Japanese policy making, given a neo-corporatist form of government, more similar to some European nations than the United States. The bureaucratic system is far less transparent and accountable, making access to it often problematic for groups seeking policy change. (See Richardson, 259.) Bureaucrats prefer informal procedures that are not documented as a way of controlling political access. Despite the passage of an Information Disclosure Law in May 1999, much information is "off limits."[7] However, we have seen that the bureaucrats' efforts to contain the formal legal decision-making processes through litigation by creating alternative mediation-based mechanisms of dispute resolution have been unsuccessful to date. By pursuing legislative agenda-setting efforts, feminists may be helping to democratize the system of policy making in Japan.

Despite key systemic and cultural differences, approaches employed by advocacy groups in both nations include litigation, lobbying and protest. Japanese feminists have become more proactive with regard to efforts to influence the national government, and, in recent years, they have made renewed efforts to create broad-based networks rather than operating solely at the local level.

The widespread use of litigation has been a strategy utilized by feminist groups in both nations. Litigation has proven to be a crucial tool for American feminists, sometimes supported by government efforts through the EEOC and other agencies. At their most effective, lawsuits in the United States have provided major tools for increasing implementation and compliance with rules and regulations, and they have functioned to benefit women collectively. Litigation has also been used more widely in Japan than many believe in order to press for women's rights. However, the results of litigation are far more limited in terms of impact on wage disparities, access to career positions and promotions than in the United States. The concept of indirect discrimination has as yet not been operationalized in a meaningful way.

This analysis has emphasized the important role played by litigation in the United States in creating gender equity policy, particularly in the employment area. But the role of a more conservative federal judiciary coupled with more complex "second generation" cases presently under review may call into question the future efficacy of feminist law suits.

Backlash in both nations. The research has demonstrated the continued vigor of the American feminist movements, though frequently constrained by hostile political environments. However, despite occasional policy victories even in conservative times, U.S.-based feminist advocates have had to expend much energy fending off the attacks of the "New Right," whose agenda has been incorporated into that of the Republican Party. Successful policy enactment, VAWA and the FMLA, has often been supported by members of both parties on issues related to broadly defined "family values" or anti-crime policies.

Political processes in both nations involve manipulation of symbols that engage both proponents and opponents of feminism and women's rights. The overt, bitter conflicts that surround in particular abortion policy in the United States have only begun to have a parallel in Japan, where in recent months "backlash" has developed to protest and limit relatively moderate approaches to gender equality. Such controversies, largely revolving around rhetorical (or "horatory") ordinances, emphasize aspects of equity for women at the prefectural and municipal level. These struggles, as well as the failure to achieve any gain with regard to the selective surname issue, suggest a continuing battle between traditional values and ideology and the alternative vision offered by feminism. It may be that the initial, more progressive local policies that were adopted reflected a lack of clear understanding by the "opposition," which has now mobilized to prevent further change (Yamashita interview). Now that attention has been heightened and the "conflict socialized," it may be more difficult to gain even limited gender equality policies. Perhaps an analogous process has been seen in the hospital merger/reproductive rights access in the United States, which created some rare efforts at compromise on this controversial issue through less visible and highly publicized solutions.

Conflict that involves strongly held societal values involving women's roles has been evident in both nations. Such values are culturally and ideologically constructed and exist on different issues in each country. This analysis has highlighted continuing cultural constraints on women's options in Japan, while suggesting that other constraints limit women's opportunities in the United States as well. In the case of Japan, conflict over traditional values has been deep seated, preventing feminist claims from even reaching the public agenda until the last several decades. Until recently, their demands were largely ignored or not given opportunity for public access. Value conflict revolves around issues of women's full participation in the work force as opposed to remaining in the private house-hold sphere, as well as seeking to seeking independence through other means, including retention of surnames after marriage. For women in the United States, there is deep-seated conflict regarding women's demands, albeit around equiva-lent but different issues. Abortions, which threaten dependent roles and challenge traditional women's place, are the most complex in terms of successful resolution and lack of compromise, with moral and religious polarization continuing unabated. The ideological struggle related to abortion rights in the United States has no Japanese parallel, although the relatively conflict-free approach there can-not be imported into the very distinct American political system. In addition, in the United States, policies that impact on what is seen as the private family structure are the subject of considerable controversy, with issues related to "family values" and "family friendly" policy highly contested as well.

Japanese women's policy success to date may be ranked in terms of ease of pas-sage: from DV law, representing women as victims, or *kawai sona hito* (in a poor and miserable situation), being the most acceptable; to vague and ambiguous pol-icy with a human rights, educational component such as the Basic Law for Gender Equal Society; to the most difficult, laws dealing with traditional and ingrained structures of inequality, including the EEOL and retention of women's surname after marriage, which challenge prevailing mores and established groups and practices (Fukushima interview).[8] In the United States, policies may be ranked from easy to difficult to attain, with one of the easiest involving "role equity"—women gaining rights similar to those enjoyed by men. More difficult issue resolution involves the role of national government in developing national family policy and the perception that women are treated preferentially or "differently." (See Gelb and Palley, 1996, for a fuller description of "role equity." See McDonagh, 2002, for a useful analysis of "sameness" and "difference.") It is evident that femi-nism is threatening to interests and traditional attitudes in both nations, so that its gains are potentially fragile.

Differences

Symbolic policy making. As demonstrated, there has been far more attention to feminist issues in Japanese politics during the past decade, although it must be cautioned that there is often a gap between rhetoric and reality, as the controversy over the EEOL suggests.

Symbolic policy making as a governmental mechanism for responding to and manipulating demands for change is well recognized. In Japan, as political scientist T.J. Pempel suggests, the answer to the question of whether or not things are changing in Japan must always be "both" (2000). However, it is possible that government efforts like the EEOL and the enactment of the Basic Law for Gender Equal Society, which lack enforcement power and sanctions, may produce effects different from their intentions. Both of these efforts appear to respond to women's demands, but are intended to blunt the edge of social change through the time-honored technique of enacting vague symbolic law but changing little. In fact, such policies may have an effect other than what was anticipated by the government. The existence of these flawed but important initiatives helps to create a more informed discourse, enhanced expectations and new momentum for change, rather than limiting options and controlling dissent and discontent, as the government may have hoped. (See Gelb, 2000, 402; also see Pharr, 1990, 216–31.)

Implementation. An important aspect of analysis of policy change, in addition to agenda setting, is implementation. There is no question that the United States has developed more (if not completely) effective systems of enforcement and sanctions to eradicate sex discrimination. The cases of the EEOL and other labor-related laws, as well as the Basic Law for Gender Equality, suggest the limitations of laws without teeth, or punishment for noncompliance. They present the image but not necessarily the reality of change, although as we have seen they can be utilized to redefine and develop policy in more meaningful ways. The policies that involve criminal prosecutions, for example, anti-stalking, anti–child prostitution and anti-pornography as well as DV laws, appear to fare better since they contain compliance mechanisms which seem to be modestly enforced if complaints are made.

It is the case that symbolic law can lead to unintended consequences including increased consciousness and "feedback" effects that produce demands for new policy. However, the often-cited idea that the Japanese obey laws even without sanctions appears to have little basis in fact as the systematic resistance of employers to ending practices of sex discrimination confirms.

Resources for policy change and implementation. One significant difference between the U.S. and Japanese systems may lie in the amount or magnitude of resources devoted to specific policies. The scope and breadth of domestic violence policy in the United States, in comparison to its Japanese counterpart, has already been noted. The case of domestic violence policy is also instructive with regard to resource commitment: the U.S. Congress authorized expenditures of $1.8 billion in 1994 and, in Japan, the equivalent of about $1 million was spent in 2001. More substantial and generous funding has been allocated to support "family friendly" policy, which the Japanese government perceives as a national priority, in the hope that the marriage and the birth rate will increase. In general, the Japanese government has favored gender policies that involve limited financial costs, although activists hope that future, more expansive policy can be built incrementally.

Conclusion

By increasing participation and representation, women's citizenship in both countries has been greatly enhanced. Women in Japan have achieved considerable success in gaining political representation and increased access in recent years. However, at this time, their access to the labor force remains problematic and lags behind their newly found political role. It has been suggested that Japanese women may choose to pursue either children and marriage or high-paying careers (Schoppa, 2001, 78). However, there is little evidence in the data presented here of the existence of these alternative options, as most Japanese women are limited in their job choices, either within or outside of marriage. Their role in politics and society will not be fully realized until they attain equity in the workplace. In the United States, women's participation through elected representatives and interest groups continues at a high level. Although economic mobility has been addressed far more successfully than in Japan (as least for educated women), the future remains unclear, given the ongoing struggle for values and expectations related to women and the family.

In both nations, advocacy and efforts to achieve gender-related policy innovation and change continue with vigor and enthusiasm. Further gains in policy impact in each nation seem assured only when changes in their respective opportunity structures affect political as well as economic and institutional circumstances.

Notes

Introduction

1. Recently, there has been attention to comparing gender and other social policies in Japan and Germany, but not comparing Japan and the United States. See Lenz Ilse (1999), Globalization and the Formation of Semi Publics. International Conference on Rationalization, Organization, Gender Proceedings. Sozialforschungsstelle Dortmund; See also Gottfried and O'Reilly and Streeck (in references).
2. I am indebted to Professor Anthony Chambers of Arizona State University for the refinement of this term.
3. This view was vigorously endorsed at the Annual Justice Ruth Bader Ginsburg Distinguished Lecture on Women and the Law, "Panel Discussion on Current Topics in International Human Rights," 13 December 2001, Association of the Bar of the City of New York and NOW (National Organization for Women) Legal Defense and Education Fund.

   As of August 2002, the U.S. Senate Foreign Relations Committee approved the Commission on the Elimination of Discrimination against Women (CEDAW), initially recommended by Democratic Presidents Carter and Clinton, but it has never been ratified by the Senate. Its political future remains unclear as of this writing. (Dao James, *New York Times*, 31 July 2002. A7–8).
4. Advocacy coalitions are closely related to "policy communities," "policy subsystems" and "issue networks" as well as epistic communities. (Lembruch, 2001, 42).
5. Frank Schwartz describes the process as "neopluralist" with small and relatively stable sets of well-organized state and societal actors dominating relatively self-contained policy domains by privatizing conflicts and resorting to informal decisions (1998, 284). However, his useful analysis is limited to issues of business and labor. In his discussion of revision of the Labor Standards Act, women do play a vocal if not decisive role.
6. Other political scientists, including Ellis Krauss, Sone Yasunori and Inoguchi Takashi, argue that Japan is pluralist. See McKean in Allinson and Sone, 1993, 78 for a review of this literature.

Chapter 1

1. The role of UN conferences and feminist networks on the diffusion of gender equity policies worldwide have been the subject of countless books and articles, including Dorsey Lenz and Sassen 1996 among many others.
2. The small decline in representation was due in part to a revised electoral system for the Upper House, limiting proportional representation which has been more beneficial to women's electoral opportunities to some extent. Through the amended system, the LDP and its coalition partners sought to enhance possibilities for political dominance.

3. This small party that existed from 1991 to 1998 was comprised primarily of reformist minded former LDP members.
4. Iwamoto Misako (2001) also suggests that women were angry because of efforts to restrict abortion access.
5. In Ueno's view, this term has less of a negative connotation than "fragmentation" and reflects a new stage in Japanese movement development in which feminists were divided into different camps or factions (1997).
6. See Sheldon Garon (1997), who contends that most large women's groups are in fact conduits for state policy. Buckley agrees on their closeness to the state and LDP but argues for their greater autonomy from state interference (1994, 159).
7. The United States, as suggested in chapter one, resistant to signing international treaties, has never become a signatory to CEDAW though over 160 nations have (Gelb, 2002, 6).
8. Hotlines have been utilized by Japanese women as a means of gauging and responding to gender-related problems including sexual harassment, domestic violence, stalking and work-related sex discrimination. Established by women's groups, government or unions, they may reach women who would normally not come in contact with one another. I am indebted to Heidi Gottfried of Wayne State University for this general observation.

Chapter 2

1. By 1983, 36 percent of 99,093 or approximately 35,000 EEOC charges or complaints were processed and 45 percent of the 209 cases filed were on sex discrimination-related issues. (Burstein, 1991, 1211).
2. Customarily, the offending company rectifies its practices rather than risking loss of contracts.
3. In her dissertation, unpublished at the University of Hawaii, 2002b, Kobayashi Yoshie argues that rather than women's movements acting as primary advocates of change regarding the EEOL both in 1985 and 1997, "femocrats," or state feminists acting through the MOL Women's Bureau, were the major architects of the new policy agendas. She points to disagreement within the ranks of such groups as the Liaison Group on the abolition of protective measures to support the view that it was female bureaucrats who led the charge for employment policy. A more traditional approach to analyzing EEOL ratification, reflected to some extent in the account presented here, emphasizes the number of factors including the role of women's NGOs such as the Liaison Group, along with the mass media, female Diet members and female bureaucrats, in persuading the government to sign CEDAW and move to subsequent adoption of the EEOL.
4. The willingness of the Shiba Shinyo Credit Union to settle the case seemed to be motivated by their merger with another credit union in July 2003, and the need to resolve this matter prior to that.
5. One factor in bringing public attention to sexual harassment was the arrest of Osaka Governor "Knock" Yokoyama, who in 1999 was ordered to pay the equivalent of $111,000 to a campaign volunteer for harassment. He was forced to resign his office although in a subsequent criminal suit in August 2000 he was given a suspended sentence.

Chapter 3

1. Efforts to "defund" the bill at the eleventh hour, during the appropriations process by conservative Republicans, were met with exposure and grassroots pressure.

2. As noted in the introduction, and to be discussed further in chapter four, the passage of the Eugenic Protection Law in post-war Japan had virtually no female input.

3. Pettman 1996 contended that violence against women has often been the catalyst for organizing within and between states. Quoted in Grubel, 2002, 7.

4. For example, the UN Commission on the Elimination of Discrimination against Women (CEDAW) observed with concern that, although Japan ranked second among the world's nations in terms of overall resource development, according to the UN, its rank was reduced to fourteenth when the socioeconomic status of women was taken into consideration. (Yoneda, 2000).

5. It should be noted that not every one agrees with this characterization of the process. Former Diet member Shimizu Sumiko takes issue with the view that the anti child pornography and prostitution law reflects a non partisan process by Diet women.

6. A formal group, Fujin Giin Kondanki, does exist but by all accounts does not play an important role in rallying legislative support by women (Moriyama interview).

7. Her research was based on examination of several internet sites, such as *http://www.clb.go.jp.english/index.htm* and the *Asahi Shimbun* "Sangiin no tsuchisho; Anata ga eranda giin nenkan no hatarakiburi" (transcripts of the Members of the House of Councilors; the way they worked for their six years), 30 April 2001.

8. Research committees were established as part of a reform effort in 1986 in the House of Councillors to provide the Sangiin, the less powerful house of the Diet in which legislation normally does not originate, with a purpose distinctive from the House of Representatives, that of engaging in long-term investigation of public policy. Research committees were given the power to recommend bills to the larger body. Earlier legislation they successfully supported included a Basic Law of Aging Society passed in November 1995 (Shiomi and Yoshioka, 2001).

9. Law professor Masuyama Mikitaka evaluates the view that the Japanese Diet may be predisposed toward unanimity, as appears to be the case in several of the policies examined in this study. In "Is the Japanese Diet Consensual?" *Journal of Legislative Studies*, winter 2000, 6, no. 1: 9–28, he concludes that it is part of a behavioral pattern that emerges from strategic interaction between the government and the opposition; that it is a manifestation of consensual policy making (28).

10. See *Nihon Keizai Shinbun*, 31 January 2001, for an article that indicates that a former NGO anti-violence activist was hired as an expert on violence prevention by the Bureau of Gender Equality.

Chapter 4

1. On February 26, 2003 the Supreme Court ruled against the pro-choice view finding that federal extortion and anti-racketeering laws were wrongly used to thwart Operation Rescue and other anti-abortion protesters. ("High Court Sides with Abortion Protesters," *Associated Press*, 27 February 2003).

2. They are subject to the Ethical and Religious Directives, issued by the National Conference of Catholic Bishops and consider reproductive health services to be "morally objectionable." Rachel Benson Gold, "Advocates Work to Preserve Reproductive Health Access When Hospitals Merge" *Perspectives on Public Policy*, Guttmacher Institute, 2000, 2: 1–4.

3. The Criminal Abortion Law provides for prison terms for women who abort and doctors who perform abortions, and it prohibits abortion regardless of the reason. Criminal Law of Japan, chapter XXIX. Made available by Ashino Yoriko.
4. In her analysis of reproductive policy in Japan, Norgren (2001) argues that unlike the case of abortion, no strong interests supported contraception and "outdated" thinking at the MHW prevailed in the absence of pro-birth control advocacy.

Chapter 5

1. The feminist groups NOW and the Fund for a Feminist Majority were advocates of paid leave but became inactive members of the FMLA coalition in deference to the dominant forces who felt that paid leave would never be accepted.
2. Berman favored a national maternity law to overturn the initial decision of the California court; he demurred at the prospect of a gender-neutral approach and therefore ultimately relinquished his lead position on this policy to Patricia (Pat) Schroeder (D-CO). In 1987, the U.S. Supreme Court upheld the California law that triggered initial interest in a gender neutral approach permitting disability law to cover pregnancy. This ruling only provided impetus for those who endorsed a broad based leave policy, which had already gained momentum (Wisensale, 2001b, 141).
3. Nonetheless, even the defeat of proposed legislation helped to spur increased attention to childcare for the poor.
4. See Peng, 2001, who believes that these are central factors.
5. According to Jeffrey Broadbent who analyzed environmental policy, the 1967 basic law on the environment was a weak bill that provided a symbolic response to a complaining public, lacking standards of regulation or sanctions for violators. It did lead to subsequent environmental ministry-based initiatives and continued domestic and international pressure led to major revisions in the "Pollution Diet" of 1970.
6. The role and status of the Office for Gender Equality has been upgraded twice, in 1997 and 2001, through action by the Diet.
7. In addition to the interview, Mr. Furuhashi supplied an informative written review of the policy process.
8. See especially Hashimoto, Danjo Kyodo, 2002.

Conclusion

1. For the first fifteen years of its existence, the caucus did not include abortion on its agenda.
2. While still a strong force in Japanese policy making, "the rapid decline of bureaucratic authority was one of the most noteworthy events of the 1990s." Takeshi Sasaki, "The Changing Shape of Party Politics and Governance in Japan" in Thomas Mann and Sasaki Taskeshi, *Governance for a New Century*, Tokyo, Japan Center for International Exchange, 2002, 103. This decline clearly contributed to the rise of Diet member's bills.
3. The Women's Bureau, a sub-agency of the Department of Labor founded in 1920, has played virtually no role in any of the policies studied here. A possible candidate for the "state feminist" role in the United States, it has never been a major policy actor.
4. Sometimes also known as "strategic partnerships"(Mazur, 190). Another similar concept emphasizes the formation of "issue networks."
5. I am indebted to Heidi Gottfried of Wayne State University for this observation.

6. The notion of the "life cycle" of an issue somewhat tepidly described as the "the climate of the times" is not quite the same as a "policy cycle" as that term is being employed here (Cobb and Ross, 1997, 10).
7. Ohmori (interview) described the "blacklining" or censorship of requested information, as the government claims the right of individuals to privacy.
8. In the United States, one compelling appeal of the VAWA as well was its framing as assisting female victims in need of protection.

Abbreviations and Acronyms

DV law	Law for the Prevention of Spousal Violence and Protection of Victims
AARP	American Association of Retired Persons
ADCC	Aid to Day Care Centers Act
AFER	Alliance of Feminist Representatives
AMPO	Japan–United States Security Treaty
CARE	Concerned Alliance of Responsible Employees
CBAS	Committee for the Betterment of Aging Society
CCDBG	Child Care and Development Block Grant
CCDF	Child Care and Development Fund
CCWI	Congressional Caucus for Women's Issues
CEDAW	Convention on Elimination of Discrimination against Women (also Commission at the UN)
CLUW	Coalition of Labor Union Women
CSW	Commission on the Status of Women
EEO	equal employment opportunity
EEOC	Equal Employment Opportunity Commission
EEOL	Equal Employment Opportunity Law
EMILY's List	U.S. women's campaign finance group
EO	equal opportunity
ERA	Equal Rights Amendment
FACE	Federal Access to Clinic Entrances Act
FIMA	Ichikawa Fusae Memorial Association
FMLA	Family and Medical Leave Act
HELP	Japanese domestic violence shelter
ILO	International Labor Organization
IWY	International Women's Year
JAC	Joint Accountability Committee
JAL	Japan Airlines
LDP	Liberal Democratic Party
MHW	Ministry of Health and Welfare
MMM	mixed member majority
MOL	Ministry of Labor
NAM	National Association of Manufacturers
NARAL	National Abortion Rights Action League now known as NARAL Pro-Choice America
NCADV	National Coalition against Domestic Violence
NCCB	National Conference of Catholic Bishops
NCPAC	National Conservative Political Action Committee
NGO	nongovernmental organization
NHK	Japanese educational television station

NOW LDEF	National Organization for Women Legal Defense and Education Fund
NOW	National Organization for Women
NRTLC	National Right to Life Committee
NWLC	National Women's Law Center
NWPC	National Women's Political Caucus
OECD	Organization for Economic Co-operation and Development
OFCCP	Office of Federal Contract Compliance Programs
PAC	political action committee
PNAP	Pro Life Non Violent Action Project
PRWORA	Personal Responsibility and Work Opportunity Reconciliation Act
RFP	Reproductive Freedom Project
RICO	Racketeer Influenced and Corrupt Organization Act
SDP	Social Democratic Party
STOP	services, training, officers and prosecutors
TANF	Temporary Aid to Needy Families
TDI	Temporary Disability Insurance
VAWA	Violence Against Women Act of 1994
VAWO	Violence Against Women Office
WAC	Women's Action Coalition
WHAM	Women's Health Action Mobilization
WINWIN	Japanese women's campaign finance group
WWIN	Working Women's International Network

References

Works Cited

Abrams, Kathryn. 1994. "Title VII and the Complex Female Subject." *Michigan Law Review.* August, 92: 2479.

Allinson, Gary. 1993. "Introduction: Analyzing Political Change: Topics, Findings and Implications; State Strength and Public Interest." In Gary Allinson and Yasunori Sone, *Political Dynamics in Contemporary Japan.* Ithaca, NY: Cornell University Press. 1–14.

American Political Network. 1995. "Abortion Report." Available online at www.nationaljournal.com. Washington, D.C. 25 October, 1–67.

Ando Ritsuko. 2002. "Dependents Forced to Limit Work." *Japan Times.* 26 June, 3.

Asahi Shinbun. 1994. "Conflict between the MOL and Office for Gender Equality." 11 December.

———. 2001. "Surname Debate Heats Up." 6 November, 22.

———. 2002. 17 December.

Asakura Mutsuko and Konno Hirano. 1997. *Josei Roudou Hanrei Guidebook.* Tokyo, Japan: Yukaku Publishing Company.

Ashino Yuriko. 1999. "Long Wait for Birth Control Pills." *Japan Quarterly.* October–December. 86–91.

Associated Press Online. 2003. Available online at http://www.ap.org. "Supreme Court Takes on Family Leave Case."

Bashevkin, Sylvia. 1998. *Women on the Defensive.* Chicago: University of Chicago Press.

———. 2002. *Welfare's Hot Buttons.* Toronto: University of Toronto Press.

Baumgardner, Jennifer. 1999. "Immaculate Contraception?" *Nation.* 25 January, 11–15.

Baumgartner, Frank and Bryan Jones. 1993. *Agendas and Instability in American Politics.* Chicago: University of Chicago Press.

Baumgartner, Frank. 2002. Unpublished paper presented at the Conference on Social Movements, Public Policy and Democracy, University of California, Irvine: 11–13 January.

Beckwith, Karen. 2000. "Beyond Compare: Women's Movements in Comparative Politics." *European Journal of Political Research.* 37: 431–68.

Beijing Joint Accountability Caucus. (Peking JAC) 1996. *Recommendations from Beijing JAC.* August 1996. Unpublished manuscript.

Bellandi, Deanna. 1999. "Catholic Deals with Non-Catholics Grow." *Modern Healthcare.* 15 March, 24–5.

Bergeson, Jan and Kaoru Oba. 1986. "Japan's New Equal Employment Law: Real Weapon or Heirloom Sword?" *Brigham Young Law Review.* 865–90.

Bergmann, Barbara. 1997. *In Defense of Affirmative Action.* Washington, D.C.: Harper Collins.

Bernstein, Anya. 2001. *The Moderation Dilemma: Legislative Coalitions and the Politics of Family and Medical Leave.* Pittsburgh, PA: University of Pittsburgh Press.

Bestor, Theodore. 1998. *Neighborhood Tokyo*. Stanford, CA: Stanford University Press.

Bevacqua, Maria. 2000. *Rape on the Public Agenda*. Boston: Northeastern University Press.

Bishop, Beverly. 2000. "The Diversification of Employment and Women's Work in Contemporary Japan." In J. S. Eades, Tom Gill, and Harumi Befu, *Globalization and Social Change in Contemporary Japan*. Melbourne, Australia: Transpacific Press. 93–109.

———. 2002. "Globalization and Women's Labour Activism in Japan." *Electronic Journal of Contemporary Japanese Studies*. 6 December, 1–19.

Blumrosen, Alfred. 1993. "Society in Transition IV: Affirmation of Affirmative Action Under the Civil Rights Act of 1991." *Rutgers University Law Review*. 45: 903.

Brenner, Joanna. 1996. "The Best of Times, The Worst of Times: Feminism in the United States." In Monica Threlfall ed., *Mapping the Women's Movement*. London: Verso. 17–72.

Broadbent, Jeffrey. 1998. *Environmental Politics In Japan*. Cambridge, England: Cambridge University Press.

Brooks, Rachelle. 1997. "Feminists Negotiate the Legislative Branch; The Violence Against Women Act." In Cynthia Daniels, ed., *Feminists Negotiate the State*. Latham, PA: University Press of America. 65–82.

Brown, Clair; Yoshifumi, Nakata; Michael Reich; Lloyd Ulman and David Stern. 1997. *Work and Pay in the United States and Japan*. New York: Oxford University Press.

Bucar, Liz. 1998. *When Catholic and Non-Catholic Hospitals Merge: Reproductive Health Compromised*. Washington, D.C.: Catholics for Free Choice.

Buckley, Sandra. 1994. "A Short History of the Feminist Movement in Japan." In Joyce Gelb and Marian Palley, eds., *Women of Japan and Korea*. Philadelphia, PA: Temple University Press. 150–88.

———. 1997. *Broken Silence: Voices of Japanese Feminism*. Berkeley: University of California Press.

Burk, Martha and Heidi Hartmann. 1996. "Beyond the Gender Gap." *The Nation*. 10 June, 18–21.

Burstein, Paul. 1989. "Attacking Sex Discrimination in the Labor Market: A Study in Law and Politics." *Social Forces*. March, 67, 3: 641–65.

———. 1991. "Legal Mobilization as A Social Movement Tactic: The Struggle for Equal Opportunity." *American Journal of Sociology*. 96, 5:1201–25.

Cabinet Office (Japan). 2001. *FY 2000 Annual Report on the State of Formation of A Gender Equal Society and Policies to be Implemented in FY 2001 to Promote the Formation of A Gender Equal Society*. Outline: Tokyo. June.

Campbell, John Creighton. 1992. *How Policies Change*. Princeton, NJ: Princeton University Press.

Carroll, Susan J. 1995. "A Mixed Verdict: The Impact of Women in Congress on the Crime Bill." Unpublished paper presented at the Midwest Political Science Association, Chicago, Illinois. 6–8 April.

———. 2002. "Representing Women: Congresswomen's Perceptions of their Representational Roles." In Cindy Simon Rosenthal, ed., *Women Transforming Congress*. Norman: University Oklahoma Press. 48–70.

Casamayou, Maureen Hogan. 2001. *The Politics of Breast Cancer*. Washington, D.C.: Georgetown University Press.

Cassellas, Gilbert. 1998. "The Equal Employment Opportunities Commission: Challenges for the Twenty First Century." *University of Pennsylvania Journal of Labor and Employment Law*. Spring: 255.

Catholics for a Free Choice. 1999. *Caution: Catholic Health Restrictions May be Hazardous to Your Health*. Leaflet. Washington, D.C.: Catholics for a Free Choice.

Center for American Women in Politics. 2001. *Women State Legislators: Past Present and Future.* New Brunswick, NJ: Eagleton Institute.

———. 2002. *Women in Elective Office.* Fact Sheet.

———. 2003. *Summary Fact Sheets.*

Chronicle of Higher Education. 1995. 15 September, A43.

———. 2002. "Sexual Harassment Cited in Japan." 5 July, A41.

Coalition on Human Needs. 2002. *CHN Issue Brief on Child Care.* Washington, D.C. April.

Cobb, Roger and Charles D. Elder. 1983. *Participation in American Politics: The Dynamics of Agenda Building.* Baltimore Md: Johns Hopkins University Press.

——— and Marc Howard Ross. 1997. "Agenda setting and the Denial of Agenda Access: Key Concepts." In Roger Cobb and Marc Howard Ross, *Cultural Strategies of Agenda Denial.* Lawrence: University of Kansas Press. 3–25.

Cohen, Sally S. 2001. *Championing Child Care.* New York: Columbia University Press.

Community Unions National Network, Edogawa Union, Nagoya Fureai Union, Senshu Union, Ohdate Labour Union, Working Women's PAW. 2001. *Reports to the Director General of the International Labor Office on the Application of ILO Convention No. 100 to Part-Time Workers in Japan.* Tokyo: 2 July. Unpublished report.

Congressional Quarterly Almanac. 1987. Washington, D.C.: Congressional Quarterly Press. 43.

Conway, Margaret, David Ahern and Gertrude A. Steuernagel. 1999. *Women and Public Policy.* Washington, D.C.: Congressional Quarterly Press.

Costain, Anne. 1992. *Inviting Women's Rebellion.* Baltimore MD: Johns Hopkins Press.

Costello, Cynthia and Anne Stone. 2002. *The American Woman 2001–2002.* New York: W.W. Norton.

Craig, Barbara Hinkson and David M. O'Brien. 1993. *Abortion and American Politics.* Chatham, NJ: Chatham House.

Creighton, Millie. 1996. "Marriage, Motherhood and Career Management in a Japanese 'Counter Culture.'" In Ann Imamura, ed., *Re-Imaging Japanese Women.* Berkeley: University of California Press. 192–220.

Curtin, Sean. 2002. "Paternal Childcare Leave in Japan," Japan Insitute of Global Communications. Available online at http://www.glocom.org. Special Topics: Social Trends. 57, 1.

Daniels, Cynthia. 1997. "The Paradoxes of State Power" in Cynthia Daniels, ed., *Feminists Negotiate the State: The Politics of Domestic Violence.* Latham, PA: University Press of America. 1–4.

Dao, James. 2002. "Senate Panel Approves Treaty Banning Bias against Women." *New York Times.* 31 July, A8.

Darcy, Robert, Susan Welch and Janet Clark. 1995. *Women, Elections and Representation.* Lincoln: University of Nebraska Press.

Disney, Jennifer Leigh and Joyce Gelb. 2000. "Feminist Organizational 'Success': The State of U.S. Women's Organizations in the 1990s." *Women and Politics.* 21, 4: 39–76.

Dobash R. Emerson and Russell P. Dobash. 1992. *Women, Violence and Social Change.* New York: Routledge.

Dodson, Debra. 1998. "Representing Women's Interests in the U.S. House of Representatives." In Sue Thomas and Clyde Wilcox, *Women and Elective Office: Past Present and Future.* New York: Oxford University Press. 130–49.

Dorsey, Ellen. 2001. "The Global Women's Movement: Articulating a New Vision of Global Governance." In Paul Diehl, ed., *The Politics of Global Governance.* Boulder CO: Lynne Rienner. 436–64.

Economist. 2002. 2 March. "Women in Suits." 60–1.

———. 2002. 29 June. "A Survey of America's Role." 24–6.

Edwards, Linda. 1994. "The Status of Women in Japan: Has the Equal Employment Opportunity Law Made a Difference?" *Journal of Asian Economics.* Summer, 5, 2: 217–40.

Equal Employment Opportunity Commission (United States). 1999a. *Equal Employment Opportunity Commission: An Overview.* Washington, D.C. 21 June.

———. 1999b. *Summary Enforcement Data. FY 1992–1998.* Washington, D.C.

———. 2003. *EEOC Litigation Statistics, Sex Based Charges. FY 1992 Through FY 1998.* Washingon, D.C.

Eto Mikiko. 2001. "Women's Leverage on Social Policy Making in Japan." *PS.* July, 241–6.

"EW = EW Tokyo" Circle. 1995. *We Are Fighting for Equality in the Japanese Workplace.* Nonpublished handout. 15 August.

Feldman, Eric. 2000. *The Ritual of Rights in Japan.* Cambridge, England: Cambridge University Press.

Ferree, Myra Marx and Beth Hess. 2000. *Controversy and Coalition.* 3rd edition. New York: Routledge.

Flammang, Janet. 1997. *Women's Political Voice.* Philadelphia, PA: Temple University Press.

Foerstel, Karen. 1999. *Biographical Dictionary of Congresswomen.* Westport, CT: Greenwood Press.

Foreign Press Center, Japan. 1997. *Public Opinion Survey on Participation of the Sexes in Society.* Available online at http://www.fpcj.jp.

———. 2000. "Social Security: A Web Guide." 27 April. Available online at http://www.fpcj.jp.

Fox, Richard. 2000. "Women and Congressional Elections." In Sue Tolleson Rinehart and Jyl J. Josephson, eds., *Gender and American Politics.* Armonk, NY: M. E. Sharpe. 227–56.

Freeman, Jo. 2000. *A Room at a Time: How Women Entered Party Politics.* Lanham, PA: Rowman and Littlefield.

French, Howard. 2000. "Women Win a Battle, But Job Bias Still Rules Japan." *New York Times.* 26 February, A3.

Fujieda Mioko and Kumiko Fujimura-Fanselow. 1995. "Women's Studies: An Overview." In Kumiko Fujimura-Fanselow and Atsuko Kameda, *Japanese Women.* New York: Feminist Press. 155–82.

Fujimura-Fanselow Kumiko. 1995. "College Women Today: Options and Dilemmas." In Kumiko Fujimura-Fanselow and Atsuko Kameda, *Japanese Women.* New York: Feminist Press. 125–54.

——— and Atsuko Kameda. 1995. "Introduction." In Kumiko Fujimura-Fanselow and Atsuko Kameda, *Japanese Women.* New York: Feminist Press. xvii–xxxviii.

Fukushima Mizuho. 1997. *Women Study in Trials?* Tokyo: Yuhikaku Publishing Co.

Fukuzawa Keiko. 1995. "Women's Hiring Woes." *Japan Quarterly.* April–June, 155–61.

Garon, Sheldon. 1997. *Molding Japanese Minds.* Princeton, NJ: Princeton University Press.

Gelb, Joyce. 1989. *Feminism and Politics.* Berkeley: University of California Press.

———. 1991. "Tradition and Change in Japan: The Case of Equal Employment Opportunity Law." *U.S.-Japan Women's Journal.* English Supplement 1. August, 51–77.

———. 1996. In Marianne Githens and Dorothy Stetson, eds., "Abortion and Reproductive Choice." *Abortion Politics: Public Policy in Cross National Perspective.* New York: Routledge. 119–40.

———. 2003. "Feminism, NGOs, and the Impact of the New Transnationalisms." In David Vogel and Robert Kagan, eds., *Dynamics of Regulatory Change: How Globalization Affects National Regulatory Policies.* Berkeley: University of California Press.

——and Marian Palley. 1996. *Women and Public Policies*. Charlottesville: University of Virginia Press.

——and Margarita Estevez Abe. 1998. "Political Women in Japan: A Case Study of the Seikatsusha Network Movement." *Social Science Japan Journal*. October, 1, 2: 263–80.

——and Vivien Hart. 1999. "Feminist Politics in a Hostile Environment: Obstacles and Opportunities." In Marco Giugni, Douglas McAdam and Charles Tilly, eds., *How Social Movements Matter*. Minneapolis: University of Minnesota Press. 149–81.

Gender Equality Bureau. Cabinet Office (Japan). 1996–2001. *Women in Japan Today*. Tokyo.

——. 2001. *Eradication of Spousal Violence: Do You Worry About It?* Handout. 13 October 2001.

——. 2002. *Steps Toward Gender Equality in Japan*. The Government of Japan: Tokyo.

General Accounting Office (United States). 2002. *A New Look at the Glass Ceiling: Where Are the Women? The Status of Women in Management*. Washington, D.C. January.

Ginsburg, Faye. 1998. *Contested Lives*. Berkeley: University of California Press.

Giugni, Mario. 1999. "How Social Movements Matter: Past Research, Present Problems, Future Developments." In Marco Giugni, Douglas McAdam and Charles Tilly, eds., *How Social Movements Matter*. Minneapolis: University of Minnesota Press. xiii–xxxiii.

Goff, Helen. 1995. "Glass Ceilings in the Land of the Rising Sons: The Failure of Workplace Gender Discrimination Law and Policy in Japan." *Law and Policy in International Business*. Summer, 26: 1147–68.

Gold, Rachel Benson. 2000. "Advocates Work to Preserve Reproductive Health Access When Hospitals Merge." *Perspectives on Public Policy*. Guttmacher Institute. April, 2: 1–4.

Goldfarb, Sally. 2000. "No Civilized System of Justice—The Fate of the Violence against Women Act." *West Virginia Law Review*. 102: 499.

Goodman, Roger. 2000. *Children of the Japanese State*. Oxford: Oxford University Press.

Gottfried, Heidi. 2002. "Network Organizations: A New Face of Union Representation in Japan." *Critical Solidarity*. 2, 1: 5–6.

——and Jacqueline O'Reilly. 2002. "Reregulating Breadwinner Models in Socially Conservative Welfare Regimes: Comparing Germany and Japan." *Social Politics*. 9, 1: 29–59.

——and Laura Reese. 2003. "Gender, Policy, Politics and Work: Feminist Comparative and Transnational Research, *Review of Policy Research*. 20; 1 Spring: 3–20.

Greenhouse, Linda 2003. "In Family Leave Case, Supreme Court Steps Back into Federalism Debate." *New York Times*. 12 January, 12.

Grubel, Ruth. 2002. "Globalization as a Catalyst for Human Rights Activism in Japan: The Case of Domestic Violence Law." Unpublished paper. June.

Gunther, Richard and Anthony Mughan. 1993. "Political Institutions and Cleavage Management." In R. Kent Weaver and Bert Rockman, *Do Institutions Matter?* Washington D.C.: Brookings Institution. 272–301.

Gupta, Sanjay. 2001. "Bush Reinstates Ban on International Family Planning Funds." Available at www.cnn.com. 22 January.

Guttmacher Institute. 2000. "Minepristone Rollout Begins: DA Okays New Contraceptive Shot." *Perspectives on Public Policy*. December: 3, 6.

Hada Aiko. 1995. "Domestic Violence." In Kumiko Fujimura-Fanselow and Atsuko Kameda, eds. *Japanese Women*. New York: Feminist Press. 265–70.

Haley, Jack. 1991. *Authority Without Power: Law and the Japanese Paradox*. Oxford: Oxford University Press.

Hall Cynthia. 2003. "The Congressional Caucus for Women's Issues at 25: Challenges and Opportunities." In Cynthia Costello, Vanessa Wright and Anne J. Stone, eds. *The American Woman 2003–2004*. New York: Palgrave Macmillan Press.

Hanami Tadashi. 2000. "Equal Employment Revisited." *Japan Institute of Labor Bulletin.* Special Topic V. 1 January. 39: W1: 1–8.

Hani Yoko. 2001. "Women's Groups Decry Foundation's Demise." *Japan Times.* December 3.

Hashimoto Hiroko. 2002. "The Basic Law for a Gender Equal Society and Local Ordinances [*Danjo Kyodo Sankaku Shakai Kihonho to Jichitai Jyorei*]—Design of Universal Services, Planning a New Local Government." Unpublished paper. Spring.

Hatch, Diane and James Hall. 2002. "The Supreme Court declares FMLA Regulation Invalid." *Workforce.* June, 81, 6: 1–3.

Hayashi Hiroko. 1991. "Legal Issues on Wages of Japanese Women Workers." *International Review of Comparative Public Policy.*

——. 1995a. "Sexual Harassment in the Workplace and Equal Employment Legislation." *St. Johns Law Review.* Winter-Spring 69: 37–60.

——. 1995b. "10 Years of the Equal Employment Law in Japan: Its Future Problems." *Jurisuto.* November, 1079:2–4.

Helweg, Diana. 1991. "Japan's Equal Employment Opportunity Act: A Five Year Look at its Effectiveness." *Boston University International Law Journal.* Fall, 293–320.

Henshaw, Stanley. 1998. "Abortion Incidence and Services in the United States." *Family Planning Perspectives.* 30, 6: 263–83.

Higuchi Keiko. 1984. "Japanese Women in Transition." *Japan Quarterly.* 312–18.

Ichikawa Fusae Memorial Association. 2001. *Japanese Women.* 1 March, 85, 1; September, 86.

——. 2002. *Japanese Women.* 1 March, 87.

Ikeya Akira. 2002. "Day Care Next On Reform Agenda." *Nikkei Weekly.* 11 February: 1, 19.

——. 2002. "Tying the Knot." *Nikkei Weekly.* 1 April.

Imada Sachiko. 1996. Special Topic V. "Female Labor Force after the Enforcement of the EEOL." *Japan Institute of Labor Bulletin.* 1 August, 35, 8:1–6.

Imano Hisako. 1996. "10 Years of the Equal Employment Opportunity Law and the Tendency of Trials." *Labor Law White Paper.* 25 January.

International Labor Organization (Tokyo Branch Office). 2001. What is "Decent Work?: Considering 'Decent Work' from the Perspective of Gender." Conference handout. Tokyo, 10 November.

——. 2001. *Yearbook of Labor Statistics.* Geneva, Switzerland: International Labor Organization.

Ishida Takeshi and Ellis Krauss. 1989. "Democracy in Japan: Issues and Questions." In Takeshi Ishida and Ellis Krauss, *Democracy in Japan.* Pittsburgh, PA: University of Pittsburgh Press: 3–16.

Iwamoto Misako. 2001. "The Madonna Boom: The Progress of Japanese Women into Politics in the 1980s." *PS.* July, 225–6.

Iwao Sumiko. 1993. *The Japanese Woman.* New York: Free Press.

Jackman, Jennifer. 1997. "Blue Smoke, Mirrors and Mediators: The Symbolic Contest Over RU 486." In Roger Cobb and Marc Howard Ross, *Cultural Strategies of Agenda Denial.* Lawrence: University Press of Kansas.

Japan Institute of Women's Employment. 1995. *Japan's Working Women Today.* Tokyo, Japan.

Japan NGO Report Preparatory Committee. 1999. *Japan NGO Alternative Report towards the Special Session of the UN General Assembly "Women 2000: Gender Equality Development Peace."* Tokyo, Japan. August.

Japan Times Weekly, International Edition. 1992. "Caught in the Crunch." 30 August–3 September.

——. 1992. "Women's Changing Workplace Role." 29 June–5 July.

——. 1993. "Workforce Is Forty Percent Female." 8–14 November.

——. 1994. "Women Job Seekers Battle Slump, Sexism." 23–29 May.

——. 1995. "Female Workers Still Face Job Bias: Government Report." 25–31 December.

——. 1996. "Labor Union to Fight For Women's Work Rules." 27 May–2 June.

——. 1996. "Number of Part Time Women Workers Up." 16–22 December.

——. 2001. "Diet Seeks to Curb Domestic Violence." 7 April.

——. 2001. "Officials Ignore Domestic Violence Poll." 11 November.

——. 2002. "Dual Surnames 'Exceptions' In New Bill." 11 April.

——. 2002. "75% Question Domestic Violence Law." 30 April.

——. 2002. "Most Hospitals Not Prepared to Handle Domestic Violence." 7 June.

Japanese Trade Union Confederation (JTUC-RENGO). 2000. *2000–2001 Women's Activities of RENGO*. Tokyo, Japan. March.

Johnston, Hank, Enrique Larana and Joseph Gusfield. 1994. "Identities, Grievances and New Social Movements." In Enrique Larana, Hank Johnston and Joseph Gusfield, *New Social Movements: From Identity to Ideology*. Philadelphia, PA: Temple University Press. 3–35.

Kaino Tamie. 2001. *Domesutikku Baiorensu Boshi-ho (DV)*. Tokyo, Japan: Kogaku-sha. 30 November.

Kajimoto Tetsushi. 2000. "Surname Law Now Said out of Sync?" *Japan Times*. 7 November, 3.

Kamerman, Sheila and Alfred J. Kahn. 1995. *Starting Right*. New York: Oxford University Press.

Kamiya Masako. 1995. "A Decade of the Equal Employment Opportunity Act in Japan: Has It Changed Society?" *Law in Japan: An Annual*. 25–40.

Karube Keiko. 1995. "The Force of Social Change: A Case Study of the Equal Employment Opportunity Law in Japan." Unpublished paper presented at the Association for Asian Studies meeting, Washington D.C. 8 April.

Katzenstein, Mary. 1998. *Faithful and Fearless*. Princeton, NJ: Princeton University Press.

Kawashima Kenji, Hiroshi Tamura, Hidetoshi Nishida, Keiko Hirakawa, Yukiko Sakai, Masako Fujisawa, Masahiko Ishiguro, Taeko Ito, Mie Watanabe. 2001. *Comments on the Application of Convention #100 in Japan*. Addressed to the Director General of the ILO (handout). 8 May. Unpublished paper.

Keck, Margaret and Kathryn Sikkink. 1998. *Activists without Borders*. Ithaca, NY: Cornell University Press.

Kelly, Erin and Frank Dobbin. 1999. "Civil Rights at Work: Sex Discrimination and the Rise of Maternity Leave Policies." *American Journal of Sociology*. September, 105, 2: 455–92.

Kessler Harris, Alice. 2001. *In Pursuit of Equity*. New York: Oxford University Press.

Kezuka Katsutoshi. 2000. "Legal Problems Concerning Part Time Work in Japan." *Japan Institute of Labor Bulletin*. Special Topic V. 1 September: 39, 9.

Kihara Masako Ono Kihara, Jane Kramer, Deborah Bain, Masahiro Kihara and Jeff Mandel. 2001. "Knowledge of and Attitudes toward the Pill: Results of a National Survey in Japan." *Family Planning Perspectives*. May–June, 33, 3: 123–7.

Kingdon, John. 1995. *Agendas, Alternatives and Public Policies*. New York: Addison Wesley.

Kirp, David L. Mark Yudof and Marlene Strong Franks. 1986. *Gender Justice*. Chicago: University of Chicago Press.

Knapp, Kiyoko Kamio. 1995. "Still Office Flowers: Japanese Women Betrayed by the Equal Employment Opportunity Law." *Harvard Women's Law Journal*. 18: 83–137.

Kobayashi Yoshie. 2002a. "Politics is Interesting: Japanese Women Member's Legislative Activity." *Hawaii Pacific Affairs*. 20 February, 13.

——. 2002b. "A Path toward Gender Equality: State Feminism in Japan." Unpublished Ph.D. dissertation. Honolulu: University of Hawaii. December.

Komesar, Neil. 1994. *Imperfect Alternatives: Institutions in Law, Economics and Public Policy*. Chicago: University of Chicago Press.

Koppelman Andrew. 1996. *Anti-discrimination Law and Social Equality*. New Haven, CT: Yale University Press.

Kotani Sachi. 1999. "Women's New Labor Movement: A Case Study of the Women's Union Tokyo" (*Jyosei no 'atarashii' rodo undou; jyosei union tokyo no jirei kenkyu. Rodo Shakaigaku Kenkyu*)." *Journal of Labor Sociology*. 1: 3–25.

Krauss, Ellis and Takeshi Ishida. 1989. "Japanese Democracy in Perspective." In Takeshi Ishida and Ellis Krauss, *Democracy in Japan*. Pittsburgh, PA: University of Pittsburgh Press: 327–42.

Kyodo News. 2001a. "Shelters for Domestic Violence Victims Facing Difficulties." 19 December.

——. 2001b. "Domestic Violence Victims Lose Trust in Police." 14 October.

Kyoto Shinbun. 2001a. "Education for Staff and Preparation for Manuals Pressing Need." 12 April.

——. 2001b. "DV Worker Hired." 19 December.

Lam Alice. 1992. *Women and Japanese Management: Discrimination and Reform*. London: Routledge.

——. 1993. "Equal Employment Opportunities for Japanese Women: Changing Company Practice." In Janet Hunter ed., *Japanese Women Working*. London: Routledge. 197–223.

Le Blanc, Robin. 1999. *Bicycle Citizens*. Berkeley: University of California Press.

Lehmbruch, Gerhard. 2001. "The Institutional Embedding of Market Economies: The German Model and its Impact on Japan." In Wolfgang Streeck and Kozo Yamamura, *The Origins of Nonliberal Capitalism*. Ithaca, NY: Cornell University Press. 39–93.

Leonhardt, David. 2003. "Wage Gap Between Men and Women Shrinks." *New York Times*. 17 February, A1.

Levy, Denise Urias and Sonya Michel. 2001. "More Can Be Less: Child Care and Welfare Reform in the United States." In Sonya Michel and Rianne Mahon, *Child Care Policy at the Crossroads: Gender and Welfare State Restructuring*. New York: Routledge. 239–63.

Liddle, Joanna and Sachiko Nakajima. 2000. *Rising Suns, Rising Daughters*. London: Zed Books.

Lijphart, Arend, Ronald Rogowski and R. Kent Weaver. 1993. "Separation of Powers and Cleavage Management." In R. Kent Weaver and Bert Rockman, *Do Institutions Matter?* Washington, D.C.: Brookings Institution. 302–44.

Ling, Yuriko and Azusa Matsuno. 1992. "Women's Struggle for Empowerment in Japan." In Jill Bystydzienski, ed., *Women Transforming Politics*. Bloomington: Indiana University Press. 51–66.

Liu, Dongxiao and Elizabeth Heger Boyle. 2001. "Making the Case: The Women's Convention and Equal Employment Opportunity in Japan." *International Journal of Comparative Sociology*. 42: 389–404.

Mackie, Vera. 1995. "Feminist Critiques of Modern Japanese Politics." In Monica Threlfall, *Mapping the Women's Movement*. London: Verso. 260–87.

Magnier Mark. 2002a. "Confronting Marital Violence Behind the Shoji Screen." *Los Angeles Times*. 11 February, 9–10.

——. 2002b. "In Japan, Women Fight for the Last Word on Last Names." *Los Angeles Times*. 10 March.

Mainichi Shinbun. 1996. *Toward a New Century of Equality and Symbiosis: Summary of Twenty Third National Survey on Family Planning.* Tokyo: Population Problems Research Council.

———. 2000. The Population of Japan: An Overview of the 50 Postwar Years. Pamphlet. Tokyo: Population Problems Research Council.

Mainichi Daily News. 15 June 1996; 27 February 2000; 29 December 2000, 9 July 2001; 30 January 2002, 5.

———. 2002. "Wife Beater First Jailed Under Law." 4 March.

———. 2001. "Domestic Violence Against Women Swells 50%." 9 July.

Mainichi Interactive. 2001. Available online at www.mainichi.co.jp. "Government Must Create Daycare." 27 June.

Marks, Michelle. 1997. "Party Politics and Family Policy." *Journal of Family Issues.* January, 18: 1: 55–71.

Matsui Yayori. 1995. "The Plight of Asian Migrant Women Working in Japan's Sex Industry." In Kumiko Fujimura-Fanselow and Atsuko Kameda, *Japanese Women.* New York: Feminist Press. 309–21.

Mazur, Amy. 1995. *Gender Bias and the State.* Pittsburgh, PA: University of Pittsburgh Press.

———. 2001. *State Feminism, Women's Movements and Job Training.* New York: Routledge. 3–30: 293–318.

———. 2002. *Theorizing Feminist Policy.* Oxford: Oxford University Press.

McAdam, Doug, Sidney Tarrow and Charles Tilly. 2001. *Dynamics of Contention.* Cambridge, England: Cambridge University Press.

McCann, Michael. 1994. *Rights at Work.* Chicago: University of Chicago Press.

McCarthy, John D. 1987. "Pro-Life and Pro-Choice Mobilization: Infrastructure Deficits and Technologies." In Mayer Zald and John McCarthy, eds., *Social Movements in Organizational Society.* New Brunswick, NJ: Transaction Publishers. 49–66.

McClachlen, Patricia. 2002. *Consumer Politics in Post War Japan.* New York: Columbia University Press.

McDonagh, Eileen. 2002. "Political Citizenship and Democratization: The Gender Paradox." *American Political Science Review.* September. 96, 3: 535–52.

McGeehan, Patrick. 2001. "U.S. Sues Morgan Stanley, Charging Sex Bias in a Firing." *New York Times.* 1 September, C1, 4.

McKean, Margaret. 1993. "Equality." In Takeshi Ishida and Ellis Krauss, *Democracy in Japan.* Pittsburgh, PA: University of Pittsburgh Press. 201–224.

McVeigh, Brian. 1998. *The Nature of the Japanese State.* London: Routledge.

Michel, Sonya. 1999. *Children's Interests/Mothers' Rights: The Shaping of America's Child Care Policy.* New Haven, CT: Yale University Press.

Mikanagi Yumiko. 2001. "Women and Political Institutions in Japan." *PS.* July, 211–2.

Ministry of Labour, Women's Bureau. 1995. *Joshi Koyo Kanri Kihon Chosa* (Basic Research of Employment Administration of Women: Report of Results). Tokyo. Unpublished.

———. 1996. *Actual Circumstances of Working Women.* Tokyo. December. Unpublished.

———. 1997. *Equal Employment Opportunity Duties at National Women's and Young Workers Offices for the Past 10 Years, 1986–95.* Tokyo. January. Unpublished.

Ministry of Health, Labour and Welfare. Equal Employment Children and Families Bureau (Japan). 2001. "An Outline of Administration of Women Workers." Kyushu International Centre, Japan International Cooperation Agency and Kitakyushu Forum on Asian Women. Unpublished.

———. 2002. *Increasing Usage of the Individual Labor Dispute Resolution System: Implementation of the Law on Promotion of Individual Labor Dispute Resolution at the Labor Bureau of the prefectural governments.* Tokyo. January–March. Unpublished.

Minkoff, Debra. 1995. *Organizing for Equality*. New Brunswick, NJ: Rutgers University Press.

Molony, Barbara. 1995. "Japan's 1986 Equal Employment Law and the Changing Discourse on Gender." *Signs*. Winter 1995, 20, 2: 268–301.

Moriyama Mayumi. 1999. *Law for Punishing Acts Related to Child Prostitution and Child Pornography and for Protecting Children*. Tokyo: Gyosei Publishing.

Morley, Patricia. 1999. *The Mountain Is Moving: Japanese Women's Lives*. New York: New York University Press.

Mueller, Carol, ed. 1988. *The Politics of the Gender Gap*. Beverly Hills, CA: Sage.

Munroe, Maurice E. R. 1995. "The EEOC Pattern and Practice Imperfect." *Yale Law and Policy Review*. 13: 19.

Murumatsu Michio. 1993. "Patterned Pluralism Under Challenge: The Policies of the 1980s." In Gary Allinson and Yasunori Sone, *Political Dynamics in Contemporary Japan*. Ithaca, NY: Cornell University Press. 50–71.

Nakajima Michiko. 1997. "*Kaisei Kintoho-Rokiho wo Do Ikasuka—Hataraku Josei no Tachiba Kara*" (How to Make the Best of the Revised EEOL and LSL—From the Standpoint of Working Women). *Jurist*. 15 July, 11–16.

——. 2000. "The Problems of the Basic Law on the Comparative Participation of Men and Women in Society." *Women's Asia, Voices from Japan*. Autumn. 8–12.

National Council of Women's Organizations. 1997. *Facts on Women: Labor Force Participation*. Washington, D.C.

——. 2001. *2001 Women's Appointments Project*. Washington, D.C. 1 February.

National Women's Law Center. 2000. *Sex Discrimination in the American Workplace: Still a Fact of Life*. 17 July.

Nelson, Barbara and Katherine Carver. 1994. "Many Voices but Few Vehicles." In Barbara Nelson and Nazma Chowdbury, eds., *Women and Politics Worldwide*. New Haven, CT: Yale University Press. 738–57.

New York Times. 12 December 1992; 27 August 1995.

Newsweek. 2001. "The War over Fetal Rights." 5 February, 27.

Nihon Keizai Shinbun. 2001. "Termed Worker Hired By The Cabinet Office." 31 January.

——. 2002. "Record Number of Women Find Themselves Out of Work." 21 June.

Nihon Jiji Hyoron. 15 March 2002, 8.

Nihon Keizai Shimbun. 23 May 1992.

Nikkei Weekly. 13 May 1992; 8 June 2001, 3; 24 June 2002; 1 July 2002, 16.

——. 2001. "Disapproval Greets Proposals for Housewife Pension Plans." 5 November, 4.

Norgren, Tiana. 2001. *Abortion before Birth Control*. Princeton, NJ: Princeton University Press.

Norton, Noelle. 2002. "Transforming Policy from the Inside: Participation in Committees." In Cindy Simon Rosenthal, ed., *Women Transforming Congress*. Norman: University of Oklahoma Press. 256–82.

O'Connor, Julia, Ann Sheila Orloff and Sheila Shaver. 1999. *States, Markets and Families*. Cambridge, England: Cambridge University Press.

O'Connor, Karen. 1996. *No Neutral Ground—Abortion Politics in an Age of Absolutes*. Boulder, CO: Westview Press.

O'Donnell, Jayne. 1999. "Catholic Hospital Deals Limit Access, Activists Say." *USA Today*. 8 April, B1–2.

Ogai Tokuko. 2001. "Japanese Women and Political Institutions: Why Are Women Underrepresented?" *PS*. June, 207–10.

Ogino Miho. 1994. "Abortion and Women's Reproductive Rights." In Joyce Gelb and Marian Palley, *Women of Japan and Korea*. Philadelphia, PA: Temple University Press. 69–94.

Ornstein, Charles. 1998. "Faith on Principal." *Dallas Morning News*. 14 June, 1H.

Orren, Karen and Stephen Skowronek. 1989. *Studies in American Political Development.* New Haven, CT: Yale University Press.

Osawa, Mari. 2000. "Government Approaches to Gender Equality in the mid 1990s." *Social Science Japan Journal.* 3, 1: 3–19.

———. 2001. "Japanese Government Approaches to Gender Equality in the mid-1990's." Unpublished paper.

Ostrom, Elinor. 1999. "Institutional Rational Choice: What Has It Done? Where Is It Going?" In Paul Sabatier, ed., *Theories of Policy Making.* Boulder, CO: Westview Press. 35–72.

Owaki, Masako. 1997. *Trials of Working Women.* Tokyo: Yukaku Publishing.

Patterson, Dennis and Misa Nishikawa. 2002. "Political Interest or Interest in Politics: Gender and Party Support in Post War Japan." *Women and Politics.* 24, 2: 1–32.

Pekkanen, Robert. 2000. "Japan's New Politics: The Case of the NPO Law." *Journal of Japanese Studies.* Winter, 26, 1: 111–49.

Pempel, T. J. 1998. *Regime Shift.* Ithaca, NY: Cornell University Press.

Peng, Er Lam. 1999. *Green Politics in Japan.* London: Routledge.

Peng, Ito. 2001. "Gender and Generation: Japanese Child Care and the Demographic Crisis." In Sonya Michel and Rianne Mahon, eds. *Child Care Policy at the Crossroads: Gender and Welfare State Restructuring.* New York: Routledge. 31–56.

———. 2002 "Social Care in Crisis: Gender, Demography, and Welfare State Restructuring in Japan." *Social Politics.* Fall, 9, 411–443.

Pharr, Susan. 1981. *Political Women in Japan.* Berkeley: University of California Press.

———. 1990. *Losing Face: Status Politics in Japan.* Berkeley: University of California Press.

Piccinino, Linda and William Mosher. 1998. "Trends in Contraceptive Use in the United States, 1982–1995." *Family Planning Perspectives.* January–February, 30, 1: 4–10, 46.

Planned Parenthood Federation of America. 2000. *Abortion after the first Trimester.* Fact Sheet. Washington, D.C. 6 January.

———. 2001. *Laws Requiring Parental Notification for Minor's Abortion.* Fact Sheet. Washington D.C. 31 July.

Prime Minister's Office (Japan). 1995. *Japanese Women Today.* Pamphlet. Tokyo, Japan.

Primmer, Lesley. 2001. "The Congressional Caucus for Women's Issues: Achievements in the 105th Congress." In Costello and Stone, *The American Woman 2001–2002.* New York: Norton. 333–43.

Putnam, Robert. 2000. *Bowling Alone: The Collapse and Revival of American Community.* New York: Simon and Schuster.

Radigan, Anne L. 1988. *Concept and Compromise.: The Future of Family Leave Legislation in the U.S. Congress.* Washington, D.C.: Women's Research and Education Institute.

Ramseyer, Mark and Frances McCall Rosenbluth. 1993. *Japan's Political Marketplace.* Cambridge, MA: Harvard University Press.

Reed, Steven and Michael Thies. 2001. "The Consequences of Electoral Reform in Japan." In Matthew Shoberg Shugart and Martin P. Wattenberg, eds., *Mixed Member Electoral Systems: The Best of Both Worlds?* Oxford, England: Oxford University Press. 380–403.

Reinelt, Claire. 1995. "Moving onto the Terrain of the State." In Myra Ferree and Patricia Yancey Martin, eds., *Feminist Organizations: Harvest of the New Feminist Movement.* Philadelphia, PA: Temple University Press. 84–104.

Reitman, Valerie. 1996. "Japanese Women Move a Step forward with Major Victory in Job Bias Case." *Wall Street Journal.* 10 December. B10.

Research Committee on a Society of Cooperative Way of Life, House of Councilors. 1999. *Research Committee on a Society of Cooperative Way of Life Summary.* Interim report. Unpublished.

Research Group of Violence Against Women. 2003. Report on Progress of the DV Law by the Gender Equality Bureau of the Cabinet Office. Available online at http://gender.go.jp

Reskin, Barbara. 1998. *Realities of Affirmative Action in Employment.* Washington D.C.: American Sociological Association. August.

Resnik, Judith. 2001. "Categorical Feminism: Jurisdiction, Gender and the Globe." *Yale Law Journal.* December, 3: 619–80.

Rice, Melinda. 2001. "Japan Adopts Tough Domestic Violence Law." *Women's E News.* Available online at http://womensenews.org. 12 December, 1–7.

Richardson, Bradley. 1997. *Japanese Democracy.* New Haven, CT: Yale University Press.

Rodosho Fujinkyoku (Ministry of Labor, Women's Bureau). 1995. *Hataraku josei no jitsujo* (Actual Conditions of Working Women). Tokyo: Rodosho Joseikyoku.

Rosenberg, Debra. 2001. "We Have to Sacrifice." *Newsweek.* 27 August, 138: 9, 46.

Rosenberger, Nancy. 2001. *Japanese Women and the Search for Self in a Changing Nation.* Honolulu: University of Hawaii Press.

Sabatier, Paul. 1999. "The Need for Better Theories." In Paul Sabatier, ed., *Theories of Policy Making.* Boulder, CO: Westview Press. 3–18.

——and Hank C. Jenkins Smith. 1999. "The Advocacy Coalition Framework: An Assessment." In Paul Sabatier, ed., *Theories of Policy Making.* Boulder, CO: Westview Press. 117–68.

San Francisco Chronicle. 24 September 2002. "Time for Families." A20.

Sasaki Takeshi. 2002. "The Changing Shape of Party Politics and Governance in Japan." In Thomas Mann and Sasaki Takeshi, eds., *Governance for a New Century.* Tokyo: Japan Center for International Exchange. 94–117.

Sasakura Naoko. 1995. "Aokage Takako: Housewife Turned Political Representative from Seikatsu Club Seikyo." In Kumiko Fujimura-Fanselow and Atsuko Kameda, *Japanese Women.* New York: Feminist Press. 374–83.

Sassen, Saskia. 1996. "Toward a Feminist Analytics of the Global Economy." *Global Legal Studies Journal.* 4, 7: 7–41.

Sato Hiroki. 2000. "The Current Situation of 'Family Friendly' Policies in Japan." Special Topic VI. *Japan Institute of Labor Bulletin.* 1 February, 39, 2:1–9.

Sato Yoko. 1995. "From Home to the Political Arena." In Kumiko Fujimura-Fanselow and Atsuko Kameda, *Japanese Women.* New York: Feminist Press. 365–72.

Schneider, Anne and Helen Ingram. 1993. "Social Construction of Target Populations: Implications for Politics and Policy." *American Political Science Review.* June, 334–45.

Schneider, Elizabeth. 2000. *Battered Women and Feminist Lawmaking.* New Haven, CT: Yale University Press.

Schoppa, Leonard. 2001. "Japan: The Reluctant Reformer." *Foreign Affairs.* September–October, 80, 5: 76–88.

Schroedel, Jean Reith and Nicola Mazumdar. 1998. "Into the Twenty First Century: Will Women Break the Political Glass Ceiling?" In Sue Thomas and Clyde Wilcox, eds. *Women and Elective Office.* New York: Oxford University Press. 203–19.

Schwartz, Frank. 1998. *Advice and Consent: The Politics of Consultation in Japan.* Cambridge, England: Cambridge University Press.

Shiomi Mayasuki and Yoshioka Seiko. 2001. *Domestic Violence Preventive Law.* Tokyo: Gyosei Publishing.

Shirahase Sawako. 2002. *Women's Working Pattern and the Support of Working Mothers in Contemporary Japan.* Working Paper of the National Institute of Population and Social Security Research. Tokyo, Japan.

Shultz, Vicki. 1998. "Reconceptualizing Sexual Harassment." *Yale Law Journal.* April, 107: 1683.

Siim, Birte. 2000. *Gender and Society.* Cambridge, England: Cambridge University Press.

Skocpol, Theda. 1999. "Advocates without Members: The Recent Transformation of American Civic Life." In Theda Skocpol and Morris Fiorina, eds., *Civic Engagement and American Democracy*. Washington D.C.: Russell Sage. 461–510.

Social Security Administration. 2000. *Social Security: A Web Guide*. Social security online is available at www.socialsecurity.gov.

Spain, Daphne and Suzanne M. Bianchi. 1996. *Balancing Act: Motherhood, Marriage and Empowerment Among American Women*. New York: Russell Sage.

Spalter Roth, Roberta and Ronnee Scheiber. 1995. "Outsider Issues and Insider Tactics: The Battered Women's Movement and the Politics of Engagement." In Myra Marx Ferree and Patricia Yancey Martin, eds., *Feminist Organizations: Harvest of the New Women's Movement*. Philadelphia, PA: Temple University Press. 105–27.

Staggenborg, Suzanne. 1991. *The Pro-Choice Movement*. New York: Oxford University Press.

Stanley, Alessandra. 2002. "For Women, To Soar Is Rare, To Fall Is Human." *New York Times*. 10 January, C1.

Stetson, Dorothy. 1991. "The Political History of Parental Leave." In Janet Shibley Hyde and Marilyn J. Essex, eds., *Parental Leave and Child Care*. Philadelphia, PA: Temple University Press.

——and Amy Mazur. 1995. *Comparative State Feminism*. Thousand Oaks, CA: Sage Publications.

Streeck, Wolfgang. 2001. "Introduction: Explorations into the Origins of Nonliberal Capitalism in Germany and Japan." In Wolfgang Streeck and Kozo Yamamura, *The Origins of Nonliberal Capitalism*. Ithaca NY: Cornell University Press. 1–37.

Sturm, Susan. 1998. "Rethinking Law in the 21st Century Workplace: Article and Essay." *University of Pennsylvania Journal of Labor and Employment Law*. Fall, 1: 639.

——. 2001. "Second Generation Employment Discrimination: A Structural Approach." *Columbia Law Review*. April, 101: 458.

Supreme Court of Japan. 2002. *Data on Domestic Violence*. October 2001–April 2002.

Swers, Michele. 2001. "Understanding the Policy Impact of Electing Women: Evidence from Research on Congress and State Legislatures." *PS*. June, 217–24.

Takai Yoko. 2000. "Survey of Shelter Support." Shelter: Domestic Violence Problem Research Conference. Yokahama City Women's Association (Yokohama Shi Josei Kyokai). Yokahama, Japan. Unpublished paper.

Takayama Hideko. 1996. "Great News for the OL's." *Newsweek*. 9 December, 22.

Talbot, Margaret. 1999. "The Little White Bombshell." *New York Times Magazine*. 11 July, 39–43.

Tanaka Kazuko. 1995. "Work Education and the Family." In Kumiko Fujimura-Fanselow and Atsuko Kameda, *Japanese Women*. New York: Feminist Press. 295–308.

Tarrow, Sidney. 1994. *Power in Movement*. Cambridge, England: Cambridge University Press.

Tatalovich, Raymond. 1997. *The Politics of Abortion in the United States and Canada*. Armonk, NY: M. E. Sharpe Inc.

Tessier, Marie. 2002. "Bush Appointments Include Fewer Women." *Women's E-News*. Available online at http://www.womensenews.org. 11 February, 1–3.

Tierney, John. 2002. "The Big City: The Truth of the Myth about Mom." *New York Times*. 26 April, B1.

Tokyo Shinbun. 1998. "Violence against Women: A Fact Finding Inquiry and Collection of Opinions." 29 November.

——. 2001. "Big Progress but Difficult in Using." 24 February.

Tokyo Metropolitan Government. 2001. *Hataraku Josei to Rodo ho*. Tokyo, Japan.

True, James, Bryan Jones and Frank Baumgartner. 1999. "Punctuated Equilibrium Theory: Explaining Stability and Change in American Policy Making." In Paul Sabatier, ed., *Theories of the Policy Making Process.* Boulder, CO: Westview Press. 99–116.

Tsunoda Yukiko. 1996. "How Japanese Working Women Have Been Struggling To Promote Equality in the Workplace." Unpublished paper, delivered at Japan Society, New York. 11 December.

Uchitelle, Louis. 2002. "Job Track or 'Mommy Track'? Some Do Both in Phases." *New York Times.* 5 July 5, C1–5.

Ueno Chizuko taidan sho. 1997. "The Myth and Reality of Japanese Women's Labor." Unpublished paper, delivered at Japan Society, New York. 21 January.

—— and Mari Osawa. 2001. "Objects which the Basic Law of Gender Equality Aims At" (*Danjo Byodo Sankaku shakai kihon ho Osawa no mezasu mon*). In Chizuko Ueno ed., *Radically Speaking* (*Radikaru ni katareba taidan sho*). Tokyo: Hiebon sha publishing. 10–92.

United Nations Department of Economic and Social Affairs. 2000. *World Women 2000: Trends and Statistics.* Table 5.

United Nations Development Fund for Women (UNIFEM) 2000. *Progress of the World's Women 2000: A Biennial Report.* New York.

United Nations. 1995. "Report of the Committee on Elimination of Discrimination Against Women to the General Assembly of the United Nations." 31 May, Fifteenth Session. A/50/38.

——. Economic and Social Council. 2001. *Concluding Observations of the Committee on Economic, Social and Cultural Rights.* Japan. 31 August 2001, E/C.12/1/Add. 67.

United States Department of Commerce News. 2001. "Labor Force Participation for Mothers with Infants Declines for First Time." *Census Bureau Reports.* Washington, D.C. 18 October.

United States Department of Health and Human Services. 1999. "Only 10 percent of Eligible Families Get Child Care Help, New Report Shows." *HHS News.* October 19.

United States Department of Labor. Office of the Assistant Secretary for Policy. 2000. "Balancing the Needs of Families and Employers—Family and Medical Leave Surveys." Available online at www.dol.gov. 2000 Update 1–81, chapter 2, appendix A-2.

——. 2001. "Family and Medical Leave Act. Leave Benefits." *FMLA Survey.* Number 2, 1–17.

Upham, Frank. 1987. *Law and Social Change in Postwar Japan.* Cambridge, MA: Harvard University Press.

Valiente, Celia. 2001. "A Closed Subsystem and Distant Feminist Demands Block Women Friendly Outcomes in Spain." In Amy Mazur, ed., *State Feminism, Women's Movements and Job Training.* London: Routledge. 111–30.

Vogel, David. 1993. "Representing Diffuse Interests in Environmental Policy Making." In R. Kent Weaver and Bert Rockman, eds., *Do Institutions Matter?* Washington, D.C.: Brookings Institution. 127–71.

Voices from Japan—Women's Asia 21. 2000. Autumn, 6: 8–12.

Wada Junchiro. 2001. "Political Economy of Nurseries in Japan." Unpublished paper prepared for Childcare Workshop at Yale University (New Haven, CT). 18 January.

Wagatsuma Takashi. 2000. "Reponse to the Oral Contraceptives." In *The Population of Japan: An Overview of the 50 Postwar Years.* Mainichi Shimbun: Population Problems Research Council. 187–98.

Waldfogel, Jane. 2001. "Family and Medical Leave: Evidence from the 2000 survey." *Monthly Labor Review.* September, 124, 9: 17–24.

Wall Street Journal. 15 August 1995; 10 December 1996.

Warren, Mark. 2001. *Democracy and Association*. Princeton, NJ: Princeton University Press.

Washington Representatives. 1995. Washington D.C.: Columbia Books.

Weaver, R. Kent. 2002. "The Limits of Institutional Reform in Japan." In Thomas Mann and Takeshi Sasaki, *Governance for a New Century: Japanese Challenges, American Experience*. Tokyo: Japan Center for International Exchange. 118–26.

—— and Bert Rockman. 1993a. "Assessing the Effects of Institutions." In R. Kent Weaver and Bert Rockman, *Do Institutions Matter?* Washington, D.C.: Brookings Institution. 1–40.

——. 1993b. "When and How do Institutions Matter?" in R. Kent Weaver and Bert Rockman. *Do Institutions Matter?* Washington, D.C.: Brookings Institution. 445–62.

Weissman, Carol; Amal Khoury; Virginia Sharpe; Christopher Cassirer and Laura Morlock. 1997. *Is There A Common Ground? Affiliations between Catholic and Non-Catholic Hospitals and the Availability of Reproductive Health Services*. Kaiser Family Foundation.

Whittier, Nancy. 1995. *Feminist Generations*. Philadelphia, PA: Temple University Press.

Wilson, Graham. 1998. *Only in America: The Politics of the United States in Comparative Perspective*. Chatham, NJ: Chatham House.

Wisensale, Steven. 2001a. "Family Leave Policy." Unpublished paper. Presented at American Political Science Association, San Francisco, California. 28 August–1 September.

——. 2001b. *Solving a Problem or Tinkering at the Margins?* Armonk, NY: M. E. Sharpe.

Wolfe, Leslie and Jennifer Tucker. 1995. "Feminism Lives: Building a Multicultural Movement in the U.S." In Amrita Basu, ed., *The Challenge of Local Feminisms*. Boulder, CO: Westview Press. 435–64.

Women for Alternative Legal System for Sexual And Reproductive Rights/Health Japan. 2000. *Proposal on an Alternative Abortion Law Based on Reproductive Rights/Health: Repeal of the Criminal Abortion Law Is a Must—A Voice from Japanese Women*. Presented for the NGO Forum on Beijing + Five, The Hague. 6–7 February, 1–3.

Women's Labor Association. (Josei Rodo Kyokai). 2001. *Women and Work*. 136, (289): 6–11 June.

Working Women's International Network (WWIN). 1999–2001. *WWIN Newsletter*. January 1999: 6; March, 2000: 8; August 2001: 10.

——. 2001. "Counter Report" to the Committee on Economic Social and Cultural Rights Concerning the State Party Second Report. 13 August. Working Women's International Network (WWIN).

——. 2003. "Counter report to the Japanese Government's Fourth and Fifth Report on the Implementation of the UN Convention on the Elimination of Discrimination against Women (CEDAW)." Unpublished letter to CEDAW from the Working Women's International Network (WWIN). February.

Yamamoto Takushi. 2001. "LDP Divorced Over Dual Surname System." *Nikkei Weekly*. 24 December.

Yamamoto Akiko and Doug Struck. 2002. "Japan's Moms Caught in Day Care Dilemma." *Washington Post*. 10 November.

Yamashita Yasuko. 1993. "The International Movement toward Gender Equality and Its Impact on Japan." *U.S.–Japan Women's Journal*. English Supplement 5:69–86.

Yomiuri Shinbun. 26 June 1995; 13 July 1999; 1 August 2001.

Yoneda Masumi. 2000. "Japan." In Marilou McPhedran, Susan Bazilli, Moana Erickson and Andrew Byrnes, eds., *The First CEDAW Impact Study: Final Report*. Toronto, Canada: Center for Feminist Research and International Women's Rights Project.

Yoshihama, Mieko. 1999. "Domestic Violence: Japan's "Hidden Crime." *Japan Quarterly*. July–September, 76–82.

Yoshihama Mieko. 2002. "Policies and Services Addressing Domestic Violence in Japan: From Non-Interference to Incremental Changes." *Women's Studies International Forum.* 25, 5: 541–53.

Young, Lisa. 2000. *Feminists and Party Politics.* Ann Arbor: University of Michigan Press.

Zahariais, Nikolaos. 1999. "Ambiguity, Time and Multiple Streams." In Paul Sabatier, ed., *Theories of Policy Making.* Boulder, CO: Westview Press. 73–96.

Zald, Mayer. 1988. "The Trajectory of Social Movements in America." *Research in Social Movements: Conflict and Change.* 10: 19–41.

—— and Bert Useem. 1987. "Movement and Countermovement Interaction: Mobilization, Tactics and State Involvement." In Mayer Zald and John D. McCarthy, *Social Movements in An Organizational Society.* New Brunswick, NJ: Transaction Publications. 273–92.

—— and John D. McCarthy. 1987. "Social Movement Industries: Competition and Conflict Among SMOs." In Mayer Zald and John D. McCarthy, *Social Movements in An Organizational Society.* New Brunswick, NJ: Transaction Publications. 161–84.

Zwarensteyn, Lena. 2001. "Battered Women, Silent Screams." Unpublished manuscript, Wellesley College. Thesis submitted in partial fulfillment of the Prerequisite for Honors in Japanese Studies. April.

Interviews

Akamatsu, Reiko. Founder WINWIN, former head, Women's Bureau, Minstry of Labor. Tokyo, Japan (October 2001).

Ando Yoshiko. Planning Director, Policy Planning Bureau, Ministry of Labor. Tokyo, Japan (October 2001).

Appelbaum, Judith. Lawyer, National Women's Law Center. Washington D.C. (1999).

Asakura Mutsuko. Law Professor, Tokyo Metropolitan University. Tokyo, Japan (October–November 2001).

Ashino Yuriko. Assistant to Secretary General, Japan Family Planning Federation. Tokyo, Japan (July 2002).

Bando Mariko. Director General, Gender Equality Bureau, Cabinet Office. Tokyo, Japan (October 2001).

Clark, Ann. Labor lawyer, Vladeck, Waldman, Elias and Englehard. New York, New York (March 2002).

Coker, Donna. Professor, University of Miami Law School. Miami, Florida (June 2002).

Fukushima Mizuho. Diet member, House of Councilors Tokyo, Japan. (November 2001).

Furuhashi Genrokuro. Bureaucrat (retired). President, Salt Science Research Foundation. Tokyo, Japan (November 2001).

Goldfarb, Sally. Law professor, Rutgers University Law School. New York, New York (June 2002).

Goodman, Janice. Labor lawyer. Goodman and Zuchlewski. New York, New York (February 2002).

Hasegawa Kyoko. Labor lawyer and founder, Japan DV Prevention Information Center. Kobe, Japan (July 2002).

Hashimoto Hiroko. Professor, Women's Studies, Jumonji University. Tokyo, Japan (November 2001; June 2002).

Hayashi Hiroko. Law Professor, Fukuoka University. Tokyo, Japan (October 2001).

Hayashi Yoko. Labor lawyer, Minerva. New York, New York (July 1997).

Hitosugi Kazuko. Bureaucrat, Women's Bureau, Ministry of Labor. Tokyo, Japan (January 1997).

Kaino Tamie. Professor, Social Science and Family Studies, Ochanamizu University. Tokyo, Japan (October 2001; June 2002).

Kawahashi Yukiko. Member, House of Councilors. Tokyo, Japan (October 2001).

Koedo Shizuko. Secretary General, Working Women's International Network (WWIN). Osaka, Japan. (October, November 2001).

Komiyama Yoko. Member, House of Councilors. Tokyo, Japan (November 2001).

Kotani Sachiko. Ph.D. student, Waseda University. Tokyo, Japan (February 2000).

Kubo Kimiko. Secretary General, Ichikawa Fusae Memorial Association. Tokyo, Japan (November 2001).

Kumazaki Kiyoko. Assistant General Secretary, RENGO (Japan Trade Union Confederation). Tokyo, Japan (January 1997).

Kuroiwa Yoko. Labor lawyer, Tomin-Soga Law Office. Tokyo, Japan (October 2001; June 2002).

Masuda Reiko. Hitachi employee, Plaintiff. Tokyo, Japan (March 2000).

Matsumoto Yuiko. Member, House of Representatives. Tokyo, Japan (January 1997).

Moriyama Mayumi. Minister of Justice, Cabinet member. Tokyo, Japan (July 2002).

Muraki Atsuko. Director, Equal Employment Policy Division, Equal Emploment, Children and Families Bureau, Ministry of Health Labor and Welfare. Tokyo, Japan (October 2001).

Nagai Yoshiko. Beijing Joint Accountability Committee (Peking JAC) Secretary General. Tokyo, Japan (November 2001).

Nagamine Yoshimi. Reporter, *Yomiuri Shinbun*. Tokyo, Japan (January 1997).

Nakajima Mitsuko. Labor lawyer. Tokyo, Japan (January 1997).

Nakanishi Tamako. Former Diet Member. President, Women's Solidarity Foundation. Tokyo, Japan (April 2000).

Natori Haniwa. Director, Prime Minister's Office for Gender Equality. Tokyo, Japan (January 1997).

Noda Seiko. Member, House of Representatives. Tokyo, Japan (July 2002).

Nohno Chieko. Vice Minister of Health, Welfare and Labor. Member, House of Councilors. Tokyo, Japan (October 2001).

Nozaki Mitsue. Showa Shell employee, plaintiff. Tokyo, Japan (March 2000).

Nuita Yoko. Former President, Ichikawa Fusae Memorial Association. Tokyo, Japan (November 2001).

Ohmori Kaori. Labor lawyer. Tokyo, Japan (November 2001).

Osawa Mari. Professor, Institute of Social Science, Tokyo University. Tokyo, Japan (November 2001; June 2002).

Outten, Wayne. Labor lawyer, Outten and Golden. New York, New York (February 2002).

Owaki Masako. Member, House of Councilors. Labor lawyer. Tokyo, Japan (January 1997; November 2001).

Sakai Kazuko. Director, Tokyo Union. Tokyo, Japan (November 2001).

Sakai Yukiko. Kanematsu employee, plaintiff. Tokyo, Japan (April 2000).

Sakamoto Fukuko. Labor lawyer. Tokyo, Japan (April 2000).

Schneider, Elizabeth. Law professor. New York, New York (March 2002).

Shiba Shinyo. Credit Union Plaintiffs presentation. Diet building. Tokyo, Japan (October 2001).

Shiga Hiroko. Research Institute for Bank Employees, GIN RO KEN. Tokyo, Japan (January 1997).

Shimizu Sumiko. Former Diet member. Tokyo, Japan (August 2002).

Shirafuji Eiko. Sumitomo employee, plaintiff. Osaka, Japan (March 2000).

Sumitomo Hearing. Osaka District Court, Japan (March 2000).

Takenobu Mieko. Reporter, *Asahi Shinbun*. Tokyo, Japan (October 2001).

Tanigawa Shizuko. Dai Ichi Kangyo bank employee, activist. Tokyo, Japan (March 2000).

Tenao Setsuko. Trade union employee; Nomura Securities, plaintiff. Tokyo, Japan (April 2000).

Terao Yoshiko. Law Professor, Tokyo University. Tokyo, Japan (November 2001).

Thomas, Sheila. Lawyer, Equal Rights Advocates. San Francisco, California (April 2002).

Tsunoda Yukiko. Labor lawyer. Tokyo, Japan (October 1997; February 2000; November 2001).

Vladeck, Judith. Labor lawyer, Vladeck, Waldman, Elias, Engelhard. New York, New York (March 2002).

Williams, Wendy. Law professor, Georgetown University. Washingon, D.C. (May 2002).

Yakabi Fumiko. Member, Onna Rodo Kumiai. Osaka, Japan (April 2000).

Yamaguchi Mitsuko. Secretary General, Liaison Group. Executive Director, Ichikawa Fusae Memorial Association. Tokyo, Japan (November 2001; July 2002).

Yamashita Yasuko. Professor, Bunkyo Gakuin University. Tokyo, Japan (February 2003).

Yoshimiya Sougo. Executive Director, Gender Equality Division, RENGO (Japanese Trade Union Confederation). Tokyo, Japan (November 2001).

Yoshioka Seiko. Member, House of Councilors Research Committee. Tokyo, Japan (October 2001).

Index